Crossing the Line

UNIVERSITY PRESS OF FLORIDA

Florida A&M University, Tallahassee
Florida Atlantic University, Boca Raton
Florida Gulf Coast University, Ft. Myers
Florida International University, Miami
Florida State University, Tallahassee
New College of Florida, Sarasota
University of Central Florida, Orlando
University of Florida, Gainesville
University of North Florida, Jacksonville
University of South Florida, Tampa
University of West Florida, Pensacola

D0880346

Crossing the Line

Women's Interracial Activism
in South Carolina during
and after World War II

CHERISSE JONES-BRANCH

UNIVERSITY PRESS OF FLORIDA
Gainesville/Tallahassee/Tampa/Boca Raton
Pensacola/Orlando/Miami/Jacksonville/Ft. Myers/Sarasota

This book may be available in an electronic edition.

First cloth printing, 2014
First paperback printing, 2015

Library of Congress Cataloging-in-Publication Data
Jones-Branch, Cherisse. author.
Crossing the line : women's interracial activism in South Carolina during and after World
War II / Cherisse Jones-Branch.
pages cm
Includes bibliographical references and index.
ISBN 978-0-8130-4925-0 (cloth)
ISBN 978-0-8130-6189-4 (pbk.)
1. Women civil rights workers—South Carolina—History—20th century. 2. Civil rights
movements—South Carolina—History—20th century. 3. African American women—
South Carolina—History—20th century. 4. South Carolina—Race relations—History—
20th century. I. Title.
E185.93.S7J68 2014
323.1196'0730757—dc23   2013034529

University Press of Florida
15 Northwest 15th Street
Gainesville, FL 32611-2079
http://www.upf.com

Contents

Acknowledgments

No one writes a book without incurring a great many debts. I would have never been able to finish my research without the diligent assistance of the librarians and archivists at Smith College, Drew University, the University of South Carolina Caroliniana Library, the South Carolina Historical Society, the Greenville County Library, the Charleston County Library, the Avery Research Center for African American History and Culture, the Sisters of Charity of Our Lady of Mercy, the College of Charleston, South Carolina State, Arkansas State (many thanks go to Michael Sheppard and Linda Creibaum in Interlibrary loan!), and Clemson, Winthrop (a special thank-you to Gina Price White for answering my many e-mail queries!), and Furman Universities. I would also like to thank the Institute for Southern Studies at the University of South Carolina for the summer fellowship I received in 2004 and the Office of Research Technology Transfer at Arkansas State for the faculty research grant I was awarded in 2007, which defrayed the costs associated with research and travel.

I am grateful to Marcia Synnott and W. Scott Poole for reading numerous drafts of the manuscript and in particular for their thoughtful and substantive feedback, which helped to dramatically improve this manuscript. I would also like to thank University Press of Florida editor Sian Hunter for her enthusiastic support.

I am immeasurably grateful to my colleagues at Arkansas State University for supporting me over the years. The sabbatical I received in the fall of 2011 provided me with the time I needed to conduct additional research and flesh out important arguments in my study. I am fortunate to have wonderful colleagues in the History Department and in the College of Humanities and Social Sciences who graciously advised me and listened to me blather on about finishing this book. I extend a special thank-you to Carol O'Connor, Janelle Collins, Pamela Hronek, Gina Hogue, and Lauri Umansky. I especially appreciate Clyde Milner and Glen Jones, who secured the indispensable services of Ona Siporin to read and critique a very early draft of my study.

This book would not have been possible without the love and support of family and friends, who encouraged me through it all, especially when my self-confidence waned. Yulonda Eadie Sano and Michael Nash took time out of their busy schedules to read and comment on various drafts. Many thanks to you both and to Deirdre Cooper Owens for your pep talks. To Amy McCandless and Susan Hartmann, who were there at the beginning of my journey as a scholar, thank you for allowing me to learn from your fine examples and for your unfailing confidence in me.

To Mom, Daddy, Audrey, Deborah, and Germain, thank you all for your love, advice, and candor. To my nieces Lauren and Lailah and my nephew JoJo, I hope one day, when you are older, you will appreciate how this book, in many ways, was a labor of love with thoughts of you always at the forefront of my mind. And finally to my husband, Ezell, thank you for loving me, and dancing for me. I dedicate this book to you.

•

Portions of this book have been adapted from the following articles, reprinted here with permission:

"'How Shall I Sing the Lord's Song?': United Church Women Confront Racial Issues in South Carolina, 1940s–1960s." In *Throwing Off the Cloak of Privilege: White Southern Women Activists in the Civil Rights Era*, edited by Gail S. Murray, 131–152. Gainesville: University Press of Florida, 2004.

"'May We Pray That We Be Given Strength and Faith To Stand Together': Conflict, Change and the Charleston, South Carolina YWCA, 1940s–1960s," *Proceedings of the South Carolina Historical Association*, 2008: 15–28.

"Modjeska Monteith Simkins: I Cannot Be Bought and Will Not Be Sold." In *South Carolina Women: Their Lives and Times*, vol. 3, edited by Marjorie Julian Spruill, Valinda W. Littlefield, and Joan Marie Johnson, 221–239. Athens: University of Georgia Press, 2012.

"'To Speak When and Where I Can': African American Women's Political Activism in South Carolina in the 1940s and 1950s." *South Carolina Historical Magazine* 107, no. 3 (July 2006): 204–24.

Abbreviations

AAUW	American Association of University Women
ABE	Adult Basic Education
AFSC	American Friends Service Committee
BUA	Blacks United for Action, Inc.
CIC	Commission on Interracial Cooperation
CORE	Congress of Racial Equality
CWC	Columbia Women's Council
CWU	Church Women United: 1966–present
GCCCD	Greenville County Council for Community Development
NAACP	National Association of For the Advancement of Colored People
NACW	National Association of Colored Women
NCC	National Council of Churches
NICC	National Intercollegiate Christian Council
PDP	Progressive Democratic Party
PSTA	Palmetto State Teachers Association
RCCC	Richland County Citizens Committee
SCCHR	South Carolina Council on Human Relations
SCCIC	South Carolina Committee on Interracial Cooperation
SCERA	South Carolina Emergency Recovery Administration
SCFCWC	South Carolina Federation of Colored Women's Clubs
SCLC	Southern Christian Leadership Conference
SCTA	South Carolina Tuberculosis Association
SNCC	Student Nonviolent Coordinating Committee
SRC	Southern Regional Council

UCCW   United Council of Church Women (1941–50)
UCP   United Citizens Party
UCW   United Church Women (1950–66)
USO   United Services Organization
WCC   Welfare Council of Charleston
WICS   Women in Community Service
YWCA   Young Women's Christian Association

Introduction

Black and white women activists of the 1940s, 1950s, and 1960s have long been the unsung heroes in the narrative of South Carolina's civil rights movement. Throughout three decades, these women reacted to the social and political climate of the time to confront racial injustice, and their efforts to foster change laid the foundation for the burgeoning mass civil rights movement that arose in the 1950s and 1960s.

The World War II years formed a critical historical watershed for black and white women's activism. They were aware of the democratic rhetoric that portrayed the United States as fighting a war not only to protect its own freedom but also to extend that prerogative to others. Many of the women understood this rhetoric to further mean the expansion of freedom and democracy to America's disfranchised and dispossessed, not only in the 1940s but in the decades that followed.

This study explores how African American and white women in all-female and mixed-gender organizations interpreted and dealt with racial issues and how individual women worked against racial injustice in South Carolina during and after World War II. It also examines the accomplishments and limitations of interracial activism as black and white women pursued sometimes similar but occasionally conflicting agendas. Although black and white women sometimes found it difficult to overcome their fear and distrust of each other to pursue activism across racial lines, they realized that doing so gave them the best opportunity to enact change. They therefore took careful but courageous steps as they embarked upon their journey to improve race relations and conditions for African Americans in their region.

The women in this study lived in a deeply divided society. Although African Americans constituted the majority of South Carolina's population, in the years after the Civil War a "master-slave" relationship persisted in the state because it depended on a plantation economy in which whites owned most of the land and blacks were reduced to sharecropping under conditions not much different from slavery.[1] By the end of Reconstruction the pattern of segregation had yet to be fully formed, although its elements were well in the making. It was not until the last decade of the nineteenth century that absolute segregation was established in practice, if not in law. Restrictions on black suffrage were codified in the state constitution of 1895, and in the following year all blacks were prevented from voting in the state. With the repeal of the state civil rights law and the establishment of absolute and legalized segregation, a racially based caste system developed that relegated African Americans to second-class citizenship.[2] Many white South Carolinians used violence and the law to maintain segregation and to keep blacks out of politics. Although racial conventions were thoroughly entrenched in the minds of both black and white South Carolinians, an undercurrent of activism in the years during and after World Wars I and II signaled the dawn of a new era in race relations.[3]

In the 1940s, most South Carolinians lived in rural areas or in towns with fewer than twenty-five hundred people. During the war, when more than 184,000 men and women were in uniform, South Carolina experienced a shortage of labor as did many other states. Textile mills upstate operated around the clock, and employment at the Naval Shipyard in Charleston increased significantly.[4] Although the war increased employment opportunities and many people supported the war effort, African Americans saw little change in racial conditions in South Carolina. Like African Americans throughout the South, South Carolina blacks escaped racial violence and poverty by migrating north, leaving the state with a white majority for the first time in a century. Some of those who remained in South Carolina, however, seized the liberal rhetoric of the war years and began to push for racial equality.[5]

According to historian Susan Lynn, black and white women had endeavored to work together even before World War II through such organizations as the Commission on Interracial Cooperation, formed in 1919. Although such organizations considered and demanded improvements for African Americans, few white women were willing to attack southern racism head-on, although some did question and challenge racial injustice. Among South Carolina white women, Alice Spearman Wright, executive director of the

South Carolina Council on Human Relations, is one notable example of open and vocal activism.[6]

In their demands for full citizenship, black women, in general, were vocal and aggressive, even before they were able to utilize the wartime atmosphere of liberation and democracy. This climate of black activism led to increased challenges to Jim Crow society by both black and white women. Although interracial activism was limited, contacts between women across racial lines created new opportunities for dialogues about race before and during World War II and in the postwar years.[7]

Despite the recent increase in scholarship on racial activism, South Carolina's case has not been examined to the same extent as those of North Carolina, Georgia, Mississippi, and Alabama. Even less work has focused on the roles of black and white women in the state. Their activism was evident even when South Carolina proved resistant to racial change. In 1944, for example, when the U.S. Supreme Court ruled that blacks could not be kept from voting in the Texas Democratic primary, South Carolina led the South's opposition to black voting rights by creating the "South Carolina Plan." This was based on the premise that if the state let political parties hold primaries as private organizations, they would be beyond the reach of federal courts.[8] When the "South Carolina Plan" was proposed, other southern states rejected it and left South Carolina standing on its own as they devised other ways to maintain white supremacy in the primaries.[9]

Not all black and white South Carolinians, however, were willing to accept the status quo, and thus a series of historical watersheds provided the impetus for racial and political activism throughout the state. In 1947, U.S. District Court judge J. Waties Waring ruled in *Elmore v. Rice* that blacks could not be excluded from the Democratic primary and that the South Carolina Democratic Party could not operate as a private club.[10] The following year, black South Carolinians stood in line for hours to exercise their newly won right to vote. In 1951, *Briggs v. Elliott,* the first legal challenge to school segregation to originate in the twentieth-century South, was initiated by African Americans in South Carolina and later became a part of *Brown v. Board of Education.* With the decision of *Brown v. Board of Education* in 1954, African Americans realized that they had a legal ally in the U.S. Supreme Court, and black leaders and their organizations intensified demands for the end of racial segregation and unjust treatment.[11] But this did not come without challenges from white southerners. There was massive resistance to the Supreme Court decision as chapters of the White Citizens' Council formed throughout the state. The first chapters in South Carolina were founded in

Elloree and Orangeburg in 1955 and were dedicated to maintaining segregated schools. By 1956, fifty-five separate councils had been formed.[12] Yet by the end of the decade their effectiveness was negated by what College of Charleston archivist John W. White describes as the "successes of the nationwide civil rights movement," which included the passage of the Civil Rights Act of 1957. Many whites stopped resisting desegregation and began to focus instead on ways to control its pace.[13]

In 1963, in the aftermath of violent opposition to the enrollments of James Meredith and Autherine Lucy, respectively, at the University of Mississippi in 1962 and the University of Alabama in 1956, South Carolina's Harvey Gantt successfully and peacefully integrated Clemson University. Quietly undergirding these efforts to ensure peace were South Carolina businessmen and political officials, including Governor Ernest F. Hollings, who had accepted the fact that segregation as they knew it was at an end. It was Hollings, in fact, who urged South Carolinians to accept the desegregation of Clemson University.[14] The Civil Rights Act of 1964 gave African Americans another tool with which to fight discrimination, and the Voting Rights Act of 1965 saw the arrival of federal marshals in several counties in South Carolina to oversee voter registration and to ensure black participation in the political process.[15]

This study brings that activism from the obscurity of a mostly androcentric version of South Carolina civil rights history and focuses on the ways in which women, through religious and secular organizations, interpreted and reacted to local and national events. African American women had a history of racial activism that extended back to the late nineteenth century. Though there are few extant records, sources indicate that over the decades black women had consistently fought for first-class citizenship for African Americans. It is also important to note that not all white women acquiesced to racial inequities. They often rejected being placed upon the pedestal of white southern womanhood, and they promoted racial improvements even as they often supported racial segregation. Furthermore, both black and white women shaped the public sphere through participation in religious and secular voluntary organizations at a time when the state government was unresponsive to the needs of its poor, dispossessed, and disfranchised citizens.

Although South Carolina's long history of racial oppression and segregation prohibited many black and white women from working together, some formed friendships during their work in shared racial and social reform organizations. Such relationships were possible because these women often came from middle-class backgrounds and had attended college, an environment that exposed some of them to women of different races and prepared them for a lifetime of activism. Improved educational access for African Americans was also a primary concern for black and white women activists.

Shared religious convictions also enabled some of these women to cross racial lines. Black and white women who were members of United Church Women were led by their belief in socially responsible and responsive Christianity. Along these lines, although there is evidence that Jewish and especially Catholic women protested racial injustice in South Carolina, my study focuses primarily on the activism of Protestant women, since they were and remain the largest religious group in South Carolina. They also demonstrated the most consistent record of activism in the state from the 1940s to the 1960s.

The names of black and white women appear throughout this study as a testament to the importance of reaching across the racial divide to tackle such issues as improved race relations, education, and voting rights. Marian B. Paul and Hattie Logan Duckett, for example, members of the South Carolina Federation of Colored Women's Clubs, an affiliate of the National Association of Colored Women, served with Eunice Stackhouse and Kate Tess Davis, members of the South Carolina Federation of Women's Clubs, on the state Commission for Interracial Cooperation and worked to procure political access for African Americans. Numerous unknown women activists played supporting roles as individuals or as members of organizations as racial, educational, and political changes occurred around the state.

This study expands on the growing historiography on racial or civil rights activism in South Carolina. Since the 1990s there has been a plethora of studies acknowledging the roles of women as activists, but few of these studies have taken an in-depth look at the activism of individual women and their organizations. The notable exceptions to this are Joan Marie Johnson's *Southern Ladies, New Women: Race, Region, and Clubwomen in South Carolina, 1890–1930*; Katherine Mellen Charron's *Freedom's Teacher: The Life of Septima Clark*; and to a lesser extent Peter F. Lau's *South Carolina and the Fight for Black Equality since 1865*.[16] My work helps to eliminate this lacuna in the history of women's activism in the Palmetto State.

This study further contributes to the growing historiography of women's racial activism by challenging the notion that women were confined to the domestic sphere both before and particularly after World War II. Despite the emphasis on domesticity after the war, recent scholarship has shown that many black and white women did everything but acquiesce to such demands. The women and organizations I discuss had activist roots that stretched back to the 1930s and earlier in some cases. Further, I argue that maternalism informed some women's activism; that is, black and white women were able to defend their public social and political involvement because they understood that they were ultimately responsible for shaping the world in which their children and grandchildren would live.[17]

An exploration of black women's activism and leadership in all-female and mixed-gender organizations in South Carolina is an important part of this study. Black women most often were not leaders of mixed-gender organizations in the traditional sense. Except in rare instances, they served in supplementary positions as secretaries or office assistants. But they were not excluded from the inner circle of decision makers. Moreover, their membership in and connections to myriad organizations were a crucial component in recruiting and mobilizing African Americans around such important causes as voting rights and equal access to education. Such positioning afforded black women closer ties to the pulse of their communities, which provided them with a level of access therein and augmented their racial and political activism in ways that male leaders were often unable to ascertain.[18]

The activism of white women was often driven by their membership in religiously based, largely Protestant organizations like United Church Women and the YWCA, which supported racial and social activism. Although such organizations were integrated nationally, as were some individual chapters in the South, this was generally not the case in South Carolina.[19] But at the very least, women's religious groups encouraged an exploration of avenues for racial improvement, thereby educating white women and their communities about racial conditions in South Carolina. As white women faced desegregation in South Carolina and in their organizations after the *Brown v. Board of Education* decision in 1954, the trajectory of their activism changed, as did their definition of socially active Christianity. While most secular organizations, already largely conservative, became even more so after the Supreme Court decision, some women's religious groups responded to *Brown* by pushing for racial change throughout South Carolina.

Black women established institutions to serve African Americans through the South Carolina Federation of Colored Women's Clubs, and they assumed leadership and subordinate roles in the NAACP and South Carolina's Progressive Democratic Party. As they grew impatient with their marginalization, they pushed for full inclusion in predominantly white organizations like the YWCA and United Church Women. Black women often founded NAACP chapters with men and were the best connection between African

American communities and black leadership. Many black women leaders also worked with white women leaders, and although these alliances were often fragile, they placed both groups of women in the best position to bring about racial and social change in South Carolina.

Chapter 1 examines the racial activism of black and white South Carolinians during the World War II years as they mobilized around such issues as political participation, education, and racial violence and combated racial injustice through a wide variety of professional, religious, and civic organizations. During these years few black and white women worked together, although they possessed similar ideas about racial and social reform. Many white women supported segregation, but their organizations responded to the liberal rhetoric of the World War II years by enlightening whites about racial injustice in South Carolina. Black women, on the other hand, interpreted this liberal rhetoric as a call to intensify their push for the equalization of teachers' salaries and voting rights for African Americans.

Chapter 2 focuses on the post–World War II years and the early 1950s and specifically on the formation and activism of women's organizations. Although the national organizations of the YWCA and United Church Women mandated integration, activism remained segregated at the local level in South Carolina. As *Brown v. Board of Education* loomed over the South and South Carolina, black and white women prepared themselves and their communities for changes that might result from the decision. Even before 1954, black women and their organizations galvanized support among African Americans and led the campaign for *Elmore v. Rice*, which helped blacks obtain voting rights and gain access to the state Democratic Party. This chapter also considers the activism of liberal whites like Judge J. Waties Waring and explores the difficulties they encountered when they challenged racial injustice and ingrained assumptions about white supremacy.

Chapters 3 and 4 highlight South Carolina's reaction to changes flowing from the *Brown v. Board of Education* decision. These chapters also explore the ways in which white and black women's organizations increased, or in some cases limited, their activism and their affiliations with national organizations in reaction to the decision and the increased racial tensions throughout the state. Finally, chapter 5 analyzes the 1960s as black women continued to focus on voting rights and educating African Americans while some white women redirected their attention to less controversial racial activism on issues such as the pervasive poverty in South Carolina. It also explores how black women carved out a more prominent space for their activism in predominantly white organizations like Church Women United.

As women of South Carolina labored to bring improvements to the state's racial social order, they understood that change was inevitable. Facing obstacles at every turn, they sought to enlighten themselves and others about the racial problems that had long existed in the Palmetto State. Their journey, successes, and failures are the subjects of this exploration.

1

"The Lord Requires Justice of Us"

Civil Rights Activism in World War II South Carolina

If we as Christians see injustices that frustrate some of God's children or hear lies that lash sensitive spirits, it is our duty under God to do our part in ending these things. Failure to do so may cause others to doubt the sincerity of our faith.

WOMEN OF ST. MICHAEL'S EPISCOPAL CHURCH, 1943

In 1943, the women of the predominantly white St. Michael's Episcopal Church in Charleston, South Carolina, addressed the inferior conditions in black schools in the city, explaining that their concern arose from the conviction that "the Lord requires justice of us." They noted that the value of all the black schools in the city was just one-fifth that of white schools, even though each educated approximately the same number of pupils. Taxpayers' money, they insisted, should be used "above all to provide adequate grammar school education for all young people of the city . . . regardless of creed and color."[1]

These women's actions demonstrated the growing attention to racial injustice in South Carolina during World War II. Although they made up a small minority of the population, some citizens of the Palmetto State—female and male, black and white—began to take action to guarantee African American citizens their rights to education, political representation, and protection from racial violence. The challenge over unequal education made by the women of St. Michael's reveals several elements of civil rights activism in South Carolina in the 1940s: the influence of religious convictions, the role and importance of women and their organizations, the possibilities and limitations of racial activism, the role of education as a key civil rights issue, and the impact of World War II's democratic rhetoric on black and white women's efforts to effect change. Although the women of St. Michael's were promoting "separate but equal" facilities, not integration, their statements provide evidence of the tentative steps some South Carolinians were taking to promote racial justice in education.

When the white women at St. Michael's challenged the inequities in public school funding, they addressed only one of the many issues that African Americans had been working on for decades. During the 1940s, predominantly black organizations like the federated black women's clubs, the YMCA and YWCA, Masonic lodges, Odd Fellows, the Knights of Pythias, fraternities and sororities, burial and benevolence societies, and various other private and professional organizations became increasingly active in African American communities throughout South Carolina. In most cases, they supported church- and education-related causes by combining their professional and social activities and giving direction to African American communities. Even though there were significant contributions from these organizations in rural areas like Clarendon County, most of the impetus and strength for activism came from blacks in Columbia, Charleston, Greenville, Orangeburg, and Rock Hill. In Columbia, for example, in 1941, the Palmetto State Teachers Association (PSTA), which had been organized in 1939, appeared before a joint meeting of the South Carolina Senate's Finance Committee and the House Ways and Means Committee to request a pay increase for black teachers.[2]

Educational institutions were also an important source of social and community leadership. In Charleston, African Americans attending such all-black schools as Burke Industrial School, Avery Normal School, and the Catholic Immaculate Conception School often worked with these organizations to celebrate black achievements to resist negative stereotypes of African Americans. The black branch of the Charleston YWCA, for example, scheduled programs focusing on African American contributions to American life and celebrated Negro History Week, whereas local schools did not.[3]

Black women also created and supported organizations to combat racial injustice throughout the South.[4] Before southern black and white women began working together, black women already had a history of organizing, developing, and leading programs to improve the quality of black communities throughout the South. Long before the 1940s, local black women's organizations—the Sunlight Club of Orangeburg, South Carolina, of which Marion Birnie Wilkinson was president; the Tuskegee Women's Club of Tuskegee, Alabama, led by Margaret Murray Washington; and the Neighborhood Union of Atlanta, Georgia, founded by Lugenia Burns Hope—provided support and services to African American communities such as health clinics, educational opportunities, and homes for black youth.[5]

Together, black club women founded larger organizations such as the Southeastern Federation of Colored Women's Clubs, the International Council of Women of the Darker Races, and the National Association of Colored Women (NACW).[6] Wilkinson, Washington, and Hope emerged as leaders in the southern black women's movement and the national black women's movement. These women, along with their husbands, often joined integrated organizations like the Atlanta-based Commission on Interracial Cooperation (CIC), an integrated mixed-gender group founded in 1919 following a spate of race riots throughout the South.[7] There they found southern white women working to improve race relations.[8]

In the Palmetto State, the South Carolina Federation of Colored Women's Clubs (SCFCWC), an affiliate of the NACW, was one of the state's most significant service groups for African Americans even before the 1940s. Founded in 1909 at Sidney Park Colored Methodist Episcopal Church in Columbia by Marion Birnie Wilkinson and Susie Dart Butler of Charleston, Sara B. Henderson and Lizella A. Jenkins Moorer of Orangeburg, and Celia Dial Saxon of Columbia, the SCFCWC's purpose was as follows:

> Promote education of colored women and to hold an educational convention annually . . . Raise the standard at home . . . Work for social, moral, economic, and religious welfare of women and children . . . Protect the rights of women and children who work . . . Secure and enforce the civil and political rights for our groups . . . Obtain for colored women the opportunity of reaching the highest standards in all fields of human endeavors . . . Promote interracial understanding so that justice and goodwill may prevail among all people.[9]

Born in 1873, Wilkinson, a descendant of one of Charleston's antebellum free black families, led a number of organizations in Orangeburg, including the Sunlight Club, an affiliate of the NACW. She was also the founder of the YWCA at South Carolina State College and had been an active member of the South Carolina Committee on Interracial Cooperation (SCCIC) since its founding in 1919, serving on its National Defense Committee during World War II.[10]

The SCFCWC developed strategies to address not only African American concerns statewide but in particular those plaguing indigent young black women. In 1917, under Wilkinson's leadership, South Carolina black club women established the Fairwold Home for Delinquent Girls (later renamed the Wilkinson Home for Orphan Girls) in Cayce to house black girls. The state government had failed to provide "separate but equal" facilities for black teenage girls, who were often placed in county jails or the state penitentiary with hardened criminals for petty crimes or antisocial behavior.[11] Fairwold was built on property secured for black club women by Episcopal bishop Kirkman G. Finlay of the diocese of upper South Carolina. Black club women raised $12,000 to build the home and also received small contributions from the Duke Foundation.[12]

Black women's clubs also supported a host of other causes, such as suffrage, health, education, temperance, and home economics. Although black women forged alliances with white women to correct racial injustice and other social ills, most of their early efforts involved African American institution building and community support as well as introducing poorer blacks to middle-class norms.[13] This activism would assume increasing importance during World War II.

African American Activism and World War II

After Europe descended into war in 1939, African Americans seized opportunities to increase their claims for equal treatment. In 1939, Walter White, executive secretary of the National Association for the Advancement of Colored People (NAACP), anticipated a significant role for the United States in the international conflict. He understood that many African Americans embraced isolationism because they could not imagine fighting a war to end fascism in Europe when they suffered the indignity of segregation in the United States. According to historian Harvard Sitkoff, militant editorials in the black press, threats by African American leaders and protest organizations, and portents of black disloyalty alongside support for the Allied cause were evident even before the war.[14] But White also recognized that black participation in the war was a propitious moment that would underscore their demands for civil rights.[15]

Nationally, African American activists were galvanized by the rhetoric of Allied forces, which invoked democratic principles in their propaganda against Nazi Germany. In turn, activists adopted this propaganda as a central argument in their campaign for civil rights, making it a moral crusade for many Americans during and after the war.[16] African Americans would not repeat the mistakes of World War I, when they had fought for democracy abroad and found it profoundly lacking at home. World War II found activists better prepared and more sophisticated, if not a little skeptical. Patriotism, therefore, was tenuously coupled with hope for the future. American involvement in World War II thus highlighted the hypocrisy of fighting a war for democracy abroad while failing to provide the same rights among the nation's own citizens. African Americans had mixed reactions to this international conflict, and as the war heightened the contradiction between white supremacy and wartime objectives, southern segregationists stepped up their efforts to justify racial policies. By 1941, the increasing political influence of blacks outside the South forced political parties and the federal government to take an interest in the plight of its most overlooked citizens.[17]

African Americans and their white supporters acknowledged the numerous injustices plaguing southern states, such as inequities in education, unequal pay for black teachers, and the denial of voting rights. For black South Carolinians, the war years represented monumental change and, for most, a heightened awareness of racial injustice throughout the state. Instead of expecting patriotism to win them respect at the war's end, African Americans began to use the rhetoric of the World War II years to advance their cause.[18]

World War II, then, not only ended the Depression and stimulated the economy but also provided new economic opportunities that encouraged increased African American migration to areas outside the South. As African American political influence expanded in northern states, the federal government, even if slowly, realized the imperative of intervention on the behalf of black South Carolinians. In 1941, Asa Philip Randolph, leader of the Brotherhood of Sleeping Car Porters, called for a march on Washington to gain equal employment opportunities.

As national civil rights leaders emphasized equal opportunities and access to democracy, black leaders and organizations in South Carolina focused on combating inequitable salaries for black schoolteachers and obtaining voting rights. In 1941, after years of inequality, black teachers asked the state for the same pay as white teachers who held the same certification. NAACP chapters in South Carolina took an active role in this fight. In Sumter, Osceola McKaine, executive secretary of the local NAACP, urged his branch to take action and obtain information about the rules and laws of the state educational system. He and local black businessmen also started a legal defense fund.[19] Given their substantial presence in the teaching profession, it is not surprising that black women featured prominently in this battle. In September

1942, when the Sumter NAACP held a mass meeting at Mt. Pisgah African Methodist Episcopal Church to mount a campaign to equalize teachers' salaries, Columbia activist Modjeska Simkins not only procured South Carolina NAACP attorney Harold R. Boulware, a Howard Law School graduate, to discuss legal procedures, but also outlined the potential social, economic, and educational effects of a salary equalization suit. Simkins had little patience for black passivity when it came to fighting for civil rights.[20] In 1943 she had lambasted members of the predominantly black PSTA when they obsequiously petitioned the South Carolina Board of Education to equalize salaries for black and white teachers with equal qualifications: "'We have come to you a powerful, influential, and authoritative group, begging you to help another group that is not so powerful.' This nauseating paragraph closing the petition presented to the State Board (of education) from the (Palmetto) teachers association fell like a stench bomb among self-respecting Negroes in all walks of life. BEGGING! One group of freeborn citizens BEGGING another freeborn, but certainly not superior group."[21] Simkins admonished African American teachers for groveling rather than fighting for the equality and the rights of full citizenship to which they were entitled.[22] In her mind, demanding that qualified black teachers receive equal payment was an extension of the overall fight for "economic security, human dignity, and for equality of opportunity."[23] Black teachers abandoned their timidity and their gradualist approach and supported the NAACP in its battle to achieve educational parity for African American educators in South Carolina.[24]

The legal fight for equal salaries intensified in 1943 when Boulware filed a suit on behalf of Viola Louise Duvall, chair of the chemistry department at Burke Industrial High School in Charleston, against the Charleston Board of Education for paying higher salaries to white teachers than it did to black teachers with similar qualifications and responsibilities.[25] According to historian R. Scott Baker, Duvall earned $645 per year, while the lowest salary paid to a white teacher with similar qualifications was $1,000.[26] The call for the equalization of teachers' salaries was too much for many white Charlestonians to bear. The city's conservative newspaper, the News and Courier, reflecting the views of many local whites, suggested that all public education be discontinued in South Carolina except for elementary "reading, 'riting and 'rithmetic" in order to forestall granting equal salaries to black teachers.[27] These stall tactics also gave them time to punish black teachers who sued for equal pay: state officials purposefully lost paperwork and unjustly attempted to revoke teachers' certification.[28] But victory was on the horizon. Duvall prevailed when NAACP lawyers, including Thurgood Marshall, convinced Judge J. Waties Waring, a federal judge in the U.S. District Court in Charleston in the case of *Viola Louise Duvall et al. v. J. F. Seignous*, that the city's school board discriminated against black teachers.[29] She won her suit in February 1944.[30] When a similar case, *Thompson v. Columbia School System*, came to trial in Columbia in 1944, Judge Waring also ruled in favor of the plaintiff and ordered the Columbia School Board to equalize the salaries of black teachers for the 1945–46 school year.[31] This would not be the last time that Waring would take on civil rights issues with African Americans.

During the World War II years, African Americans were emboldened by a newfound sense of their equal entitlement to democracy. However, most white southerners were not ready for black assertiveness and responded with intimidation and violence. South Carolina was no exception. In 1940, Ku Klux Klan violence and intimidation increased in upper South Carolina when African Americans registered to vote. Race riots ensued in Greenwood in 1942, when a white man slapped an African American whom he accused of cursing him.[32] In 1943 in Rock Hill a black army lieutenant was addressed as "nigger" and placed under arrest by a bus driver after he had taken the only vacant seat on the bus. In the same year, Ben F. Kirkley Jr., a convict on a Florence County chain gang, was beaten by prison guards when they suspected that he had reported prior physical abuse to the NAACP. The guards asserted that he was the "only god damned nigger" on the gang who "had sense enough" to write a letter of complaint to the NAACP.[33]

The NAACP in South Carolina

Although southern NAACP chapters were often the only means of resistance to segregation and discrimination in African American communities, the threat of racial violence kept many blacks from joining such organizations. Yet, many South Carolina African Americans were not deterred by such atrocities, and their efforts to combat violence against African Americans increased as NAACP membership numbers grew. The first chapters of the NAACP in South Carolina had been founded in 1917 in Charleston and Columbia. By 1938 fewer than twelve hundred African Americans in eight different South Carolina communities belonged to the NAACP. Between 1939, when the South Carolina Conference of the NAACP was founded, and 1948, membership in the organization increased to fourteen thousand. NAACP meetings in the 1940s often considered such themes as "The Negro in the Present Crisis" and "Working toward Democracy in America." In 1941 a "Citizens' Mass Meeting" was held at Zion Baptist Church in Columbia where members of the Interdenominational Ministerial Union, the Civic Welfare League, the NACW, the National Negro Business League, and the NAACP discussed such issues as old-age pensions, discriminatory wages, the need for African American policemen in Columbia, and the need for playgrounds and recreational facilities in black neighborhoods.[34] In June of that year, the NAACP met at Sidney Park Colored Methodist Episcopal Church in Columbia to consider the equalization of school facilities, equal employment in the wartime defense industries, and the right to the franchise. Modjeska Simkins was present at this meeting and was elected corresponding secretary of the state NAACP.[35]

The NAACP's existence was clearly, according to historian Bryant Simon, an "act of defiance" by the "disenfranchised against Jim Crow."[36] Black women, in particular, used the NAACP to gain access to the franchise and entry into the Democratic Party. Lottie Polk Gaffney, the principal and a teacher at Petty Town School in Cherokee, tested the limits of democracy in August 1940 when she and several other African Americans from Cherokee County in upper South Carolina went to register to vote in the presidential election being held that year. When their turn came, the registrar informed Gaffney and those with her: "Darkies ain't never voted in South Carolina and especially Cherokee county. I will not register you." Gaffney and her party promptly went to see the county attorney, who told them that they should have had no trouble voting. Although the attorney informed the registrar that African Americans were eligible to vote, Gaffney and her party were still not allowed to register.[37] Gaffney then sought the assistance of the NAACP and brought suit against the Cherokee County Registration Board, but her efforts were to no avail. After deliberating for thirty minutes, the Spartanburg County federal court jury acquitted the officials of the charge of refusing to register African Americans, citing insufficient evidence; thus, the case, *United States v. Ellis et al.* was lost. The decision had further repercussions for Gaffney, however. Because she had appeared as a witness, she not only lost her position as a teacher but also found that she could no longer obtain employment in any Cherokee County school district.[38] This would not be the last time a black schoolteacher would lose her position due to controversial racial activism.

Throughout the 1940s, the South Carolina NAACP continued to fight to obtain black voting rights in South Carolina.[39] African Americans understood the obstacles they faced. After the U.S. Supreme Court declared the white primary unconstitutional in Texas's *Smith v. Allwright* in 1944, however, white southerners became determined to prohibit black political involvement.[40] Voting-age blacks comprised the majority in approximately half of the Palmetto State's forty-six counties, and white Carolinians were disturbed by this threat to white supremacy. Governor Olin D. Johnston, an avowed white supremacist, was particularly dedicated to ensuring that the vote was limited to white men and declared that the state would use every means at its disposal to stop blacks from voting.[41] In 1944 he called a special session of the legislature and attempted to push through a bill to keep the Democratic primary "pure," that is, white, and to "maintain white supremacy."[42]

Although some white South Carolinians decried the atrocities of racial injustice and discrimination during the war years, state legislators expressed their concern about increasing demands for black civil rights. A statement from the March 16, 1944, edition of *The State*, a Columbia newspaper, outlined the three major fears of many whites. First, the out-migration of blacks to places where their "unalienable rights" were more respected would result in labor shortages for whites, who had always depended on a cheap and compliant labor force. Second, African Americans had become more aware of the legal channels through which they could move toward fuller participation and integration into American economic, educational, and political life. And third, as the abolition of the poll tax qualification for voting became imminent, South Carolina legislators and congressmen feared political liquidation.[43]

White Liberals, Black Activists, and the Progressive Democratic Party

Although racial demagoguery appealed to many in South Carolina who wanted to keep blacks from voting, some whites found it counterproductive to their efforts to improve race relations. Hence they organized in 1944 to "ask white South Carolinians for a drastic revision in our attitudes toward our colored citizens."[44] The group, which was made up of professionals, educators, and community leaders from around the state, including white women leaders like Clelia Peronneau McGowan (a member of the Charleston Interracial Committee) and Wil Lou Gray (the state supervisor of adult schools), issued an appeal, titled "A Statement on the Race Problem in South Carolina," which denounced the "segregation evils inflicted upon the Negroes, apostles of social equality, and supporters of white supremacy."[45] The group did not endorse ending segregation, but rather advocated what it perceived as equitable treatment for African Americans under that system.

Some black leaders attacked incendiary and racist political rhetoric head-on. Modjeska Simkins challenged Governor Johnston to a debate, asserting, "the time has come for a showdown on the white supremacy issue. Demagoguery, haranguing, supposition and emotionalism must be pitted against logic, common sense, science, and the teachings of Jesus Christ."[46] She asked him to prove conclusively that whites were superior to blacks and other people of color. This challenge came a short while after Johnston's declaration to maintain white supremacy in the state Democratic Party. Simkins gave the governor until midnight on April 22, 1944, to accept her challenge. In her estimation, his failure to do so "could be considered as conclusive proof that you and your fellow travelers realize that you have been bluffing yourselves all along."[47] Johnston never replied, but Simkins' vehemence demonstrated that she, like other black women activists, had no qualms about challenging racial injustice, even if it meant confronting officials at the top levels of South Carolina's state government.[48]

In an effort to counteract black exclusion from the state Democratic Party and South Carolina's political arena, activists Osecola McKaine and John McCray, editor of the *Lighthouse and Informer* in Columbia, founded the South Carolina Colored Democratic Party in 1944, after the state legislature converted the Democratic Party into a private club to preserve its racial exclusivity. In July 1944, members of the South Carolina Colored Democratic Party, which was renamed the Progressive Democratic Party (PDP)[49] in April 1944, attended the Democratic National Convention in Chicago to support President Roosevelt's nomination for a fourth term in office and to attempt to unseat the all-white delegation from South Carolina.[50] The very presence of PDP members at the convention embarrassed the state's white power structure by revealing its failure to encourage the practice of democracy among all South Carolinians.[51]

Black women like Sarah Z. Daniels and Dr. Annie Bell Weston had helped to found the PDP. Historian Vicki Crawford has argued that the marginalization of black women in the civil rights movement obscures an understanding of their participation and leadership at the local level. Although men dominated at the national and regional levels, black women's activism was strongest on the local level, where they were able to extend their roles within church communities and secular organizations.[52] This was no less the case among black women in South Carolina.

Daniels and Weston were leaders and members of the NAACP and the SCFCWC, where they had blazed a path of activism. When the PDP established a woman's auxiliary in 1945, black women jumped at the opportunity to serve in leadership positions within it and the main body of the organization. In 1945, Daniels, president of the Manning NAACP, was appointed auxiliary chairman of the PDP. An educator, home demonstration agent, and president of the Clarendon County Teachers Association, Daniels had organized PDP auxiliaries in Manning and Summerton.[53] She was enthusiastic about accepting the position and about her efforts to get eligible blacks to register to vote: "I consider my appointment to speak when and where I can for the Progressive Democratic Party a privilege and I am glad to accept."[54] Using her leadership in the Manning NAACP, Daniels made voter registration "the number one objective."[55]

Like Daniels, Annie Bell Weston held membership not only in all-female organizations but also in mixed-gender groups. Born in Columbia in 1894, Weston graduated from the historically African American Benedict College in Columbia and was the first woman to receive the Doctor of Humanities degree from the institution. She served as secretary and women's director for the PDP during and after World War II.[56] Also a member of the SCFCWC, Weston urged women to increase their demands for access to the ballot. Like many other black leaders of the time, she made references to African Americans who had fought for democracy abroad during World War II but were denied such rights at home.

Like other women activists, Weston made connections between women's right to vote and their roles as wives and mothers. In doing so, Weston urged black women to put the welfare of African Americans before their individual concerns: "Women must think of their people [and] then of themselves. Think what it will mean to our families to help elect those who govern us. Think women what it means to have your G.I. Joe come back from the battle having given Democracy to others, but denied it himself. If this prevails blame yourselves. If they lose hope blame your own lack of integrity. Women, let us register! Women, let us register everyone else that we can. Then let us all vote!"[57] Weston insisted that black women had to expand their domestic responsibilities to help their spouses and their children, whose futures were tied to obtaining full citizenship for African Americans.[58]

As state secretary of the PDP, Weston was committed to harnessing black women's skills as political activists. In October 1945, African American representatives met at an afternoon session of a meeting of the National Council of Negro Democrats at Benedict College in Columbia to discuss the role of blacks in southern politics. Weston moderated a panel titled "Women's Place in the Political Life of the Democratic Party."[59] In January 1946, at the PDP's state committee meeting, members recommended that "women be appointed in each precinct, city, and country organization to direct activities among women."[60] Throughout 1946, black women from around the state sought Weston's advice as they formed PDP auxiliaries in their towns. But Weston placed particular emphasis on black men, who continued to doubt women's political efficacy. In May 1946, at the PDP's biennial convention, she gave a talk titled "Some Pointers on Organizing Women," which was clearly designed to impress upon men the importance of women's activism in gaining political access for all black South Carolinians. Such canvassing also held great potential for increasing the black electorate, because women were not required to pay a poll tax in South Carolina.[61]

As black South Carolinians struggled for political access in the early 1940s, they found meager but significant support from small numbers of whites. A group of prominent Columbia whites, including club women Eunice Stackhouse and Charlotte Stevenson, both of whom were also members of the United Council of Church Women (UCCW) and the Southern Regional Council, attempted to get black voters on the rolls by petitioning the Democratic State Convention to appoint a committee to study the issue of black suffrage and make plans to allow qualified blacks to vote in the Democratic primaries.

Stackhouse, in particular, had long worked to improve conditions for African Americans in South Carolina. Like many liberal and reform-minded southern whites, she was aware of how unpopular her ideas were; in 1969 she recalled that "a lot of my friends thought I was very strange."[62] Born in Blenheim, South Carolina, in 1885, Eunice Temple Ford Stackhouse was a 1904 graduate of Limestone College in Gaffney and had attended the University of Chicago and later the University of South Carolina School of Social Work. She was interested in improving adult education for all South Carolinians. Governor Johnston appointed her to serve on the state advisory committee on adult education in 1943. As a member of the South Carolina Federation of Women's Clubs, Stackhouse worked to improve conditions at the Colored Boys Industrial School and to found a similar institution for black girls in 1949.[63] She cultivated working relationships with African Americans throughout the 1940s, 1950s, and 1960s through her involvement in such organizations as the South Carolina State Probation, Parole, and Pardon Board (she was the first woman to serve on this board), the South Carolina Conference of Social Work, the South Carolina Citizens Committee on Children and Youth, and the South Carolina Council on Human Relations. She also served on the board of trustees of Columbia's Good Samaritan Waverly Hospital for Negroes.[64]

Other activist white South Carolinians also demonstrated that they recognized the hypocrisy of war rhetoric that coexisted with the denial of African Americans' right to suffrage. These white Democrats acknowledged that many blacks shared with them similar class and educational backgrounds that had prepared them for full citizenship. Hence, they urged the South Carolina Democratic Party's leadership to permit African American membership:

> Many of our Negro citizens are keenly desirous of exercising their rights of citizenship. We believe that they are now fitted by education and experience to assume the responsibilities that go with citizenship. We do not believe that it is either necessary or advisable that the Democratic Party be thrown open to Negroes indiscriminately. Nor do we believe that anything but good would come from establishing minor educational and character qualifications for membership for whites in the party. We believe that carefully considered qualifications of this kind, applied to whites and blacks, might result in a definite improvement in our political institutions.[65]

Many white South Carolinians had long been invested in limiting African American access to the franchise. Although blacks had attempted to vote in the primary since 1934, Democratic Party rules had prohibited them from doing so unless they had cast their ballots for the party since 1876, an act most South Carolina blacks found difficult to prove.[66] Moreover, in 1944 the South Carolina House of Representatives defeated a bill to abolish the poll tax as a prerequisite for voting in the state. One representative claimed that abolition of the tax would only serve "to ram the Negro down our throats." Integrated organizations like the South Carolina division of the Southern Regional Council (SRC), which replaced the State Interracial Committee in 1944, helped blacks register to vote as a result of a resolution adopted by the group's executive committee in 1945. According to Marion A. Wright, state chairman of the organization, it was "felt to be the duty of white members of our committee to lend assistance to South Carolina Negroes seeking to register for voting purposes where such Negroes meet all legal qualifications." Wright called on liberal white members to uphold their commitment to racial justice in the state.[67]

Many southern whites resisted challenges to the racial order, but those concerned with solving racial problems in South Carolina realized that blacks and whites had to work together. Women proved especially amenable to activism across racial lines in these early years. In 1940 in Florence, members of the State Interracial Committee met to discuss organizing a county interracial committee. This meeting included black and white women in addition to representatives from various denominations, civic and service groups, and the white City Federation of Women's Clubs.[68] The founders of these interracial committees realized the importance of encouraging mutual understanding to address pressing social and racial problems. The Richland County Interracial Committee urged members to present issues of concern to both races.

South Carolina white women like Adele Minahan of Charleston, Mrs. Leon S. Holley of Aiken, and Kate Tess Davis of Orangeburg, who were also members of the UCCW, had a history of involvement in integrated organizations. Kate Tess Davis had been involved in interracial activism at least since the 1920s.[69] In the 1930s she was a member of the South Carolina Council for the Common Good (SCCCG), a coalition of white women's organizations founded in Columbia in 1935 and dedicated to the "betterment of living conditions in South Carolina."[70] Members addressed such issues as housing shortages, conservation, tuberculosis, infant and maternal mortality, and interracial problems.[71] In the 1940s, Davis, who also served on the state executive board of the Southern Regional Council, chaired the SCCCG's Interracial Committee, whose members were primarily interested in studying conditions among black Carolinians. With only vague objectives, Davis urged a "program of education and cooperation."[72] These women did not espouse social equality between blacks and whites in South Carolina. When it came to race relations, SCCCG members' attitudes were often paternalistic. During World War II, for example, they argued that the eradication of syphilis was necessary so that more black men would be able to assume military service, thereby lessening the demand for white men. However, the organization also supported the creation of industrial schools for African Americans and permitted a guest to give a presentation titled "Problems of Inter-Racial Relations" at their annual meeting.[73]

Black and white women also worked together through state and local branches of the Committee on Interracial Cooperation. The SCCIC and the Charleston Interracial Committee formed subcommittees to study the principles of federal aid to education, to find ways to extend public library services to both races, and to obtain longer school terms and more vocational training for blacks. At this time, however, the goal of these efforts was not racial equality but the creation of equal facilities for both races.

The SCCIC included such black women officers as Marion Birnie Wilkinson, who headed the organization's National Defense Committee during World War II, and Georgetown native Marian Baxter Paul, who served as secretary of the SCCIC in 1941 and 1942. These women often cooperated with white women leaders like Mary E. Frayser, chairman of the Planning Committee, who formed a "Leisure Time" committee to support the development of state parks and to establish municipal playgrounds for blacks. The interracial commission also established a committee to create a State Industrial School for Negro Girls.[74] In 1943, at the annual meeting of the SCCIC, for which the theme was "Tensions, What We Can Do to Relieve Them," members were encouraged to urge the black and white newspapers throughout the state to ease racial tensions.[75] Even as they sought solutions to South Carolina's racial problems through the SCCIC, some black women questioned whites' commitment to substantial and lasting change. Modjeska Simkins recalled that some white SCCIC members were "well-meaning people, but for the most part they were paternalistic. . . . [I]t was, as they say now, more 'rhetoric' than anything else. . . . Whenever it got right down to where we said, 'Now, what action should we take?,' usually there was a back out. Not only on the part of paternalistic whites, but on the part of the blacks who had called themselves those who wanted to do something."[76]

Women, Religiously Inspired Organizations, and the United Council of Church Women

It was religion that most often provided a foundation for southern black and white women to come together. For example, the founder of the all-white Association of Southern Women for the Prevention of Lynching (ASWPL), Jessie Daniel Ames, had a history of not only working in integrated organizations like the Committee on Interracial Cooperation but also using the best resources of black and white women's religious organizations like Methodist missionary societies, the UCCW, and the YWCA to combat lynchings throughout the South.[77] In 1942, when a black man suspected of assaulting a white woman was taken from a city jail in Sikeston, Missouri, and dragged through the African American district and then set on fire, a group of Methodist women wrote to Missouri governor Forrest C. Donnell expressing their satisfaction that he had formed an investigative committee: "We join in your sorrow over the tragedy of the lynching." The letter was signed by Methodist women from North Carolina, Georgia, and South Carolina.[78]

Ames worked closely with the SCCIC and often attended its annual meetings and corresponded with its members. Ames was schooled in what historian Jacquelyn Dowd Hall called "the politics of interracialism," and her tactics were perhaps too aggressive for more conservative South Carolinians.[79] When she attended an interracial conference in Sumter in 1941, she angered local whites by pointing out their failures in front of an integrated audience. One local Sumter white woman referred to Ames as a "rabble-rouser" whose remarks to the group only served to "pour oil on troubled waters."[80] Although Ames criticized southern racial injustice and attended integrated meetings, she did not consider the African American leaders she encountered to be her equals. Nor did she invite black women to become members of the AS-WPL. According to historian Bettye Collier-Thomas, Ames, like many other white liberals of the time, often dealt with African Americans in a patronizing manner.[81]

Efforts to forge interracial projects were characterized by timidity on the part of both black and white women activists. For many years, black and white southern church women had established educational programs dedicated to developing church and community leadership among black women, but with the understanding that those women would work with fellow African Americans, not with white women. Summer schools with black and white facilities and day-long interracial forums in southern states were sponsored by white Baptist, Methodist, and Presbyterian women in cooperation with black women and their churches. For southern women activists, maintaining segregated living facilities at these forums and working through separate organizations was the best way to enact change without raising the suspicion and animosity of their local communities. But more than that, it again reified some white women's reluctance to understand and work with black women as their social equals.

Efforts to improve conditions for African Americans throughout the South were the mainstay of black and white women's organizations throughout the war years. In 1943, eighty southern Methodist women met in Atlanta and declared: "The denial of equality of opportunity between races in America, particularly in the South, is a denial of the Christian faith in the unity of all mankind." This declaration from the Southeastern Jurisdiction of the Woman's Society of Christian Service of the Methodist Church was signed by women from Virginia, Kentucky, Tennessee, North Carolina, South Carolina, Georgia, Florida, Alabama, and Mississippi.[82] In this same year, the South Carolina Conference Central Jurisdiction of the Woman's Society of Christian Service of the Methodist Church invited Thelma Stevens, executive secretary of the Department of Christian Social Relations and Local Church Activities, Woman's Division of Christian Service, in New York City to speak at an integrated meeting at Bethel Methodist Church in Greer, South Carolina. The theme of the meeting was "Planning for Peace," which quite likely included racial peace in addition to military peace.[83] The theme may have been informed by increased racial tensions as African Americans intensified their demands for civil rights.

As we saw at the beginning of this chapter, the women of St. Michael's Episcopal Church, one of Charleston's most prominent white churches, declared in 1943 that "the Lord requires justice of us." These Charleston blue bloods acknowledged the inferior quality of the city's black schools and recognized their civic duty to all children in the city and declared that taxpayers' money should be used to educate all young people of the city and county of Charleston "regardless of creed and color." These women clearly saw their duty and that of taxpayers in Christian terms and asserted, "God loves all men and desires that all men fulfill their lives. If we as Christians see injustices that frustrate some of God's children or hear lies that lash sensitive spirits, it is our duty under God to do our part in ending these things. Failure to do so may cause others to doubt the sincerity of our faith."[84] Although committed to Christian doctrine as a mandate for racial justice, these women did not challenge segregation itself. They wanted adequate funding for black schools, but their sense of justice did not extend to the integration of black and white children.[85] Like many southern whites, these women focused on an improved version of Jim Crow, not its eradication.

Other religiously based organizations in South Carolina expressed concern about the education and welfare of the dispossessed and disfranchised around the state.[86] Although members of the United Council of Church Women were committed to improving conditions for blacks in South Carolina, their racial work also reflected a commitment to maintaining segregation in South Carolina. "Separate but equal," with an emphasis on "separate," most often dictated the extent of their activism. The extension of library services for both races clearly meant access to different facilities. Vocational education was most often located in predominantly African American schools, and the sentiment of the time was such that school administrators, who were mostly white, did not see the need for more substantial training for South Carolina blacks. It also appears that black and white women differed in their opinions on the use of federal aid for education. White women, like most whites in the state and, indeed, the South generally, favored federal aid to support an educational system that was truly "separate but equal." However, black women and many black South Carolinians wanted not only improvements in black schools but also access to predominantly white ones.

Church women's most vital activism often occurred not in individual

churches or denominations but in female-led Protestant ecumenical organizations with religious foundations. The purpose of the UCCW, which was
founded in 1941 as an interdenominational organization and affiliated with
the National Council of Churches (NCC), was to "unite church women in
their allegiance to their Lord and Savior, Jesus Christ, through a program
looking to their integration in the total life and work of the church, and to
the building of a world Christian community."[87]

The UCCW, which included millions of Protestant church women world-
wide, never questioned black women's inclusion in the organization. At its
founding, when the national assembly debated whether such a stipulation
should be included in the new constitution, the consensus was that "interdenominational unquestionably meant interracial." As a matter of course,
annual and regular meetings were integrated. But the national UCCW,
which welcomed members who did not represent a denomination, understood that many women struggled with their own perceptions about race.
Hence, its members were urged to first examine their own attitudes about
race relations in the United States and then to expand their knowledge
of other cultures and races.[88] The national organization also insisted that
membership in local councils include women from black churches, and in
the 1940s it refused to recognize local chapters that were not integrated.
Consequently, many local chapters of UCCW were not officially affiliated
with the national council.

During World War II, the national organization's primary focus was on
the war effort at home and abroad, although a 1943 article in UCCW's magazine, *The Church Woman*, acknowledged that Christian women had a duty to
recognize and confront the problem of race relations in America. The author
asserted that

> existing attitudes and practices toward racial groups in America tend
> to wipe out the sacredness of individual personality; that they open the
> way to dangerous propaganda; that they create unsalutary reverbera-
> tions around the world; that they hamper the possibility for America's
> effective leadership among the nations; that they hinder democracy
> from being exemplary; that they are stumbling blocks for a just and
> durable peace; that they threaten the Christian movement around the
> world; and finally, that unless changed, they may become the grounds
> for an even greater war for the supremacy of the races.[89]

In 1944 the UCCW proved its commitment nationally by supporting the
establishment of a permanent Fair Employment Practices Committee in the

federal government to protect black workers from discrimination in companies with government contracts. In 1945 the board of the UCCW held a meeting in Washington, D.C. Even though advance preparations had been made, black women's hotel reservations were not honored. In response, all of the participants withdrew from the hotel and chose instead to board with Washington residents.[90] At this same meeting, UCCW delegates met with U.S. senators and representatives to press for civil rights legislation, specifically an anti-poll-tax bill. Both of these events were covered by the national media, a method the organization used effectively to further their cause for racial equality.[91]

The UCCW of Columbia, originally founded as the Woman's Interdenominational Missionary Union, first proposed an affiliation with the national organization in early January 1944. Even before the organization changed its name and became officially affiliated with the Council of Church Women in 1946, most of its efforts in the 1940s focused on public welfare, migrant workers, and Native Americans.[92] It is likely that its members chose to focus on these very specific issues because they did not want to challenge the prevailing social order. During their World Day of Prayer in March 1943, members voted to give Christian literature to Native American students in government schools and to lend assistance to workers in migrant camps throughout the state.

Simply affiliating with the national UCCW did not mean that the local chapters were prepared to implement its racial agenda. UCCW of Columbia did not actively welcome black women, and it addressed social issues primarily by providing funds for segregated institutions. Its members supported the resumption of the Annual Christian Conference of Negro Women at Benedict College in 1947, voting to sponsor three women at the conference.[93] They also supported a day nursery at the college. However, black women were hesitant to make use of it, a point white women made note of in their minutes. Understandably, black women probably did not trust their intentions and turned to predominantly black women's organizations for assistance. This tension was not unusual among black and white southern women. Black women believed that southern white women often sought to usurp their authority over their children and that they did not have a clear understanding of the particular trials that black women faced in the Jim Crow South. They further felt that white women's efforts for "Negro betterment" often amounted to nothing more than a concern for "better" servants.[94] Despite this, black women understood that dismantling racism required establishing working relationships with white women who were amenable to the righteous cause of racial justice and who, according to historian Bettye Collier-Thomas, most often had the ears of and influence with powerful white men, "their fathers, husbands, brothers, sons, and lovers."[95]

In keeping with the support of segregated institutions, UCCW of Columbia also assisted the Girls Industrial School and the Negro Boys School by establishing youth programs. Both were created for wayward black youth and to fight juvenile delinquency in the state. Juvenile delinquency was a consistent issue for both black and white women throughout the 1940s. Members were concerned about juvenile delinquency because many women and men were employed at Fort Jackson, the city's army base, or were serving in the armed forces during the war. The federal government had made few provisions for child care assistance, and recreational activities in community facilities had been reduced to meet the demands of wartime production and the armed forces, thus removing an outlet for youthful aggression. Concerns mounted about women deserting domestic life and their children, thereby contributing to juvenile delinquency. Church women particularly wanted to curb delinquency among young women who lived near wartime production centers. The national UCCW addressed this issue in tandem with the federal government, waging a campaign to end sexual delinquency in war production areas. Accordingly, UCCW of Columbia members pressured their city officials for action, including writing to the mayor regarding the seriousness of this issue.[96]

UCCW of Columbia was also committed to fighting illiteracy in the state and supported "opportunity schools." Originally developed by Wil Lou Gray, supervisor of adult schools in South Carolina and a member of both the UCCW and SCCIC, opportunity schools were state-supported institutions designed to allow adult students to earn a high school diploma and learn a vocation simultaneously. These schools were particularly beneficial to returning World War II veterans, who had often left high school to enlist in the military.[97]

Gray, often referred to as the "First Citizen of South Carolina," was a pioneer in adult education. Born in Laurens County in 1883, she earned an A.B. degree from Columbia College in 1903. She later attended Winthrop College in Rock Hill, where she studied the latest teaching methods and was inspired to create educational opportunities for illiterate South Carolinians.[98] Like other white South Carolina women, Gray aimed not to obtain social equality but rather to establish educational equality, leading to improvements for both races. Education, in her estimation, was an important part of teaching the disadvantaged how to behave more like the privileged class. Gray, who was later a member of the South Carolina division of the Southern Regional Council, did not challenge segregation; rather, she worked within its confines for racial and social improvements. Indeed, she believed that desegregation should occur slowly.[99] UCCW of Columbia followed in her footsteps in supporting an all-black opportunity school in Seneca, South Carolina.[100] Some African American women, however, took issue with Gray's limited agenda and remained skeptical of her intentions for decades. When the first opportunity school opened in 1921 in Tamassee, South Carolina, in the foothills of the Blue Ridge Mountains, it was for whites only. Modjeska Simkins recalled that she had "never forgiven [Gray] for calling her school the Opportunity School and opening it only to whites." She further asserted that although a black opportunity school was organized in 1932 with the same facilities and resources as the white school, Simkins believed that Gray should have realized sooner that "black youth needed opportunity as well as white youth." She declared, "I've never forgiven her for not being able to see that."[101]

Members of UCCW of Columbia, then, did not ignore racial issues, but they did uphold Jim Crow by advocating only slow and conservative changes. Throughout most of the 1940s their agenda was limited to efforts that merely informed its membership about racial injustice in South Carolina. But even these tentative steps were important, because they reveal that some progressive-minded white church women bravely and sometimes stealthily encouraged their community to question and analyze the state's racial status quo.

The Young Women's Christian Association in South Carolina

Like the UCCW, the YWCA recognized black and white women's interaction as a conduit for solving many of society's ills in the 1940s.[102] From the time of its national organization in 1906, the YWCA offered the potential for women to cooperate across racial and religious lines. Its purpose was as follows:

> To unite in one body the Young Women's Christian Associations of the United States; to establish, develop, and unify such Associations; to participate in the work of the World's Young Women's Christian Association; to advance the physical, social, intellectual, moral, and spiritual interests of young women. The ultimate purpose of all its efforts shall be to seek to bring young women to such a knowledge of Jesus Christ as Saviour and Lord as shall mean for the individual young woman fullness of life and development of character, and shall make the organization as a whole an effective agency in the bringing in of the Kingdom of God among young women.[103]

The organization took this task seriously. Southern white women who worked to improve race relations and conditions for African Americans were often able to trace their activism back to some exposure to the YWCA, an experience that often included working with black women. In April 1940, the YWCA's National Student Council asked the YWCA to appoint a commission to study its interracial experience. One of the commission's recommendations was that all local associations include African American women and girls in the mainstream of association life. They were also not to plan separately for any group of women, be they white, African American, or other, and all salary and wage differences for whites and African Americans doing the same work were to be eliminated.[104] According to historian Judith Weisenfeld, YWCA delegates voted at the national convention in 1940 to form a commission for interracial concerns. Four years later, the commission's findings were published in *Interracial Practices in Community YWCAs*, by Juliet Ober Bell, a white researcher, and Helen J. Wilkins, a black woman who helped conduct the study. Bell and Wilkins conceded that YWCAs were indeed segregated and that members needed to work to make the organization and its activism more inclusive.[105]

In communities with rigid patterns of racial separation, the national YWCA still urged local associations to use the Interclub Council or other intergroup activities to bridge gaps between different groups of women. The objective was to bring these groups "progressively closer to inclusive functioning," and the national YWCA suggested that in some communities "individuals who are ready for participation in joint clubs be given that opportunity, even though the general constituency may not be ready for such experience."[106]

Black and white women were drawn to the YWCA for a number of reasons. The YWCA was the largest and one of the most influential liberal women's organizations of the twentieth century. It offered social and recreational activities often not found in other organizations, and it provided opportunities for women to exercise their leadership abilities. Integrated at the national level, the YWCA was one of the few national women's organizations to accept black women, who made up approximately 10 percent of its membership before the founding of groups like the UCCW.[107] Unfortunately, local YWCAs in the South were often insensitive to the needs of black women, because white women did not understand or ignored the depth of the problems in black communities.[108] Moreover, black women who held leadership positions within their segregated YWCAs did not wish to have their authority usurped by white women or have white women work on their behalf. Rather, they wanted to develop equal and mutually respectful working relationships with them.

In many southern states, student YWCAs took on the cause of interracial activism even before the local branches did. Race was an important subject of discussion in student YWCAs between the 1930s and the 1950s.[109] By the end of the 1930s, young college women encouraged the YWCA to examine the effects of discrimination on the organization and to consider the possibility of integration. Funded by the National Board, student YWCAs in southern states attempted to alter the racial practices by introducing college women to social Christianity, with the hope that its message would inspire these students to reshape southern society. Referred to as the Social Gospel in the late nineteenth century, with origins in the Second Great Awakening, social Christianity encouraged believers to apply Christian teachings of brotherhood to daily relationships.[110] It inspired a new understanding of religion that emphasized using Christian activism to ameliorate the physical, spiritual, and social ills of American society.[111] Although urban and labor conditions comprised the student YWCAs' agenda at first, the topic of race relations was later included.

The development of a religious philosophy of life within the student YWCA enabled young white women, according to scholar Frances Sander Taylor, to "acknowledge and overcome the racism ingrained in them since birth and to advocate radical changes in the fabric of southern life." Taylor went on to say that "this religious philosophy of life entailed the creation of an active, critical role of women in a society which still clung to a strong tradition of genteel southern womanhood."[112] On northern college campuses, YWCAs and YMCAs invited African American students to become members, although most blacks did not participate fully in their programs.[113] White women often came quite willingly to the student YWCA, because they realized that the pedestal upon which white southern womanhood was placed was more often than not a lie constructed by white men who sought to retain control over them.[114] Involvement in student YWCAs prepared many of these women for lifelong careers as social activists.

In South Carolina, the YWCA chapters in Rock Hill, Charleston, and Columbia struggled to address racial issues. The YWCA established at Winthrop College for Women in Rock Hill in 1899 demonstrates how attempts at activism became manifest in an all-female collegiate environment. Winthrop's student YWCA endeavored to exert religious influence on its students. In the 1930s it established a committee on race to "seek wisdom and guide our students in action on this most pressing and burning problem."[115] To this end, Winthrop sponsored a series of on-campus intercollegiate meetings on race relations in 1940 and 1941. This was a radical move for the time in South Carolina.[116]

Mary E. Frayser, the white faculty adviser of the Interracial Affairs Committee, who organized the meetings, did so cautiously. Born in 1868, Frayser had been predisposed to social activism by her parents, who participated extensively in business, social, civic, and church work. A well-informed activist, Frayser became involved in many efforts for reform in child labor, legislation, education, recreation, feminism, world peace, and race relations.[117] White women activists like Frayser realized the controversial nature of their activism, and their motive may very well have been to promote increased racial understanding rather than justice.[118] In a letter to Frayser in 1940, Elizabeth Stinson, secretary of the Winthrop YWCA, wrote, "I believe we are agreed on the fact that only the white race will attend the meeting in as much as we feel it wise to move not too rapidly in the direction of race relations."[119]

The "interracial" conference, thus, was meant only for white college students and black and white leaders. White women's cautious tones are evident in their correspondence.[120] When advertising for the meeting, Frayser and Thelma Hicklin, president of the Winthrop YWCA, emphasized that it was not to be "radical"; rather, it would question the social and economic progress of the South as it pertained to better educational opportunities for low-income blacks and whites. By including low-income whites and focusing on improvements for all impoverished South Carolinians, white women activists sought to defuse the racial implications of their agenda. The letter was carefully constructed so as not to raise the suspicion or ire of Rock Hill's white community. According to Hicklin:

> No emotional or radical presentation is proposed but the question of social and economic progress for all in the South is intimately associated with better educational opportunities for whites and Negroes in the lower-income or no-income brackets.
>   This question will receive consideration as will the matter of what constitutes adequate education for both races of the underprivileged and the inequalities of rural and urban educational opportunity for both.[121]

Although the conference was not open to black students, it brought together influential white and black leaders such as Jessie Daniel Ames, president of the ASWPL and executive secretary of the CIC, and Dr. W. A. Whitaker, president of South Carolina State College, who lectured on portions of the general topic "Providing Adequate Educational Opportunities at All Levels and to Both Races." It also included local white women like Laura Smith Ebaugh, a sociology professor at Furman University, and Kate Tess Davis, who at the 1941 forum gave talks on "Proven Methods for Developing Negro Leadership" and "The Working Relationship between College and Adult

Interracial Committees."[122] The Findings Committee, entirely female save one, found that a number of changes and improvements were necessary in educational resources and race relations in South Carolina. Committee reports also included "accepting the responsibility of interesting others in the study of interracial relations and problems of justice and fair dealing to the underprivileged whites and Negroes." They also opposed the unequal dissemination of funds appropriated for black and white schools, encouraged the impartial enforcement of laws without regard to race, and favored fair representation of blacks and their role in American culture in print matter, screen, and radio.[123] Thus, the committee did not alienate reform-minded whites by emphasizing racial equality in its findings, but rather advocated improvements in conditions and facilities for African Americans and whites alike.

Although the conference was clearly a step in the right direction, some Winthrop YWCA members wanted the organization to go further in its efforts to eradicate racial and economic inequalities and wanted to act in tandem with black students. A 1941–42 report submitted by Caroline Marion, president of the Winthrop YWCA, reveals that although white students found the conference "very enlightening and very worthwhile," they saw it as "only a small beginning of a slow climb to what they hoped would some day be a large and powerful conference which would be truly interracial."[124] While they appreciated being educated about South Carolina's racial problems, they recognized the hypocrisy of focusing on "interracial relations" when there had been no black students in attendance with whom they could discuss the topic.

Even these tentative efforts on the part of the Winthrop YWCA were cut short by the very racial conventions the organization sought to eradicate.[125] In a 1944–45 report, the president of the Winthrop YWCA, Dorothy Kirkley, was distressed that the discussions about interracial activism in Winthrop's YWCA program had not developed into integrated activism. The Findings Committee faced strong opposition in efforts to get school officials to allow integrated meetings. Their petition to the trustees of Winthrop College to repeal the ruling forbidding such attendance had been denied. Moreover, Kirkley was disappointed when Dr. Benjamin Mays, a black Baptist minister and president of Morehouse College, was rejected as a vesper speaker. A Greenwood County native, Mays was a sharecropper's son with a doctorate from the University of Chicago Divinity School. In 1944 he was elected vice president of the Federal Council of Churches (FCC), an interracial Protestant organization founded in 1908, and influenced members to assume an active role in combating southern racial issues. His position in the FCC, its liberal policies, and the fact that Mays was openly critical of segregation made it dangerous for him to come to Winthrop as a vesper speaker.[126] In fact, in the mid-1940s, few southern white churches would have dared to invite a black man to speak to their congregations about segregation.[127]

Kirkley and other Winthrop YWCA members had been motivated by the discussions about race to which they had been exposed. They wanted to act on their newfound knowledge and form close working relationships with students at Friendship and Clinton Colleges, predominantly black institutions in Rock Hill. Winthrop YWCA members met with advisers and faculty members from these institutions and discovered that black students were amenable to working with them to improve race relations in South Carolina. However, Kirkley and others had met with them as individuals, not as representatives of the college.[128]

Winthrop YWCA members believed that "a more liberal step forward" was necessary. Many of Winthrop's students had been informed and inspired by the Social Gospel and were ready to challenge racial injustice. But the times in which Kirkley and other like-minded students operated prevailed. Students who were motivated by their convictions often found themselves acting without the explicit approval of their colleges. In 1944, when Kirkley was invited to attend the annual meeting of the National Intercollegiate Christian Council (NICC) at Atlanta University to study racial problems in the South, she did so as a representative of the NICC, not Winthrop College.[129]

Although significant changes would occur in other YWCAs in the state much later, the timing for such activity at Winthrop was unpropitious. The interracial programs of the YWCA varied with the locality. In many states, interracial student YWCAs gave students of both races a chance to gain familiarity with one another, not to promote racial justice. In the Deep South, the only vigorous work among students of both races was in Atlanta.[130] When a regional meeting of student YWCAs was held at Atlanta University in 1944, for example, a delegation from Winthrop attended.

In South Carolina, merely using the term "interracial" did not mean that black and white college students would work together to bring about change. In fact, the majority of southern white students in the 1940s adamantly supported segregation. The precarious position of the Winthrop YWCA was further exacerbated by the policies at the national level. At the Seventeenth National YWCA Conference, which met in Atlantic City in 1946, the national body issued an Interracial Charter in which it pledged to eradicate racial segregation and discrimination within its organization and society at large by integrating African American women and girls into the full program of the YWCA. It further mandated that local organizations do the same, particularly in communities where the races were rigidly separated.[131]

Some members found the national YWCA's declaration not only problematic but also un-Christian. In 1946, Eleanor V. Nichols, the acting general secretary of the Winthrop YWCA, was convinced that an organization dedicated to a "combining of the religious forces on campus" was necessary. She further felt, as did Winthrop president Henry R. Sims, that the national YWCA's Interracial Charter, its support of social, economic, and political reforms, and the campus YWCA's focus on racial activism were not in keeping with the tenets of a Christian education.[132] This thinking was shared by many other historically white colleges throughout the South. They consequently rejected the national YWCA's Interracial Charter and forbade their students from participating in integrated meetings. Others banned the YWCA, and the YMCA for that matter, from their campuses entirely because of its policy on integration.[133]

Winthrop YWCA members debated retaining their membership in the national body, which supported its programs financially, and accepting its mandate, but ultimately they succumbed to pressure from the local Rock Hill community. Although Winthrop members acknowledged the organization's importance, most of its members were unwilling to directly confront South Carolina's racial hierarchy and assume the social risks that would ensue from challenges to deeply entrenched patterns of racial segregation and discrimination. Indeed, the angst among members is clear in the Winthrop YWCA's minutes when they referred to the controversial nature of national mandates. Furthermore, the Winthrop YWCA was controlled by the college administrators, who made it clear that compliance with the national YWCA's Interracial Charter was impossible.

Mary Ellen Jackson, president of the Winthrop YWCA in 1946, revealed the fears of many members when she said that "the secrecy that surrounds the telling of what schools in the southern region subscribe to the YWCA is only one of the unfavorable questions that cloud our minds." One can only surmise what these "unfavorable questions" were. At an all-white and female institution, racial integration was not a primary concern. And, some of the Winthrop YWCA members' increased interest in racial activism and the likelihood of working with African American students, particularly males, did much to heighten the southern whites' fears of any challenge to South Carolina's racial hierarchy.

After much consideration, Winthrop College disbanded its YWCA and reorganized as the Winthrop Christian Association in September 1947. For many members, the formation of the new association meant the advent of "a more effective religious organization" for the Winthrop student body.[134] It also meant writing a new constitution that excluded any references to racial harmony and focused instead on the less controversial benefits of Christian harmony.

Although the Winthrop YWCA's end placated the local community, and perhaps even some students, many of its members found their exposure to the pressing racial and social issues of the time rewarding. As other local YWCAs began to see the tide of change and as the national YWCA began to push its policy supporting racial equality, white women realized that racial activism through community branches could not be put off indefinitely. While this change had occurred in other parts of the nation, such inclusiveness would not be forthcoming in South Carolina YWCAs until decades later.[135]

The Charleston and Columbia YWCAs

YWCA chapters in Charleston and Columbia demonstrate both the possibilities and the limits of integrated activism in South Carolina and the ways in which black and white women interpreted their obligation to uphold the dictates of the national YWCA in the 1940s. The Charleston YWCA, organized in 1903, initially served as a women's aid society. At different times it helped white women develop marketable skills, find housing, and attend night school. The Charleston YWCA had also used the name "YWCA" before the national YWCA adopted it in 1907. This would later become a contentious issue both nationally and locally.[136]

Although white women were able to form YWCA chapters at will, black women were not. When they approached the national YWCA to organize branches in the early decades of the twentieth century, it determined that black branches in southern cities had to be supervised by an existing "central" YWCA. "Central" clearly meant "white." The central YWCA had to agree to start a black YWCA; the latter was overseen by a management committee of three white women and two black women.[137] According to historian Marion W. Roydhouse, the reality was that African American women who worked in branches of the central YWCA often did so in isolation.[138]

The predominantly black Coming Street YWCA was formed by the Women's Auxiliary of the Young Men's Christian Association in 1907 because black women in Charleston felt that although the YMCA was helping black men save black boys, it was neglecting black girls. Thus, the auxiliary formed the YWCA to "look out for the future mothers of the race."[139]

During World War II, the Charleston YWCA paid scant attention to southern racial problems and instead focused on supporting the war effort. However, racial tensions existed between black and white YWCA members, particularly surrounding civil rights issues such as voting rights for African Americans. Because African Americans made up such a large portion of the population, whites in Charleston, more so than other parts of South Carolina, were committed to maintaining a carefully crafted racial hierarchy. The city also had a very small black middle class and no black institutions of higher learning. Thus, the effectiveness of black activism for equal treatment in Charleston was extremely limited.

When Belle Ingels of the national YWCA staff visited Charleston in 1944, she noted the slow progress in race relations and reported that when the issue of blacks gaining the right to vote came up it was disregarded as "a straw in the wind."[140] During her visit to the predominantly black Coming Street YWCA, Ingels discovered that black women leaders were suspicious of white co-members because they felt that the latter kept them in the dark about YWCA affairs.[141] When Mamie E. Davis,[142] also of the national YWCA staff, visited the branch in 1946, she noted the hostility between black and white women. When the branch chairman, chairman of the house, and acting secretary of the Coming Street YWCA asked the white leadership at the central YWCA about the status of their building, they were told that the central YWCA was the landlord and they were tenants. That is, white YWCA leaders could enter the building at any time, without the branch officers' knowledge, and could do as they so chose.[143] Such demeaning attitudes continually scarred the relationship between black and white women members in the 1940s and beyond.

The Columbia YWCA, unlike the Charleston YWCA, at least attempted to educate its members about racial conditions in South Carolina and had more interaction with black members than did other South Carolina YWCAs in the 1940s. The Columbia YWCA (white) was founded and chartered by the national YWCA in 1914. It is unclear when the Phyllis Wheatley branch was organized, although some sources argue that it might have been as early as World War I or in 1921.[144] However, both the Columbia YWCA and the Phyllis Wheatley branch provided housing and social services to young, single working women who came to the city from rural areas.[145] In the early 1940s, Columbia YWCA members recognized black women's agency and acknowledged their efforts to increase branch membership. Indeed, black women focused on improvements within their own communities by sponsoring programs like Negro Health Week.[146]

Columbia YWCA members participated in national events in the early 1940s. Members attended conferences and returned with reports highlighting the international and interracial aspects of the YWCA's work. They were also influenced by the democratic fervor of the World War II years and appeals to the duty of Christians during those years. One member, Alves Long, stressed this point after returning from a conference on world fellowship in 1943. The conference, she asserted, "defined the responsibility of Christians as citizens of country and state" and "the duties of the citizen as concerned with one's attitude to all public questions."[147] More than those of other South Carolina YWCAs, Columbia YWCA meetings in the 1940s focused explicitly on racism and interracialism. Its meeting in March 1944 was devoted to a discussion: "Is There Race Superiority?" At subsequent meetings in 1944, members considered interracial activities and the YWCA's possibilities with younger women.[148] In October 1944, members were challenged to examine themselves and their commitment to interracialism when Mrs. J. Roy Jones, chairman of the interracial committee, gave the devotional, using as her subject "Brotherhood the World Over."[149]

Because Columbia had a larger, more active, and better-educated African American community, numerous black civic and political organizations, and several black institutions of higher learning, white women of Columbia were more inclined to consider racial change than their counterparts in Charleston were. Columbia's small black middle class was also much more vocal. Furthermore, some white women had made contacts with black women activists and resolved that it was best to work for reforms that would benefit South Carolina as a whole.

In the mid-1940s, in response to the national YWCA's commission to study interracial policies and practices in community YWCAs, the Columbia association wrote a letter to Mary Shotwell Ingraham, president of the National Board, about recommendations passed by the board "concerning interracial study."[150] Although there is no extant information to illustrate what these recommendations were, the fact that the Columbia YWCA bothered to send anything to the national YWCA demonstrates that, even in these tense years in South Carolina, these women were willing to consider the problems plaguing the South.[151] Nor did their efforts stop there. They recognized that the black branch was at a decided disadvantage in terms of finances and leadership. Consequently, in 1945 the interracial committee gathered material for a study to present to the Community Chest, a local fund-raising agency for Columbia's organizations that wielded considerable control over those it assisted, in order to procure a trained worker at the branch YWCA.[152] The study, which demonstrated a need for a black worker for women and girls in Columbia, convinced YWCA members as well as Community Chest officials. The committee then contacted the national YWCA about obtaining an experienced worker. In September 1945 the Community Chest gave $1,800 to the Columbia YWCA for a program director at the Phyllis Wheatley branch.[153]

Conclusion

During the World War II years, black South Carolinians focused their efforts on issues of political representation, education, and racial violence, and they encouraged those relatively few white South Carolinians who spoke out on racial issues to do the same. These black and white activists combated racial injustice through a wide variety of professional, religious, and civic organizations. Black women and their organizations were able to procure equal salaries for black teachers and the beginnings of access to the franchise for African Americans throughout South Carolina.

These years evidenced activism from South Carolina women and revealed patterns that would characterize their efforts for racial change in the decades to come. Although black women often had different goals and separate facilities from white women, many black and white leaders shared similar socioeconomic backgrounds, and this facilitated interracial cooperation, the building of institutions to help African Americans, and eventual educational access for all South Carolinians. Nonetheless, white women's organizations did not usually include black women. And although many black women denounced white women's racism, they recognized the expediency of pursuing interracial activism to bring about important changes for African Americans.[154] Even though such opportunities were rare and limited, black women, fueled by the democratic rhetoric of the World War II years, most often found support and leadership roles within their own organizations and male-led organizations like the NAACP and the PDP. They were further influenced by the social Christianity of organizations like the YWCA.

Understandings of how racial and social improvements would benefit blacks varied greatly during these years. Clearly, most white women activists favored "separate but equal" improvements for blacks. Unfortunately, the paucity of black women's records prohibits an extensive analysis of their activism during these years. Yet, enough is available to demonstrate their frustrations with white women's unwillingness to confront South Carolina's power structure directly to enact positive changes for blacks. These black women had limited contact with white southern women, and when they did have contact, those relationships were at times fraught with tension and often revealed skepticism on the part of black women and paternalism from white women. As African Americans secured important political concessions in South Carolina after World War II and into the 1950s, some of these already fragile relationships would become increasingly strained.

2

"The Negro Only Wanted a Chance to Live"

Civil Rights Activism in Postwar South Carolina

The Negro only wanted a chance to live, feed his family, minister to his sick and to educate his children so that they might be law abiding citizens.

CHARLESTON METROPOLITAN COUNCIL OF NEGRO WOMEN, 1950

In 1950, Elizabeth Waring, a white woman and the second wife of Judge J. Waties Waring, gave a controversial speech at the Coming Street YWCA in which she lambasted white Charlestonians who resisted desegregation efforts and interracial activism. She described them as a "sick, confused, and decadent people . . . full of pride and complacency, introverted, morally weak and low," while black Charlestonians were "building and creating."[1] Afterward, the Charleston Metropolitan Council of Negro Women applauded her "unfaltering courage, strength, and integrity." This group of black women supported increased interracial cooperation promoting "justice, amity, understanding, and cooperation among women regardless of race, creed of people or color."

Black women understood that their organizational affiliations were crucial to the enactment of reforms at the local level. They were also less likely to encounter racial violence than men. Thus black women were often better positioned to effect change throughout South Carolina. More than this, however, they also asserted a shared heritage and pride as American citizens and South Carolinians and underscored their claim to the benefits of full citizenship by declaring their desire to live free of racial segregation, to care for their families and their communities, and to educate their children.[2] In the years following World War II, black women, as individuals and as members of mixed-gender and integrated organizations, continued to focus on issues that disproportionately affected their communities. In doing so, they found that some white women supported their increasingly aggressive racial agenda.

Although black women welcomed white women's efforts for interracial understanding and cooperation in the 1940s, they increasingly sought more tangible change, including obtaining the long-sought-after right to vote. After *Smith v. Allwright* in 1944, which ruled that blacks could not be prohibited from voting in Texas Democratic primaries, black women supported similar legal changes in South Carolina in *Elmore v. Rice* and *Brown v. Baskins*.[3] The impact of these cases in South Carolina and throughout the nation further ignited organizational and individual activism among black women.

Elmore v. Rice had particular importance in South Carolina, where white women and especially black female and mixed-gender organizations had fought for access to voting since the 1930s. The South Carolina Democratic Party controlled state, county, and city governments throughout the state and had excluded blacks from participation in the primary. Although the Republican Party had some small successes in South Carolina, it had gained such a bad reputation during Reconstruction that it was too weak to have any major impact on local politics.[4]

In 1946, when George Elmore went to the voting precinct office and presented himself to John I. Rice, chairman of the Richland County Democratic Executive Committee, he was not permitted to vote. According to Rice, Elmore was not a member of the Democratic Party, and "no Negroes were permitted to vote in the Democratic Primary."[5] Elmore, a Columbia taxi driver and secretary of the Richland County Progressive Democratic Party, had met all of the voting requirements for the city and state. The following year, a black citizens' committee from Richland County, backed by the NAACP, sued for the right to participate in the Democratic primary, claiming that it, whether supported by state law or by party rules, controlled the choice of officeholders in South Carolina.[6]

Judge J. Waties Waring and African American Voting Rights

Elmore v. Rice was tried before federal district court judge J. Waties Waring, who decided in favor of the plaintiffs in 1947. Blacks could not be excluded from the primary, he ruled, and the South Carolina Democratic Party could not operate as a "private club" and restrict its membership as it pleased. Waring added pointedly, "It is time for South Carolina to rejoin the Union. It is time to fall in step with the other States and to adopt the American way of conducting elections."[7] Waring's decision was upheld by the Fourth Circuit Court of Appeals, and the U.S. Supreme Court refused to review the decision.[8]

Black women played key roles in *Elmore v. Rice,* and none more so than Columbia native Modjeska Simkins. Born in 1899, Simkins, a teacher, social worker, and longtime civil rights activist, gave her personal support during the development of this case. Her mother, Rachel Evelyn Hull Monteith, had been a member of W. E. B. DuBois's Niagara Movement and was among those African Americans who founded a branch of the NAACP in Columbia in 1917. Already a skilled activist, Simkins had sharpened her abilities as a leader and fine-tuned her racial philosophy in the 1920s during the nadir of civil rights activism.[9] During the 1920s, 1930s, and 1940s she participated in several integrated organizations dedicated to racial, social, and educational improvement, such as the Commission on Interracial Cooperation, the Southern Conference for Human Welfare, the Southern Negro Youth Congress, the Southern Regional Council (SRC), and the Southern Conference Educational Fund.[10] Later, on the local level, she was a member of black and integrated organizations such as the South Carolina Tuberculosis Association (SCTA), the Civic Welfare League, the Columbia Women's Council, the Columbia Town Hall Congress, and the Richland County Citizens Committee, of which she was publicity and public relations chairperson.[11]

Simkins, who often traveled around the state on behalf of the South Carolina NAACP, became its secretary in 1941 at its annual state conference.[12] Thurgood Marshall, lead counsel for the South Carolina NAACP and a graduate of Howard University Law School, recognized that Simkins, because of her travels throughout the state and her positions in the NAACP and the SCTA, had firsthand knowledge of the racial injustice South Carolina blacks endured. He asked her to sit close to him and the other attorneys so she could advise them during the in-court proceedings of *Elmore v. Rice.* In response, she offered him a note about an argument from *Brown v. Baskin* that he later used as a part of his case.[13] Also, Simkins contributed financially to the cause by helping George Elmore, who had fallen into economic distress and faced losing his home. Simkins gave him a personal loan and arranged for him to manage one of her husband's businesses.[14]

This litigation did not stop white attempts to limit black voting rights. In May 1948 the Democratic State Convention adopted a new set of rules designed to discourage most black voters. The rules required all would-be voters to sign a discriminatory oath declaring themselves in favor of "separation of the races" and "States Rights" and opposed to the "proposed Federal so-called F.E.P.C. law." Created by President Franklin Roosevelt in 1941, the Fair Employment Practices Committee prohibited racial discrimination during World War II.[15] President Harry S. Truman wanted to make it permanent in 1948.

Some white Democrats repudiated the oath, however. The Greenville County Democratic Executive Committee broke with the state organization and set aside the registration oath, allowing blacks to register, as did Richland, Marlboro, Darlington, Spartanburg, and Laurens Counties.[16] In June, other liberal whites, including ministers, members of the SRC, Alice Norwood Spearman, and Susan Fitzsimmons, a former president of the South Carolina League of Women Voters, formed the Citizens Democratic Party and threatened to send an alternative delegation to challenge the South Carolina Democratic Party at the national convention in Philadelphia.[17]

At the same time, members of the Progressive Democratic Party were making their own preparations to attend the Democratic National Convention at their annual meeting in Columbia. They again argued that the South Carolina Democratic Party had been illegally chosen to represent the state because it did not represent all of its citizens.[18] The positions that black women held in the PDP make it clear that they were just as invested as men in procuring full citizenship for black Carolinians. Annie Bell Weston was not only reelected to a third term as PDP secretary and elected national committeeperson; she was also unanimously selected as secretary of the convention.[19] Mrs. L. M. Williams from Spartanburg and Mrs. Lottie P. Gaffney from Gaffney were chosen as her assistants. Mrs. M. A. Morgan from Mullins acted as chief of the registration staff along with two coworkers, Rhea Stewart and Gloria Means. Both Weston and Gaffney were among the twenty-eight delegates chosen to attend the Democratic National Convention in Philadelphia.[20] Unfortunately, in July 1948 the Credentials Committee of the national Democratic Party voted to seat the all-white South Carolina delegates, who were led by Senator Olin Johnston.[21]

Black South Carolinians' determination to gain access to the ballot proved victorious in July 1948. In *Brown v. Baskin*, Judge Waring threw out the discriminatory oath, abolishing the white primary in the process. The U.S. Supreme Court refused to review either of Waring's decisions, thus allowing them to stand.[22] The following month, African Americans voted in the presidential election in large numbers for the first time since Reconstruction.[23]

While African Americans were largely responsible for pushing for voting rights, *Elmore v. Rice* would not have been possible without J. Waties Waring's burgeoning civil rights consciousness. Waring, a member of Charleston's aristocracy whose English and Episcopalian ancestors could be traced back eight generations, had never questioned southern racial practices before he was sixty-five years old. His awareness of racial injustices had developed over the course of several years, influenced by events that also reshaped his political outlook. This new consciousness and his personal family decisions invited the ire of the white Charlestonians he had known for most of his life. In 1945, Waring forced his wife of twenty years, also a Charleston blue blood, to obtain a divorce in Florida. Just over a week later, he married Elizabeth Avery, a divorcée fifteen years his junior and a northern "rabble-rousing" socialite. The divorce alone was controversial for Charleston whites, but fuel was added to the fire when the new Mrs. Waring moved into the judge's house on Meeting Street almost immediately after Waring's ex-wife exited to New York City.[24] Elizabeth Waring would later be known as the "the witch of Meeting Street."[25]

The Warings' social isolation was further intensified by the fact that, by the late 1940s, Judge Waring had begun to seriously question segregation and white supremacy. Both had read works examining American race relations, including W. J. Cash's *The Mind of the South* and Gunnar Myrdal's *An American Dilemma*.[26] Waring's actions further demonstrated the evolution of his thoughts on these matters. He desegregated the seating and jury roster in his courtroom, demanded that lawyers address blacks with courtesy titles, and hired a black bailiff.[27] In 1946, while Waring was on the bench in Columbia, the policeman who had blinded war veteran Isaac Woodard was acquitted. Woodard, who had just returned from service in the South Pacific where he had been stationed in New Guinea and the Philippines, had gotten into an altercation with a white bus driver in Batesburg, South Carolina, and was later severely beaten by local police chief Linwood J. Shull and his deputy.[28] Waring's wife, who had been in the courtroom, went to her room in tears, while white Carolinians cheered the decision. This event further influenced the judge's break with his southern racial heritage.[29] According to historian David W. Southern, once converted, Waring became more radical on the race issue than many northern liberals.[30] However, most of Charleston's white elite considered him a traitor. It was not long before both Warings were estranged from Charleston society, and by the late 1940s they were verbally attacked and harassed for defying South Carolina's racial status quo by embracing civil rights.[31]

Unlike her southern-bred husband, Elizabeth Waring had championed black civil rights from an early age. Born into privilege in Grosse Point, an exclusive suburb of Detroit, Michigan, Waring had attended all the right schools: Liggett in Grosse Point Woods, Michigan; Sacred Heart in Paris; and the Westover School for Girls in Middlebury, Connecticut.[32] Because of her activism, her hometown newspaper likened her to Harriet Beecher Stowe. Elizabeth and her second husband, Henry Hoffman, an industrialist, met Waring at a bridge game during World War II, while they were wintering in Charleston. In 1945 she divorced Hoffman, and in June of that year she married the sixty-five-year-old judge.[33]

Elizabeth Waring's activism fomented in Charleston when she addressed the Coming Street YWCA at their annual meeting on January 16, 1950.[34] She chastised white southerners, describing them as a "sick, confused and decadent people . . . full of pride and complacency, introverted, morally weak and low," while black southerners were "building and creating."[35] She acknowledged the risk black women had assumed by inviting her to speak at the YWCA, as well as the risk taken by those who came to hear her speak. Waring also acknowledged the price she and her husband had paid for their controversial positions. Invoking Cold War terminology, she pointed out that it was fear that drove the white supremacist machine in South Carolina:

> We to them are like the atom bomb which they are afraid we will use to destroy their selfish white supremacy way of life. And they are quite correct. That is exactly what the judge and I are doing, and they know it and see the writing on the wall. But you know and we know and they should know that there is another use of atomic energy, and that is for building and healing and restoring a civilized way of life. That is what the judge is trying to do for the good of the white people down here as well as the Negro.[36]

Waring's speech set off a tidal wave of resentment, harassment, and an impeachment drive against her husband. Governor Strom Thurmond quipped that her remarks were "beneath answering," and Thomas Hamilton, grand dragon of the Associated Klaverns of the Carolinas (Ku Klux Klan), declared that he would "answer Mrs. Waring later."[37] However, the couple received endless support from African Americans. Thurgood Marshall sent his regards to Elizabeth following the speech, at the same time admonishing white South Carolinians: "Congratulations on your speech and the coverage it has received in the press up here. You did a swell job. Of course, all of us expected the reaction from [Strom] Thurmond, *The Charleston News and Courier*, Hamilton, and the rest of that group. The least that they could have done would have been to give credit to your courage even though they did not agree with what you said. On the other hand, I guess we should not expect even that much decency from them."[38]

To say that Elizabeth's speech to the YWCA was controversial is an understatement. In response, the white-controlled central YWCA drafted a statement repudiating Waring's speech. Even before this, after its members learned that the Coming Street branch had invited Waring to speak, the chairperson of its board of directors called a special meeting demanding that Septima Clark, chairperson of the Coming Street YWCA's Committee on Administration, withdraw the invitation.[39] Members of the central YWCA offered spurious reasons for withdrawing the invitation: Waring had been born in the North and was the judge's second wife after he had been previously married for thirty years. The members also felt that if Waring spoke to the Coming Street YWCA it would sully the reputation of the entire organization in the eyes of white Charlestonians.[40] This, of course, meant that organizations such as the United Givers Fund of Charleston might withhold funding from the YWCA.[41] Despite the pressure and threats, Clark and other members refused to sign the statement. Not to be deterred, the executive director of the central YWCA later prepared a statement for the newspapers saying that the Charleston YWCA did not wish Elizabeth Waring to speak at the Coming Street YWCA; the director asked Clark to sign it. Again, she refused.[42]

Some black leaders believed that whites had placed informants in the Coming Street YWCA to determine who had attended the speech.[43] Reportedly, two employees were paid extra money by whites to report on what went on in the black YWCA's meetings. This information also made it to the national NAACP's leadership. Walter White wrote to John H. McCray, editor of the *Lighthouse and Informer*, "I do not know whether these reports are accurate but I have been told to avoid talking to them as they will not only give a distorted and inaccurate picture but will promptly run to the white folks with the story."[44] Waring would later be featured on *Meet the Press*, where she further attacked white South Carolinians' racism.[45]

Black women's organizations supported Waring for her stance in her speech at the YWCA. The Charleston Metropolitan Council of Negro Women applauded her "unfaltering courage, strength, and integrity." They supported interracial cooperation promoting "justice, amity, understanding and cooperation among all women regardless of race, creed of people or color." The council proclaimed its commitment to racial justice in South Carolina while recognizing the efforts of Waring and other liberal whites throughout the South:

As time goes on may others join you in helping to bring about the type of world that He has left us, that all men are brothers under the skin. The Negro wants only a chance to live, feed his family, minister to his sick and to educate his children so that they might be law abiding citizens. We felt that there are other members of your race who feel as you do but there are not as many who have the courage to stand as you did. Christ had only twelve and some of them faltered; but as His eternal word stands today we know yours will stand.[46]

In their response to the speech, the council also connected Christian duty with racial activism.

Elizabeth Waring's social isolation among whites was somewhat mediated by the friendships she formed with members of Charleston's black elite. She and Judge Waring became close associates of activist Septima Clark, Rev. Frank Veal, pastor of Charleston's Emanuel African Methodist Episcopal Church, and his wife, Maude Thomas Veal, a Boston native and graduate of Boston University who in 1952 became the first black member of the Charleston chapter of the League of Women Voters.[47]

The judge and his wife believed their activism had given African Americans the "key to open the door" to full citizenship. But they also felt that blacks in Charleston were unwilling to work for civil rights unless influenced by whites.[48] Despite the fact that they had invited blacks into their home and formed friendships with many of them, their social isolation from Charleston's white society became too much. In March 1950 a group of white Carolinians met with members of the South Carolina delegation in the state house of representatives and presented a petition with twenty thousand signatures demanding that Waring be impeached.[49] In 1952, Waring retired from his seat on the federal bench to which he had been appointed by President Franklin Roosevelt in 1942.[50]

Civil rights activism proved both physically and psychologically overwhelming for the Warings, who left Charleston in 1952. They returned two years later when Judge Waring was honored at a testimonial dinner hosted by the Charleston NAACP.[51] Alice Norwood Spearman attended the dinner and recalled that while she "realized the value [of the judge's views on racial inequality] to the negro community" she was also aware that the address honoring Judge Waring's dissenting opinion on racial segregation in Clarendon County public schools, given by Marion A. Wright, an attorney and president of the SRC, alienated some prominent white Charlestonians.[52] Spearman quipped "that it no doubt placed an additional hurdle in our way as far as the white community is concerned." The Warings made their home in New York until their deaths in 1968.[53]

African American Women's Voting Rights Activism

While Judge Waring's decisions were crucial to the advancement of black political rights, so were the efforts of black women's organizations.[54] In 1946, under the leadership of its newly elected president, Hattie Logan Duckett of Greenville, the SCFCWC launched a voter-registration drive among black women. Members not only distributed registration bulletins all over the state but also voted to require black women to present a valid registration card before being admitted to club conventions.[55] In 1947, when Ethelyn Murray Parker, publicity chairman of the South Carolina and Charleston federations of black women's clubs, invited John H. McCray to speak to the organization about voter registration, she also informed him that delegates had been given ten thousand bulletins about voter registration to distribute in their communities.[56] She impressed upon him the strength of black women's commitment to gaining first-class citizenship and the role of the SCFCWC in its facilitation. "The president of every club is being urged to keep before her members the importance of the ballot, and to have every member registered," Parker asserted. "Some clubs have already registered one hundred percent."[57]

The SCFCWC prided itself on its efforts to transform politics in South Carolina.[58] When black leaders organized on a state level, black women's organizations such as the SCFCWC and the Columbia Women's Council were particularly involved in political activism on the local level.[59] Many of the SCFCWC's meetings focused on encouraging women to become leaders and on African Americans' efforts to exercise the rights of full citizenship in South Carolina. Accordingly, then, it was important to expose club women to national black women leaders. The SCFCWC invited speakers such as former president Marion Birnie Wilkinson and Dr. Charlotte Hawkins Brown of Sedalia, North Carolina, who also urged black women to assume leadership roles in African Americans' fight for the ballot in South Carolina. They further called upon adults, young people, institutions, schools, and churches to do their part in promoting full citizenship for African Americans.[60]

Because some of its members were also affiliated with the Progressive Democratic Party, the SCFCWC called upon John H. McCray in 1947 to speak to their organizations to galvanize support among women for voter registration. They linked the push for voting rights with the encouragement of leadership skills and civic responsibilities. Hazel O. Reese, chairman of the program committee for the Orangeburg district of the SCFCWC, asserted: "We are desirous of having someone bring a message which would deal with civic affairs which might be of interest to women." McCray recognized the impact of organizations like the SCFCWC, whose members' community activism was a necessary part of efforts to procure voting rights: "It is comforting to note that our women, 60 percent of the voting population, are giving serious thought to the role they should play in governmental affairs. And it is even more heartening when so powerful and useful and potent an organization as the Federation is pushing the interest."[61]

Black women like Annie Bell Weston and Modjeska Monteith Simkins, who were members of the SCFCWC, were able to use their membership and their leadership in male-led organizations to promote their political agenda. In a 1947 speech titled "Women Fail to Use Their Political Power," Weston, secretary of the PDP, focused on women's ability to makes changes in South Carolina. She argued that they had the power not only to obtain the vote for African Americans but also to "challenge the corrupt practices of the courts, the sadistic tendencies of the law enforcement officer, the inequalities of the educational systems and the unwholesome recreation conditions."[62] These issues concerned black and white women's organizations alike in the 1940s. Weston asserted that black women were best able to improve African American conditions generally only if they worked to obtain registration and voting rights for blacks in South Carolina.

Although Modjeska Simkins was a well-known Republican who had worked with the South Carolina Republican Party, she maintained a close relationship with PDP founders John McCray and Osceola McKaine, planned the organization's conventions, and wrote its statements and resolutions.[63] As state secretary of the NAACP, Simkins traveled with other women activists to black communities throughout South Carolina to advance the organization's political agenda. In 1947 she spoke at a meeting of the Sumter NAACP and she urged African Americans to "put up an all out fight" against discrimination, positing that "discrimination and segregation are the most poisonous of American life."[64] Other female NAACP members also continued to utilize the liberal rhetoric of the war years. Flosteen Tarleton spoke to the Sumter NAACP on the subject "America Is Willing to Try Democracy," which was clearly designed not only to inspire African Americans but also to gauge how willing the postwar nation was to eradicate racial injustice.[65]

Black women also promoted black voter participation through nonpartisan political organizations like the Columbia Women's Council (CWC).[66] Founded in 1947 under the leadership of Mrs. Horatia D. Nelson, another black activist from Columbia, the CWC aimed to make "Every Qualified Woman a Registered and Intelligent Voter." Like other black women's organizations, it touted itself as a "non-partisan, political action and civic uplift organization." The CWC, like the Women's Political Council established two years later in Montgomery, Alabama, harnessed the skills and political astuteness of professional, educated, middle-class women whose organizational networks brought much-needed attention to racial injustice and community concerns.

One of the CWC's major objectives was to increase the number of African Americans registered to vote and to promote voter education as they discussed such issues as the City Manager Plan and the methods for registering and qualifying to vote properly.[67] Between 1947 and 1949 the group's activities included citizenship training projects for its members, mass gatherings for the dissemination of information on current civic and political problems, citizenship discussions with students from local historically black institutions of higher learning such as Allen and Benedict Colleges, special city block drives to increase registration, and an annual social held in May for registered voters who offered proof of registration. In 1948 the CWC also sponsored Charleston activist A. J. Clement, executive secretary of the PDP and the first African American to run in the South Carolina Democratic primary, to talk to the group about the importance of voting in the presidential election. Another of the CWC's projects was a political action mass meeting, held in December 1949 at Bethel African Methodist Episcopal Church in Columbia, to encourage pastors of churches in Columbia and Richland County to inform their congregations and the public at large about the upcoming election. The main speaker for the event, Rev. Maxie C. Collins Jr., a white minister and political activist from Lake City, was executive director of the Christian Action Council, a group of moderate South Carolina clergymen. Introduced by Simkins, Collins led a discussion titled "South Carolina and the 1950 Election" and a roundtable discussion, "Your Importance in the 1950 Elections."[68]

In 1950 the CWC sponsored a political action rally at Benedict College that focused on black community problems in Columbia. CWC members addressed such issues as street and traffic lighting, lack of public restrooms and drinking facilities for African Americans, police protection, slum clearance, inferior public facilities for blacks, the lack of paved streets in black areas of the city, and integration in municipal government and service. Utilizing members' connections, the CWC presented African American former congressman Arthur W. Mitchell from Illinois at a program at Zion Baptist Church in 1951 to encourage more black participation in the political process.[69]

The CWC did not collect membership dues, but it presented plays in order to raise money for its efforts. These performances stressed black women's contributions as a force for change and a conduit for better race relations in South Carolina. In 1950 the CWC sponsored *Women's Role in American Life* and in 1951 *The Twentieth Century Woman*. Simkins was an important part of both of these activities and chaired a discussion on "Women in Civic and Political Life." Like many other women's organizations, the CWC paid particular attention to the integral role that women played in politics and social and racial reform.[70]

The UCCW and the YWCA

Although timid in contrast to black organizations, some predominantly white women's organizations, notably the UCCW and the YWCA, turned their attention to pressing civil rights issues such as voting rights for all Americans in the postwar years. In 1946, at a session in Washington, D.C., the UCCW opined that "a free vote" should be guaranteed to all citizens of the United States. It is unclear whether women from southern states were present. A session of the annual meeting of the United Council of Churches in 1946, held in Grand Rapids, Michigan, was devoted to the consideration of "the equal but separate tenets of some states and the segregation practices in states that have civil rights laws on their statute books." Two recommendations came from this session: first, that in states having civil rights laws, church women encourage the acceptance and practice of the laws; and second, that church women continue to bring pressure to bear on government powers against the undemocratic practices in the administration of city affairs in the nation's capital.[71]

Like the national organization, the Columbia branch of the UCCW began to pay more attention to racial injustices and child welfare issues after World War II. Meetings embraced the theme "My Community Begins with Me, Just as My World Begins at My Door." Yet it appears that throughout most of the 1940s, members pursued racial changes slowly and conservatively, if at all.[72] But, at the very least, they discussed the topic in their meetings. In 1946, a minister spoke to the group on "Christians and Race." The lecture provided information about the conditions between the races in South Carolina.[73] Thus, as these women worked for improvements in South Carolina, they did so cautiously within the confines of the UCCW, where their activism was less likely to be considered controversial. Although they supported missionary efforts and schools for African Americans, the Columbia group avoided discussing racial integration and other such issues until the 1950s and 1960s.

On a regional level, black and white women increasingly worked together in efforts to promote racial justice. In June 1947 a gathering of more than two hundred black and white southern women met at a "Conference on Human Rights and World Order" held in Atlanta. The conference, a joint project of the Georgia Council of Church Women, the Woman's Society of Christian Service of the Methodist Church, and the Southern Regional Council, brought together women from thirteen southern states and represented eleven different religious denominations, in addition to fifty-five nonreligious organizations and institutions. Many recommendations resulted from this meeting, providing evidence of the possibilities of interracial activism. Conference attendees offered recommendations in support of the "unalterable opposition to the 'white primary' because it is in direct violation of the Constitution of the United States and the U.N., of the Social Creed for the Churches and the principles of the Christian religion." They also advocated better training of public officers, particularly policemen, to ensure fair treatment and the observance of civil rights for all persons and groups, especially blacks.

In a section titled "Human Rights in Earning a Living," conference attendees recommended that local organizations of church women conduct community surveys to identify the economic, educational, and recreational activities available to all people in the local community; that they work for federal aid to education and vocational education for all races and classes; that they advocate better employment practices and work for civil rights as embodied in the Fair Employment Practices Committee; and that they advocate for the basic protection of domestic employees and others not covered by Social Security.[74]

Southern white church women continued this attention to racial issues when delegates from twelve states attended a two-day meeting in Atlanta in 1949, sponsored by the SRC. At this meeting they vowed to go to registration and voting centers with their cooks and maids in order to safeguard their right to the franchise. They pledged to make voting "legally and actually safe for all" and affirmed their belief that "all men, white and Negro, are entitled to equal justice."[75]

Dorothy Tilly, a prominent Methodist church woman and a field secretary for the SRC, played a key role in this endeavor. In 1949 she issued "An Urgent Call at an Urgent Hour to Women Leaders of the South," calling for women's church groups and the YWCA to meet in Atlanta to discuss "spiritual approaches to social problems." Tilly, who had also been a member of Harry S. Truman's Committee on Civil Rights, had long been involved in reform activities, and she believed that integration was inevitable and that southern church women should play prominent roles in the process.[76] In attendance at the conference was Eleanor Roosevelt, who addressed the audience about the recent U.N. Declaration of Human Rights and its significance to local communities.[77]

At the meeting, the women adopted a plan of action titled "What Can the Press, the School, the Church, and Women's Organizations Do to Make for Better Human Relations?" Among those in attendance were presidents of state Councils of Church Women. Mrs. C. C. Whithington of Greenville, South Carolina, participated in planning "A Program of Action" to implement changes in her community. Among the most important elements of this planning was the attendees' assertion that women take the initiative in examining race relations and cooperating with local authorities to repel racial violence in their communities.

Church women in Atlanta, led by Tilly, formed a "Fellowship of the Concerned" and pledged to "enlist the aid of others in putting the following program of action into effect in our communities." They outlined church women's commitment to change in the South and to ensuring that "opportunity for registration and voting is legally and actually secure for all." They advocated affiliating with other groups working for the same objectives. And they supported urging local schools "to cooperate in using existing materials to build better human relations," "to affirm in personal relations and religious and civic work the conviction of the dignity of all human beings and the ideal of equal justice," and to conduct a "Home Town Self-Survey" to force their respective communities to examine race relations. The fellowship also sponsored interracial meetings to promote racial understanding. They expressed concern about better law enforcement and the appointment of African American policemen. Furthermore, Eleanor Roosevelt and Dorothy Tilly urged southern church women to visit courts and use their influence in the interest of equal justice.[78]

Greenville YWCA

Just as the Truman administration's stand on civil rights stirred some southern white liberals to activism, the national YWCA continued to pressure South Carolina YWCAs to take action on racial injustices. After the national YWCA passed its Interracial Charter in 1946, mandating integration in local YWCAs, black women increasingly demanded the end of their second-class status in southern YWCAs.[79] Black women in Greenville recognized and took advantage of an auspicious moment as they sought to become members of their city's YWCA.

Incorporated in 1917, the Greenville YWCA made the strongest efforts of the South Carolina YWCAs to improve conditions for African Americans and women in the state. It joined the national YWCA in 1920. In keeping with national YWCA mandates, by 1929 the central YWCA was propelled by Christian doctrine to at least question the "race problem" in South Carolina.[80] These efforts expanded in subsequent decades, particularly after World War II.

Greenville County was heralded by many as more progressive than other South Carolina counties. The county was located in northwest South Carolina, where slaveholding never flourished, and its percentage of African Americans was low compared to other parts of the state. However, its citizens could not boast of better race relations than existed in Charleston or Columbia.[81] In the years following the Civil War, Greenville became the capital of South Carolina's textile industry. Local whites considered the presence of job-seeking African Americans, though few in number, a threat to the social order. After the proliferation of textile mills, poorly paid white mill operatives, often referred to as "lintheads" and "bobbindodgers" and also considered a threat to the social order because of their lower-class status, were added to this category.[82] Still, they were white in a state that embraced white supremacy and segregation, and when faced with the threat of black advancement, they reacted violently. Despite this, the business elite in Greenville wanted to promote a progressive image of the city in order to encourage investment.[83]

Olive H. Walser of the national YWCA believed this progressive image to be accurate when she visited Greenville in 1946. Although Walser was sensitive to community mores, she recorded that Greenville was "more democratic than many in this area." She also noted that while Greenville YWCA members were often annoyed by local business leaders' conservatism, they were generally able to "count on a good deal of cooperation and common sense" when it came to procuring concessions for its black residents.

In contrast to the YWCAs at Winthrop College and in other parts of South Carolina, the Greenville YWCA responded positively when the national YWCA issued its mandate to integrate its organizations nationally and locally in 1946. Many members had attended workshops and conferences where they had worked with women of different races. In 1947, members also praised Governor Strom Thurmond for his handling of the case when Willie Earle, a twenty-five-year-old epileptic from Pickens County, was lynched the previous year. Although the perpetrators were acquitted by an all-white jury, the Greenville YWCA asserted its belief in color-blind justice and democracy: "The Y.W.C.A. being an organization dedicated to the promotion of democratic and Christian ideals for all people is most interested in seeing that justice is properly administered. We commend your efforts in that direction not only in this case, but in any which shall occur."[84]

Although the white Greenville YWCA had been established some thirty-one years earlier, it was not until 1948 that black women, emboldened by the national YWCA's mandate for integration, approached white women and asked them to help set up a branch for the black community. Before this point, black women had assisted their community through the Phillis Wheatley Association, which was founded by Hattie Logan Duckett in 1919 and housed the African American branch of the Greenville County Public Library.[85] Named for the eighteenth-century enslaved African American poet, the association had received its certificate of incorporation in December 1920 and provided social, educational, and recreational activities to Greenville's black community.[86]

Duckett, who was born in 1885, was a Greenville native and the daughter of a Methodist minister. Like many of South Carolina's black women activists, she was well educated, having received a bachelor of arts from Claflin College in Orangeburg. A former teacher who had taught elementary school in Greenville, Duckett had always dreamed of opening a social service agency for African Americans in South Carolina, particularly after she visited the Phillis Wheatley Association in Cleveland, Ohio, in 1918, which had been founded in 1911 by Pendleton, South Carolina, native Jane Edna Hunter.[87] It was this combination of what she saw in Cleveland and her desire to do something similar to help African American women in Greenville that compelled Duckett to form her own Phillis Wheatley Association.[88]

Understandably, Phillis Wheatley members were reluctant to join forces with white women. When teenage girls from the black community asked for Girl Reserve club work, a junior version of the YWCA established in 1918, the central YWCA was happy to oblige them.[89] Black women feared that white women would find it difficult to work with them as equals and would not fully understand and appreciate the difficulties that they and their communities faced.[90] But Duckett, who was also a member of the Negro Council of the Greenville County Council for Community Development (GCCCD), the SCCIC, and the SCFCWC, realized that African Americans' resources were limited and that only with the help of local whites would much-needed improvements come to the black community.[91] Thus, she was among the first to reach out to the central YWCA and Greenville's white community to establish a two-hundred-member biracial committee to study and ameliorate conditions in the black community.[92]

As part of this effort to improve conditions for blacks in Greenville County, the central YWCA turned to the Greenville Community Council for advice. The result was a county-wide survey on the conditions of black citizens in Greenville County in 1949 titled "Everybody's Business: Greenville's Big Idea."[93] Representatives from both races worked for more than ten months to prepare the survey. Mrs. C. C. Whithington, who became president of the South Carolina Council of Church Women, led the committee.[94]

The results of the survey highlighted the pervasiveness of discrimination against blacks in Greenville. It included such recommendations as allowing African American doctors to practice at Greenville General Hospital and inviting them to attend meetings of the Greenville Medical Society.[95] The study also supported the creation of a city park and state park for blacks. The Greenville YWCA, more proactive than other local civic organizations, assisted this effort by establishing a typing course for African American girls when no business training was available for them and, with the help of the Kiwanis Club, establishing a day camp for black children.[96]

This self-contained, local survey had larger implications for race relations in South Carolina. Many black and white South Carolinians recognized the benefit of interracial cooperation as a means to community improvement. According to one committee member, "The best thing about the survey was that it got people together. We didn't know each other well enough. Now we do. Meeting and working together—not as people of two races, but as citizens with a common purpose—has been a release and a relief."[97]

White Greenville YWCA members clearly wanted to improve race relations in South Carolina. When Mrs. E. A. Mudge, a YWCA National Board member, visited Greenville and asked what YWCA members saw as their greatest need, they responded, "More courage in moving forward in race relations."[98] Greenville YWCA members also voiced concern about other political, social, and educational issues facing the black community, such as the city council's failure to appoint African American policemen, its failure to respond to the drowning of a man at the state park for blacks, and the unequal investment in black and white education.[99] These concerns prompted members to send a letter to Governor James Byrnes explaining the inadequacy of the parks facilities and asking him to earmark funds for improvement. Unfortunately, the governor responded that nothing could be done to procure additional funds. The Greenville YWCA also assumed a fairly aggressive political stance and heralded the achievements of African Americans and women, supporting Rev. W. R. Martin, a black candidate for school trustee, and Mrs. Girard C. Rippy, candidate for alderman and the first woman to ever run for office in the Greenville City Council.[100]

Though more progressive on racial issues than some other South Carolina YWCAs, the Greenville YWCA approached the topic cautiously. Its members worked to improve conditions for African Americans but not to integrate them into the larger society. They did not mention African Americans specifically in their minutes, and their meetings were held with no publicity because they feared angering local whites. However, Greenville YWCA members were aware of the changes taking place nationally. In November 1953, members Mary Slattery and Mrs. Joseph H. Cook attended a meeting sponsored by the SRC and the Fellowship of the Concerned in Atlanta that dealt with the possibilities for educating the public concerning the anti-segregation suits pending before the U.S. Supreme Court. The consensus of the meeting was that "all interested persons should do everything possible to help prepare the people of the South for a Court decision outlawing segregation in the public schools." Members of the Greenville YWCA had discussed this issue in September, November, and December 1953 when rough drafts of two letters and materials dealing with segregation were prepared by the secretary and forwarded to Greenville County ministers and all members of the Greenville County delegation.[101] By reaching out to local black and white ministers, Greenville YWCA members stressed the importance of their roles as leaders in the Christian community during this difficult time. "Whatever the Court's decision may be," they asserted, "it will all be accepted in a manner befitting Christian people who live in a democratic society under laws interpreted by the Courts."[102]

The Columbia and Charleston YWCAs

The Columbia YWCA also had a pattern of interracial activism that dated from the early 1940s. Although the Interracial Committee, also known as the Public Affairs Committee, had always existed, it often did not have a structured program or course of action. It is quite likely that white members feared risking the ire of the local white community if it challenged racial mores and discussed racial discrimination or held integrated meetings.[103] However, Columbia YWCA members did not completely marginalize black women. Their meetings always included reports from the Phyllis Wheatley branch. White members also acknowledged black women as members of the Columbia YWCA and, unlike other central YWCAs, acknowledged the autonomy of the Phyllis Wheatley branch. By 1950, the branch had a separate budget and its own employees and volunteers. It also sponsored its own adult night school, which opened in 1949, offering courses in reading, writing, history, arithmetic, geography, letter writing, parliamentary procedures, health, and art.[104] By 1953 the central YWCA and the Phyllis Wheatley branch were moving toward becoming one association. According to a 1952–53 report to the National Board of the YWCA, the board of directors of the Columbia YWCA voted to invite representatives from Phyllis Wheatley to attend board meetings. This resulted in a "close and cooperative relationship." Elizabeth C. Ledeen, executive director, asserted, "We are now moving in the direction of an integrated Association." Unlike the white leadership of the Charleston YWCA, Ledeen was hopeful about the outcome of desegregation: "The process of integration is beginning and it is our hope that we will move steadily in that direction though no doubt it will be a gradual process."[105]

After Elizabeth Waring's incendiary speech to the Coming Street YWCA, race relations were tense not only in the Charleston YWCA but throughout Charleston. Attempts for interracial activism came to a screeching halt. When Kathleen Carpenter of the national YWCA visited the city in March 1950, she reported that the Charleston association felt "very strongly now that further progress interracially will have to wait a period of time until the Waring incident has blown over."[106] When Pauline R. Schaedler of the national YWCA visited the Charleston chapter in 1950, she noted that the Charleston YWCA and the Coming Street YWCA continued to operate as two separate organizations. However, during her visit she noted in her report how much more effective and successful the Charleston YWCA could become if it operated as a "total Association."[107]

In 1954, the Charleston YWCA showed some interest in examining racial tensions in South Carolina when it invited Mrs. F. P. Byrd, who led a discussion on "Creating a Climate for Good Human Relations through the YWCA." The importance that members of the Coming Street YWCA gave to integrated meetings was demonstrated in their minutes, which meticulously reported whether or not YWCA events were integrated. After the 1954 meeting at which Mrs. Byrd spoke, the secretary noted "black and white women in attendance." Although many of the Charleston YWCA's events were not integrated, black members planned events with white members in mind. In 1955, Mrs. Tracy, chairman of the Hospitality Committee for the Coming Street YWCA, who was planning a flower show for September or October, said that "we are hoping to make it interracial."[108] Despite the eagerness of some black women to integrate YWCA activities, such goals would not be realized until the 1960s.

Conclusion

The pre-*Brown* era saw a new commitment to racial harmony on the part of national women's organizations, most notably in the YWCA and the UCCW. Reactions to this varied on the local level in South Carolina. While black and white women in the Greenville and Columbia YWCAs worked for changes in black communities and attempted to move closer to becoming one association, the Charleston YWCA found any discussion of racial and interracial activism severely limited after Elizabeth Waring's speech in 1950. The UCCW was still unable to achieve real racial integration to solve local ills, but they too paid more attention to racial injustices than before. While some individual black and white women formed interracial alliances, and even friendships that facilitated racial understanding, the tinge of paternalism and in some cases disillusionment continually rendered such relationships fraught with tension. But in the end, all of these women and their organizations had a similar goal: to comprehend and foster racial change statewide.

In South Carolina during the years before the Supreme Court's *Brown v. Board of Education* decision, voting-rights activism intensified. After *Elmore v. Rice,* black organizations rallied to the cause of voting rights, leaning heavily on the capabilities of women and their organizations to bring about change with the least amount of radicalism and retaliation. Black women's organizations like the South Carolina Federation of Colored Women's Clubs and the Columbia Women's Council, and black women's leadership in the South Carolina NAACP evidenced a consistent pattern of racial activism, and when the momentum of the civil rights movement increased, so too did their efforts to bring about changes in the racial order.

3

"How Shall I Sing the Lord's Song?"

Reactions to *Brown v. Board of Education* in South Carolina

> We came from seventeen states, represented many denominations, and faced multiple problems. But one question drew us close together: How shall I sing the Lord's song?
>
> THE CHURCH WOMAN, 1954

Caroline Gillespie, a white woman from South Carolina, expressed these sentiments after attending a conference of representatives of the Christian Social Relations Departments of United Church Women from southern, border, and midwestern states in Atlanta on June 21, 1954. The church women had met to discuss the implications of the *Brown v. Board of Education* decision, issued by the U.S. Supreme Court on May 17, 1954. UCW members throughout the South faced not only the task of dealing with school desegregation but also that of fighting their states' pervasive racial discrimination. The racial work of southern white women found much of its inspiration from religion, as Gillespie made clear when she asked, "How shall I sing the Lord's song?" She recognized that similar problems concerned white women in other southern states and emphasized the "courage" of those who had found the "power" to pursue changes throughout the South.

Whites and blacks throughout the South struggled to find the courage to understand the implications of the Supreme Court decision. However, this further provided women's organizations with opportunities to assume more active roles in improving race relations and providing equal educational access throughout South Carolina. Although many women's organizations and individual women suffered personally for their activism, and in some cases even withdrew from it, those who persevered were determined to use the significance of the decision to bring change in the Palmetto State.

Briggs v. Elliott

South Carolina played a pivotal role in *Brown v. Board of Education* in a case that originated in Clarendon County as *Briggs v. Elliott*. Almost three-quarters of Clarendon County and its school population was black, yet the all-white school board allocated more than 58 percent of public school funds to white schools. Thirty buses transported white children to school, but there were no buses for black children. In 1947, when a group of concerned black residents petitioned the school board for buses to transport their children, the chairman of the school board replied: "We ain't got no money to buy a bus for your nigger children."[1] Rev. Joseph A. DeLaine, an African Methodist Episcopal pastor and schoolteacher, encouraged black residents of Clarendon School District 26 to speak up for themselves and their children. In 1948, one of those parents, Levi Pearson, temporary president of the Clarendon County NAACP, filed suit to obtain school buses, which, according to the *Plessy v. Ferguson* doctrine of "separate but equal," should have been provided. The suit was dismissed on a technicality, and Pearson soon began to experience retaliation from whites. He was no longer able to obtain credit at any store in the county.[2] Rev. DeLaine, his wife, two sisters, and a niece lost their teaching positions in the Clarendon County and Summerton school districts.[3] Clarendon County NAACP vice president Sarah Z. Daniels lost her position as a home demonstration agent.[4]

In 1949, DeLaine met with Thurgood Marshall and other NAACP officials in Columbia to decide on a course of action. They began to circulate a petition for twenty names in order to go to court. On December 20, 1950, Harry Briggs, a thirty-four-year-old navy veteran, and twenty-four other Clarendon County residents signed a petition and filed suit against the Summerton School District.

Briggs v. Elliott was the first legal challenge to school segregation in the twentieth-century South. The case came to federal trial in 1951 in Charleston, where the state's legal counsel, Robert McCormick Figg Jr., admitted that black and white schools were unequal. However, he also argued that the state had just begun a $124 million program to create a school system that was equal and separate.[5] The court ruled two to one against the plaintiffs, who then appealed to the U.S. Supreme Court.[6] This case and the four others that joined it became the Supreme Court case of *Brown v. Board of Education of Topeka*.[7]

Like DeLaine, Briggs and his family suffered greatly for their part in this case. His wife, Eliza, who worked as a chambermaid at the Summerton Motel, was pressured by her employer to have him take his name off the petition, because otherwise the motel would not be able to obtain supplies. She refused, citing her husband's ability to decide to remove his own name if he so chose. The motel gave her a week's notice and terminated her employment.[8] Harry Briggs also lost his job at Summerton's Sinclair gasoline station and found it virtually impossible to find employment anywhere in South Carolina.[9] He attempted to grow cotton on rented farmland, but he could not get it ginned. Nor could he obtain credit at any bank in Summerton.[10] Like many other black women, Mrs. Briggs realized that her husband needed her strength to see him through this difficult time. When he considered removing his name from the petition, she threatened to leave him.[11] Financially prostrate, Harry Briggs first moved to Miami and then with his family to New York City in 1961, where the NAACP helped them reestablish their lives.[12]

When the Supreme Court decision outlawing segregated public schools was handed down in 1954, it was met with varied reactions throughout the nation and the South. Although President Dwight D. Eisenhower had outlawed segregation in the District of Columbia's public schools by executive order, he privately felt that the *Brown* decision had set back progress in the South.[13] Furthermore, many liberal whites who had been sympathetic to African Americans' call for justice perceived integration as a threat to white supremacy and summarily withdrew their support.

In South Carolina, an atmosphere of "shock, disbelief, anger, rage" reigned as whites were confronted with the *Brown* decision. In 1955, a "Committee of 52," which included prominent white businessmen, authors, clergy, and politicians, published a declaration supporting separate schools to preserve "public education and domestic tranquility."[14] Members of this group called on state officials to "take steps as may be necessary or desirable" to "interpose the sovereignty of the State of South Carolina between Federal Courts and local school officials."[15] They vowed to resist the "clear and present danger" to state sovereignty "without resorting to physical strife, but without surrender of our position." They also claimed that the Supreme Court had relied "not upon the body of established American law, but upon the dubious conclusions of sociologists and psychologists whose number include persons tainted with Communism" and that pressure from NAACP and other "self-serving organizations" had "lowered the will of politicians and the public generally to resist encroachments upon the sovereign rights of states."[16] The term "communism" was often bandied about, particularly after World War II, as the NAACP increasingly challenged segregated education and racial discrimination throughout the South.

The extent of shock in South Carolina over the *Brown* decision led to the emergence of white citizens' councils, whose members were convinced that the NAACP and its civil rights victories were communist influenced.[17] First organized in South Carolina in 1955, white citizens' councils exerted political and economic pressure on blacks who participated in desegregation cases or signed petitions.[18] As branches formed throughout the state, its leaders held a rally at Township Auditorium in Columbia in 1956. Among the featured speakers were former governor Olin Johnston and Senator J. Strom Thurmond from South Carolina, who had run for president on the Dixiecrat ticket in 1948, and Mississippi senator James O. Eastland, who would later call for an investigation of Supreme Court justices who had been "influenced" by Communist doctrine. The first branch of the white citizens' council had been established in Elloree in Orangeburg, South Carolina, in early August 1955, following a petition by African Americans for school integration. Its goal was to destroy "the financial backbone of the blacks in the community." This included loss of jobs, evictions from farms, withholding personal credit, and denying home mortgages and installment loans.[19]

Many white women responded in kind to the *Brown* decision. Not all religious women heard the scripture in the same way that Caroline Gillespie did. Some of them also associated civil rights activism with "Godless" communism. In 1955, Episcopal women's auxiliaries throughout the state approved a resolution upholding segregation in the state's public schools. They declared: "integration is a plan of the Communist party . . . communism acknowledges no God except communism. . . . It is our duty to see that those in high offices in our government are not influenced by Communist doctrine."[20] Thus, these women saw integration as many whites did, as a threat to racial security and to American religious traditions.

Individual white women also felt that southern desegregation efforts were subversive. Cornelia Dabney Tucker of Charleston, a militant lobbyist for women's suffrage who also fought against subversive influences in school textbooks, was particularly critical of the Supreme Court's decision. Born in 1881 in Charlotte, North Carolina, Tucker was a conservative activist and a member of the South Carolina Republican Party, which had crusaded for the secret ballot in the state.[21] She considered school desegregation akin to forced racial amalgamation and association with the "unmoral character of mongrel races."[22] Tucker also questioned the qualifications of the Supreme Court justices when she supported Senator Eastland's 1955 resolution that called for a Senate investigation of the sources upon which the decision was based.[23] Tucker later sent letters to state and national commanders of the American Legion claiming that the "desegregation edict of the Supreme Court of the United States has become a matter of national security."[24] In the letters she enclosed marked copies of a recent speech in the Senate by Senator Eastland, which included assertions that some of the authorities cited by the Supreme Court had past affiliations with socialist organizations.[25] Tucker circulated a petition calling on South Carolina senators to investigate these authorities, obtaining four hundred names. She was supported by many whites in South Carolina, including Senators Thurmond and Johnston. Thurmond forwarded Tucker's petition to Johnston, who then, presumably, passed it on to Eastland.[26] Accounting for her actions, Tucker maintained that she was acting "because I hope it will not become necessary to close our schools, which are essential to the education of both white and black children."[27] Finally, Tucker wrote to President Eisenhower urging him to support Senator Eastland and describing her purpose as "an earnest endeavor to call to the attention of the nation the Communist angle" of the Court's decision. She also wrote the editor of the *American National Research Report* and asserted that "should the investigation prove 'authorities' cited by the Supreme Court in any way be connected with Communist front movements, no iron curtain should hide this fact from the American people."[28] According to historian Jeff Woods, Eastland's resolution never made it out of committee.[29]

Tucker was not alone in her crusade to maintain racially segregated schools in South Carolina. No one in the state's political leadership had supported segregated school systems more staunchly than Governor James F. Byrnes, who had spoken for many white South Carolinians in early 1951 when he asserted, "We will, if it is possible live within the law, preserve the public school system, and at the same time maintain segregation. If that is not possible, reluctantly we will abandon the public school system. To do that would be choosing the lesser of the two great evils." That year, Byrnes sponsored legislation that authorized the selling or leasing of public school facilities to private individuals or groups in the event that segregation was ordered to end.[30]

South Carolina's white leaders saw that change was on the horizon and that their failure to provide equal education to black students was being scrutinized. After Byrnes became governor of South Carolina in 1950, the legislature, in an attempt to forestall integration, offered him a legislative sanction for an initial $75 million bond issue and a 3 percent sales tax to finance a broad school construction program designed to equalize physical facilities in public education.[31] This would have resulted in a $130 million expenditure by 1971.[32]

Segregation's strict maintenance in South Carolina was also evident by the way the state's politicians managed to avoid school integration from 1956 to 1963. Governor Byrnes had previously supported controversial New Deal legislation in South Carolina and had established himself as a political moderate in doing so. He did not, however, support the *Brown* decision, and upon leaving office in 1955 he urged white South Carolinians to engage in massive resistance.[33] Legal barriers erected to prevent school integration in South Carolina were the longest standing of any southern state.[34] No African American student in South Carolina was enrolled in a white public school until nine years after the *Brown* decision, although black parents in Charleston initiated a petition to transfer their children to District 20 schools in the 1950s. Most of the petitioners were federal employees, independent businesspeople, ministers, and unionized dockworkers who had little reason to fear white economic reprisals. School officials refused to offer transfer requests for almost a year. The *Charleston Post and Courier* published the petitioners' names, using information as intimidation. After this affront, the numbers of African American parents attempting to secure entry into all-white schools for their children decreased.[35]

As white resistance grew, African Americans in South Carolina worked to ameliorate the oppressive conditions in which many blacks found themselves after the *Brown* decision. As the South Carolina Conference of the NAACP counteracted white citizens' councils' efforts to ruin black citizens, black activist Modjeska Simkins was at the forefront, participating in relief work in Orangeburg and Clarendon Counties.

Because blacks in the city of Elloree and in Clarendon County did not have access to adequate financial resources and were the victims of white citizens' councils' economic reprisals after the *Brown* decision, Simkins and her brother Henry Dobbins Monteith, president of the Victory Savings Bank, the only black-owned and black operated bank in South Carolina, helped them secure much-needed financial support. This included extending loans to qualified blacks and initiating boycotts of businesses owned by council members.[36] Simkins was determined to ensure that the white citizens' councils' economic penalties would not devastate local blacks, asserting that "anywhere the councils get ready to put on the squeeze, we stand ready to put on a boycott."[37]

Simkins also secured donations from blacks outside South Carolina. In 1955 an article in *Jet Magazine* about the economic reprisals brought donations from across the country as well as from abroad.[38] In particular, Simkins received funds from individual women and women's organizations. A December 1955 letter from Loreice Hackney, president of the Young Women's Civic League of Abyssinian Baptist Church in New York City, galvanized the community to help blacks facing whites' economic sanctions and boycotts in South Carolina and Mississippi.[39]

In contrast to other women connected to organizations implementing much-needed change in the black community, some African American women in South Carolina withdrew their support from civil rights organizations like the NAACP, particularly after facing economic reprisals. In 1955, Rosa Brockington, a practical nurse in Lake City, renounced her membership in the association after discovering what she claimed were the organization's "real motives":

I formerly was a member of that organization but neither I or any of my children are at present associated in any way with that group or association. I have only recently become aware of the real motives and aims of the NAACP, the complete integration of the races. I do not agree with their program of forcing inter-mixture of white and colored children in the public schools. I have complete faith in the colored race and the integrity of my race and am not ashamed to associate with them. Had I realized what the true motives of the NAACP were, I would have never become affiliated with them.[40]

Brockington further asserted that she had spoken her true feelings on the matter and had not been coerced in any way.[41]

When some African Americans disavowed any association with the NAACP, they did so much to the glee of white politicians. Indeed, Senator Thurmond asserted that he was "glad to see a great many Negro people beginning to recognize that they are being misled and are removing their names from petitions asking for integration in schools." Thurmond led the resistance to the *Brown* decision in the Senate.[42] In March 1956 he authored a "Declaration of Southern Principles," also known as the Southern Manifesto, which denounced the *Brown* decision and threatened to defy the

Supreme Court.[43] When the document was published, 19 of 22 southern senators and 82 of 106 representatives had signed it.[44]

While national and local black organizations throughout the South were attacked for their activism, in 1955 at least three state legislatures considered bills to ban public employees from membership in the NAACP. South Carolina governor George Bell Timmerman Jr. led the fight against desegregation throughout the state, asserting that it was the "will of the people of South Carolina to continue to provide good, equal and separate school facilities."[45] Determined to maintain segregation in South Carolina, in 1956 he signed a law barring NAACP members from state, county, or municipal public employment.[46] This new law affected seventy-three hundred African Americans and allowed them four months to petition a state circuit court for a hearing.[47] The law was later repealed under threat of court action and black teachers' appeals to the Supreme Court that it was invalid.[48] Timmerman also pressured local black colleges, such as South Carolina State College in Orangeburg and Allen University and Benedict College, both in Columbia, to purge faculty members who supported desegregation.[49] When Allen University refused to comply, Timmerman had the state Department of Education withdraw its educational program's accreditation. But this punishment gave African American students a legal reason to apply to the segregated educational program at the University of South Carolina.[50]

NAACP membership and racial activism had a particularly negative effect on Septima Clark.[51] When she signed her name to 726 letters that were sent to black teachers urging that they protest the law barring NAACP members from state, county, or municipal county employment, only 26 answered. Some blacks and most whites considered Clark's interracial activities too aggressive.[52] Further, many thought she was a Communist because of her association with the integrated Highlander Folk School in Monteagle, Tennessee. Because of her uncompromising nature, her membership in the NAACP, and her having invited an integrationist to speak at a Parent Teacher Association meeting, the Charleston County school system did not renew her contract in 1956. Along with her livelihood, Clark also lost her retirement pension; she had taught in South Carolina public schools for four decades. She never taught in South Carolina schools again, but she had taken an important stand against racial injustice that would continuously fuel her activism.[53]

Clark was not the only black teacher to lose her job because of NAACP membership. In May 1957, Charleston County Schools superintendent Gordon A. Garrett informed Jessica Pearson Brown that she would not be rehired to teach at Liberty Hill Elementary School. Having received ten years of satisfactory annual ratings for her performance, Brown, who held memberships in such associations as the National Presbyterian Women's Organization, Alpha Kappa Alpha Sorority Inc., the Palmetto Education Association, the YWCA, and the Phyllis Wheatley Literary and Social Club, believed she had been fired because of her NAACP membership. Yet, she stood her ground, asserting, "I had made up my mind long ago that if the question ever came up, I would never deny my membership in the NAACP."[54]

Family members of local activists were targeted as well. Charleston County civil rights activist J. Arthur Brown's sister, Arthurlee Brown McFarlane, who lived and taught in a neighboring county, was blacklisted from teaching and library positions. Another black teacher, Ethel Jenkins Grimball, was not allowed to teach anywhere in the Ninth District in Charleston County because her father was Johns Island activist Esau Jenkins.[55]

Black leaders and their families were also subjected to reprisals. St. James African Methodist Episcopal Church in Lake City, the church of Rev. Joseph A. DeLaine, who had initiated school desegregation proceedings in Clarendon County, was burned. Whites also fired several times on DeLaine's home.[56] As a result of these incidents, according to one report, Mrs. DeLaine was placed "under medical treatment and prostrate at the residence of her parents in Columbia" and was afraid to return home.[57] This also happened to South Carolina NAACP president James Hinton and his wife. Nine bullets were removed from the couple's home, and Mrs. Hinton reported seeing a car speed away after the firing. Hinton, who was in Augusta, Georgia, when the incident occurred, refused police protection, asserting, "Mrs. Hinton is not afraid." When asked if he thought the NAACP's stand on desegregation was a cause, Hinton replied, "You can have your own thoughts."[58]

Reactions to the *Brown* decision did not result solely in the intimidation of blacks. Many whites also faced ostracism and violence for their activism, which did not escape notice inside or outside the South. A 1955 article in the *New York Times* reported that a pro-segregation group was meeting secretly in Memphis to form a national organization to fight racial integration and "other efforts to destroy the Constitution." This meeting included such individuals as Senators Thurmond and Eastland, who called on the new group to "fight the C.I.O., fight the N.A.A.C.P. and fight all conscienceless pressure groups who are attempting our destruction."[59]

Such feelings were only the tip of the iceberg of reactions in South Carolina. In 1955, Dr. Chester C. Travelstead, dean of the School of Education at the University of South Carolina, delivered a speech to summer school faculty titled "Today's Decisions for Tomorrow's Schools" in which he declared: "I find no conclusive evidence that any one group of men is foreordained to be superior or inferior to other groups of men. For races or nations to think and act upon the assumption that theirs is the superior race or nation and that all other groups are inferior is to invite disaster and downfall. None of the great religions dictates such a creed."[60] University officials wasted little time dismissing Dr. Travelstead.[61] Commenting on his dismissal from the university, Travelstead described it as "a result of my views."[62]

Newspapers throughout the country reported an increase in racial violence after the *Brown* decision. In Kershaw County, South Carolina, in 1956, fifty-two-year-old Guy Hutchings, a white Camden High School band director, was beaten by hooded locals who accused him of favoring integration. In 1957, a cross was burned in Camden mayor Henry Savage's yard after an interracial group was driven out of the community under anonymous threats of force after he failed to uphold laws requiring segregation.[63] In 1959, a report published jointly by the American Friends Service Committee (AFSC), the racial and cultural relations department of the National Council of Churches, and the Southern Regional Council listed 530 specific cases of violence, reprisal, and intimidation as well as widespread erosion of civil liberties.[64] In fact, the AFSC established a program, the Rights of Conscience Committee, providing legal fees and financial assistance for those affected by white economic reprisals in the South.[65]

Even women's organizations serving the public welfare were held suspect. In 1956 a private interracial luncheon at a restaurant in Aiken, South Carolina, sponsored by the YWCA, generated a number of complaints to the police department by local whites. The group of eighteen women, eight of whom were black, included representatives from Aiken, Columbia, Charleston, and Greenville. In the meeting's defense, Mary Reed Cook, executive director of the Aiken County YWCA, asserted that she had made the luncheon reservations with the understanding that the group would be integrated and that the restaurant manager had agreed to services on that basis. Although Aiken police chief E. M. Hanna admitted that he had received a number of complaints, he adopted a "hands off" policy because he found no state law prohibiting interracial groups from dining together in private facilities.[66] Whites in Aiken were incensed. In a letter to the editor of the *Aiken Standard and Review* titled "Discretion Lacking," whites emphasized the YWCA's dependence on the funds donated by local citizens to the Community Chest and urged YWCA members not to forget that "it certainly leaves a bad taste in the mouths of the proponents of segregation to have money donated by them be spent to break down the racial barriers."[67]

Individual white women were not exempt from suspicion and reprisal as a result of their activism. One woman subjected to severe reprisals was Claudia Thomas Sanders, who argued that desegregation could be accomplished in the public schools of the state by starting with the first grade. "Children are not born with prejudice," she declared. "If adults could only learn from children their ability to judge character and worth without regard for externals," the desegregation process "would be immeasurably lighter." Sanders was also a contributor to a pamphlet titled *South Carolinians Speak: A Moderate Approach to Race Relations*, which was published in 1957 to "promote free and reasonable discussion of the problems involved in race relations."[68]

A native Charlestonian who could trace her ancestry to the early colonial period, Sanders was a member of the Episcopal Church of the Incarnation in Gaffney and the American Association of University Women. Her public support for integration was informed by her religious beliefs. Sanders argued that "social conscience" and "Christian ethics" left southern whites no other choice but to embrace the reality of desegregation.[69]

Sanders eventually faced retaliation for her activism. In November 1957 an explosion rocked her home, tearing a hole near the chimney, breaking six windows, and cracking a wall in the living room. Fortunately, Sanders, her husband, and a guest escaped injury.[70] Five local men were arrested for their involvement in the bombing. One of them, Robert P. Martin Jr., a white machine operator, eventually confessed to the crime.[71] To his credit, Martin was remorseful about his role in the bombing: "It was the awfullest feeling I ever had in my life. I have been sick and worried to death ever since it happened. I feel better now since I have told the truth."[72] Two months after his confession, he was crushed to death by an automobile. He was quite possibly murdered by Ku Klux Klan. The other participants in the bombing were later acquitted.

Not only had Sanders's home been bombed, but all of her friends and several members of her family had deserted her. She further had to endure harassing phone calls and, according to Sanders, "the feeling that I was hated."[73] For Sanders and her family, challenging South Carolina's racial structure brought about severe social and physical consequences.[74] But she had few regrets about her activism. As Sanders recalled in 1974, "As I think about the status of blacks then and now I am encouraged by the progress that has been made."[75]

The South Carolina Council on Human Relations

By the late 1950s, South Carolina public schools had not integrated despite the Supreme Court's decision. However, many South Carolina whites urged compliance with the *Brown* decision. Among the organizations formed in South Carolina after the Supreme Court decision, the most prominent perhaps was the South Carolina Council on Human Relations (SCCHR), formerly the South Carolina division of the Southern Regional Council. Founded in 1955 as an affiliate of the SRC, the SCCHR was dedicated to "equal opportunity for all peoples of the South." It severed its financial affiliation with the SRC in 1963, becoming an independent organization and adopting a mandate "to carry on an educational program for the improvement of educational, economic, civic, and racial conditions in the state in an endeavor to promote greater unity in South Carolina."[76] Even so, the organization acted conservatively and touted itself as "making no pronouncements of what should or should not be done." According to a 1955 statement by SCCHR president J. Claude Evans, the organization's position on racial activism was moderate; rather than immersing itself in activism, it emphasized "establishing more and better communication between the races, for finding out the facts involved in each local situation and for making biracial studies of local involvements and possibilities." The organization's executive state director, Alice Norwood Spearman, who was also former executive secretary of the South Carolina Federation of Women's Clubs, expressed much the same sentiment, arguing that the SCCHR "contribute[d] more by stressing processes rather than panaceas."[77]

In February 1955, Spearman, aware of the impact the *Brown* decision had on South Carolina, wrote to Esther Cole Franklin of the national YWCA requesting an annual statewide conference for local YWCAs to devise strategies for continuing change in the state. Passionate about the need for racial progress in South Carolina, Spearman wrote, "I feel there is no more vital issue in South Carolina at the present than public response to the Supreme Court ruling against segregation."[78]

After taking over as executive director of the SCCHR, Spearman encouraged liberal white women to become members. In 1955 she asked her friend Harriet Porcher Stoney Simons, a civic and women's rights activist and president of the League of Women Voters, to become an SCCHR board member, asserting, "I do not see how we can do without you."[79] Born in Charleston in 1896 to a prominent South Carolina family, Simons had been educated at private schools in Charleston and Philadelphia. Long interested in interracial activism and the impoverished and unequal conditions among Charleston's African Americans, she had served on the board of the Welfare Council of Charleston (WWC). In 1946 she chaired the Urban League Survey Committee, which, under the auspices of the WCC, conducted a survey of poor housing and education in black communities. Like many white South Carolinians, she supported state's rights, but when she ran for the Charleston City Council in October 1948 Simons emphasized her commitment to interracial cooperation: "I have tried to do my share of working for the welfare of all members of the community, regardless of creed or color. All people who live in Charleston are citizens of our city and it is my firm belief that many of the difficult problems which confront us can be solved by understanding and cooperation." To this end, Simons was also a member of the state division of the interracial SRC in the early 1950s.[80]

Like many liberal whites who had been open to interracial cooperation in the 1940s, Simons was very cautious about participating in the SCCHR after the *Brown* decision, and she declined Spearman's invitation. According to historian Marcia Synnott, Simons was among those southern whites who found it difficult to overcome their paternalism and rejected aggressive activism—be it black or white—and federal intervention in what they considered southern and local matters.[81] Although Simons recognized that school integration in South Carolina was inevitable, she feared that forcing the issue would seriously "retard" white children's education because black children had been so poorly educated.[82] As a result, she and other whites either shied away from civil rights activity or stressed moderation and patience in racial change. This was particularly the case after Marion A. Wright's keynote address at the 1954 NAACP testimonial dinner honoring Judge J. Waties Waring. Wright's speech pleased black board members, most of whom were also members of the NAACP. Unfortunately, most white SCCHR members perceived the NAACP as a radical organization whose demands for racial justice were too aggressive, and thus they discouraged those affiliated with the NAACP from becoming members of the organization. This angered SCCHR black members such as Modjeska Simkins and Robert Hinton and intensified racial tensions. As a consequence, Simkins and Hinton resigned from the SCCHR board.[83]

Unlike Simons, Spearman had long recognized the importance of understanding and working with African Americans as equals. Indeed, her activism was part of a pattern that dated back to the 1930s. Born in Marion, South Carolina, in 1902 to a wealthy planting and banking family, Spearman had spent a year in the 1920s at the YWCA's National Training School while earning a master's degree in religious education from Columbia University. Her attendance there and earlier at Converse College for Women in Spartanburg, South Carolina, facilitated her move into a circle of liberal thinkers. During her time at Converse, Spearman was a member of the student YWCA's interracial council. This involvement was a fundamental part of her introduction to interracial activism in South Carolina.[84] While attending Converse she had been elected by the student body to represent them at the southeast regional summer conferences that the national student YWCA held at Blue Ridge, North Carolina. It was there that she first met educated blacks on an equal basis. She delighted in telling her family that while there she had met blacks who were superior to them intellectually, culturally, and spiritually.[85]

In the years that followed, Spearman maintained close ties to such organizations as the YWCA. She later served as the education director for the Germantown YWCA in Philadelphia, where she joined the Philadelphia race relations committee.[86] Spearman, executive director of the SCCHR, was a member of the South Carolina Council for the Common Good and a lifetime member of the National Association of Colored Women. At the latter organization's annual regional conference in 1957 in Greenville, she moderated a discussion titled "The Council Woman at Work in Her Community for Changing Frontiers in Our Present Day."[87] The theme for the conference was, rather fittingly, "Education a Force for Changing Frontiers in Human Relations." Also in attendance was Sarah Z. Daniels, who would later become the first African American president of United Church Women in South Carolina.[88]

Spearman became the mainstay of the SCCHR until the mid-1960s. She had long had a history of reaching out to black women and to women generally in pursuit of an alliance against racial injustice. In the 1930s she and Modjeska Simkins had worked together on the New Deal public works projects and had protested the planning committee's practice of giving menial jobs to blacks and professional jobs to whites. Spearman had further been selected as one of the first women to head the South Carolina Emergency Recovery Administration (SCERA).[89] Afterward, she became the district supervisor for social services, which included Lee, Sumter, Clarendon, Williamsburg, Georgetown, and Berkeley Counties.[90]

Spearman's politics while working for the SCERA proved problematic, however. In 1935 an anti–New Deal newspaper charged that she was teaching Communism in her adult education classes. According to South Carolina historian Jack Irby Hayes, Spearman's travels to Russia in 1931 and 1932 and the fact that she was active in the Socialist Party lent credence to these claims. Also, she later told a convention of African American teachers in Mullins, South Carolina, that "the Negro should work for social equality as was their due."[91] As a southern white woman, Spearman indeed held controversial political views for the time. Simkins once recalled that Spearman "exemplified the bull in the china closet type. She never took back water about anything."[92] Simkins further saw a kindred spirit in Spearman with her formidable and unflappable commitment to racial equality when she recalled: "Alice is a type of person like I am; she just doesn't give a damn."[93] Spearman refused to curb her attacks on racism and inequality in South Carolina, and her commitment to organized labor continued even after the head of the state Works Project Administration asked for her resignation. She was promoted to state supervisor of education for federal programs in October 1936.[94]

Although they often fought against paternalism, Simkins and Spearman were able to cooperate because both believed that black and white women working together should play a prominent role in political and civic action programs and racial cooperation in the state.[95] Spearman fervently appealed to black women affiliated with the YWCA in the Charleston area in order to solicit participation for an open meeting of the SCCHR in May 1955. In this same year, Spearman wrote to Anna DeWees Kelly, branch executive of the Coming Street YWCA in Charleston, asking her to support the SCCHR. Always concerned about the nature of interracial work in South Carolina, she inquired about the YWCA in Charleston as well as the existence of other interracial organizations in the area.[96] She learned from Kelly that some black women had long sought full integration in the Charleston YWCA and truly equal working relationships with white women.[97] However, Spearman's attempts to reach out to white women were often met with excuses and evasion because the SCCHR and interracial activism were deemed too controversial. Spearman also found this to be the case when she issued an invitation for membership in the SCCHR to the South Carolina Educational Association. The association graciously declined her offer.[98]

The Greenville YWCA

Like Alice Norwood Spearman, some white women increasingly embraced the tide of change in South Carolina through their organizational affiliations. The Greenville YWCA, for example, discussed moderate racial and social activism in South Carolina at gatherings with such women's organizations as the Greenville Social Worker's Club and the local council of United Church

Women.[99] Greenville YWCA members spent considerable time discussing the Supreme Court case in their meetings and prepared themselves to aid blacks and whites in South Carolina regardless of the decision. Many of them wrote letters to state legislators advising them that "whatever the Supreme Court holds to be the law with reference to the segregation suits now pending must be accepted and adhered to both as to letter and spirit." Greenville YWCA members were also concerned about the possibility of state officials closing public schools in opposition to the Court's decision and the impact this would have on children throughout the state. The Greenville YWCA asserted that "the public school system of S.C. must be maintained and that any tampering with it in an attempt to circumvent a Court decision will do irreparable harm to the educational opportunities of South Carolina's boys and girls."[100]

This sentiment was not unusual among white women's organizations in South Carolina. The South Carolina Federation of Women's Clubs voted to offer an award to the organizations that worked to develop citizen participation to preserve the state's public school system. The federation also felt that abandoning separate public school systems—something that many whites supported as an alternative to desegregation—should only be used as a last resort.[101]

Further evidence of the Greenville YWCA's stance on desegregation was its opposition to repealing the compulsory school attendance law. In 1951 the South Carolina legislature formed a fifteen-person committee chaired by Senator Marion Gressette of Calhoun County. When the Gressette Committee, also known as the "Segregation Committee," issued a report urging the adoption of new measures to defend segregation, Greenville YWCA members were incensed. Among the committee's proposals was a call for a referendum to delete the constitutional provision that required the state to provide public schools. Although educators and civil leaders around the state protested, the measure passed. Of the forty-six counties in South Carolina, only five opposed the amendment, as did such organizations as the South Carolina League of Women Voters, the NAACP, and the Public Affairs Committee of the state YWCA.[102] For some members of the Greenville YWCA, this only intensified the problems facing the Palmetto State. According to the Greenville YWCA president, "the repeal of the law will do nothing about solving our racial problems and will be detrimental to the welfare of South Carolina's children."[103]

This certainly was not the limit of the Greenville YWCA's fight for justice in South Carolina. In 1956, members of the board of directors of the Greenville YWCA spoke out against the South Carolina General Assembly because it had proposed bills prohibiting municipal, county, or state employees from holding membership in the NAACP and depriving churches accommodating NAACP meetings of their tax-exempt status. The board called efforts to suppress the NAACP a violation of "the democratic and Christian ways of life."[104] Members of the Greenville YWCA saw the NAACP as an organization "committed to the defense of civil liberties and religious freedom." They also understood that in order to ensure religious freedom, it was imperative to maintain separation between church and state: "If the General Assembly can dictate to Negro churches what meetings may be held in their church buildings, it can dictate to white churches what meetings may be held in theirs. If it has a right to legislate concerning one policy of a church, it has the right to legislate concerning all other church matters."[105] Board members carefully stated that although they did not endorse the NAACP, its leaders, or its activities, they strongly supported the principles of religious freedom and democracy for everyone, regardless of organizational affiliation or race. For members of the Greenville YWCA, this was especially true in the aftermath of the *Brown* decision: "The continuation of full realization of both democracy and Christianity require that we hold fast to these principles at all times, but especially so now that we are in a period of stress and tension."[106]

While the Greenville YWCA supported *Brown* and attacked efforts to resist desegregation, it moved slowly toward integration in its own organization. As autonomous organizations, local YWCAs were not legally bound to uphold the policies of the national YWCA. Southern YWCAs asserted their Christian beliefs in their pronouncements, describing their local YWCAs as "a fellowship of women and girls dedicated to realizing in our common life those ideals of personal social living, to which we are committed by our faith as Christians. The YWCA is essentially interested in helping each individual to develop her greatest potential . . . in realization of self, in service to others and in knowledge and love of God."[107] Despite this sentiment, some white women still adhered to local customs and traditions that made it difficult for them to imagine dismantling segregation in southern YWCAs.

The physical facilities of the YWCA reveal the spatial nature of race relations in local YWCAs throughout South Carolina. The Greenville YWCA facilities report listed a building at 118 West North Street, which included a residence for sixty-seven young employed women, a dining room, office space, and meeting and recreational rooms. However, there is but sparse mention of the facilities for black women and girls: "The cottage at 106 North Calhoun Street is currently rented to bring programs to Negro women and girls."[108] Although they maintained separate facilities, the Greenville YWCA participated in efforts to obtain a new and modern facility for blacks that enabled them to receive distinguished African American visitors and provided a segregated indoor swimming pool. However, the indicators of paternalism were always present. The YWCA campaign for the new building was presented to African American men and women in Greenville as "a test, keenly watched, of the progress of the Negroes toward full civic maturity."[109]

The Greenville YWCA's interracial activism was consistently tested by the pervasive racism in 1950s South Carolina. However, one Greenvillian proved the YWCA to be a conduit for such activism when she informed her sister, a newcomer interested in working with black women, "if you must work interracially, do it through the YWCA. Working there, people in the community will not consider you a 'crackpot.'"[110] Thus, the Greenville YWCA provided opportunities for black and white women to work together for racial change, not only in Greenville but throughout the state. At some points, however, Greenville YWCA members were apprehensive not only about asserting the civil rights agenda but also maintaining their affiliation with the national YWCA. In a 1958 report of the Capital Fund Committee to the United Fund of Greenville County, when the YWCA listed its community associations it stressed that "though there is no official connection, the Executive, four Board members, and one Young Adult leader have been active in this organization." Also, the Greenville YWCA reported its relationship with the national YWCA as "excellent" during a time when many southern YWCAs were questioning their affiliation with the national YWCA because of its position on civil rights activism.[111]

The Charleston YWCA

The Charleston YWCA moved more timidly than Greenville's in the wake of *Brown v. Board of Education*. While the Greenville YWCA attempted to make peace with the decision, relationships between black and white members of the Charleston YWCA became increasingly contentious.[112] In 1955, Carrie Lou Ritchie, executive director of the Charleston YWCA, invited Virginia Prouty, a Charleston native and a member of the Charleston YWCA who was also part of the national staff, to speak to the board of directors and membership about the World Fellowship Observance, which was supposed to bring together women of all racial and ethnic backgrounds in prayer once a year. Prouty agreed to speak, and her report commented on the angst among whites after the Supreme Court decision:

> The tension which is felt by the board and staff members is understandable and very real. Having been away from Charleston for some time, I was shocked when I saw and heard the "tumult and shouting" due to the Supreme Court decision. I feel that Miss Ritchie needs all the support that we as a National staff can give. She is desirous to do all that she can to move the Association ahead, and I am sure she will succeed in her efforts eventually.[113]

Although the Greenville YWCA made slight progress in interracial relationships, for the Charleston YWCA all progress in that direction stopped after the *Brown* decision. In 1955, the fear of integrated attendance at the World Fellowship Observance reached crisis proportions. In previous years, the World Fellowship Observance had been held at the Greek Orthodox Church in Charleston and planned jointly by the central and Coming Street branches of the YWCA. After the *Brown* decision, fear prevailed among white members of the central YWCA. Many white members on the World Fellowship Committee suddenly decided that they could not participate in an integrated meeting and consequently resigned. Board members of the YWCA feared any publicity, especially from local papers like Charleston's *News and Courier*.[114]

When Hattie Droll of the national YWCA visited Charleston in 1956, she noticed that most of the members of the YWCA board took great pride in "keeping alive the historical atmosphere of Charleston," or rather, maintaining the status quo. Yet she noted that younger people had grown bored with Charleston's traditions and wanted to "emphasize the present rather than the past."[115] When she returned in 1957, Droll noted that there was only token representation of blacks on the central YWCA's administrative committees and that the few integrated affairs, such as the World Fellowship Observance, were held with as little publicity as possible. Droll revealed the damage done to already fragile interracial relations in the Charleston YWCA when she reported that the "subject of desegregation is almost unmentionable in Charleston and the Citizens Councils have become more active there as it has in all South Carolina." She further recorded the YWCA's reaction to recent events: "Interracial gatherings are more conspicuous. Fear is greater. The Board of the YWCA follows the community trends and attitudes."[116] Unfortunately, the Charleston YWCA's relations with the national YWCA would become increasingly strained over the next decade.

The United Council of Church Women of South Carolina

Unlike the Charleston YWCA, the United Council of Church Women of South Carolina, founded in 1948, assumed the lead in preparing for the *Brown* decision. Publicity chair Edith Dabbs of Mayesville wrote *The Church Woman*, the national UCCW's magazine, acknowledging church women's commitment to Christian democracy and to changes yet to come. According to Dabbs, "The Council of Church Women of South Carolina is two years old but at the state meeting recently the skeleton organization was finally completed with constitution and working regulations. It is still in the throes of its infancy but the women enlisted hold the conviction that Christianity is the only answer to world confusion and are ready to meet the challenge."[117]

One obstacle to the UCCW's progress was white and black women's fear of attending integrated meetings. Born in Dalzell in Sumter County in 1906 to a Southern Baptist family, Dabbs envisioned an organization that was more than "one more stodgy, complacent, burdensome organization of women doing what we had already been doing all the time." That is, she understood that in order for Christian women to effect change in South Carolina, black and white women had to work together. Dabbs and some of the other founding members of the South Carolina UCCW invited black women church leaders to its state meeting shortly after its founding. Only one attended, and her presence revealed the angst surrounding integrated meetings. Dabbs recalled that when she and the other women entered the Columbia YWCA building, where the meeting was being held, someone called the secretary to protest the presence of one black face in the group.[118]

Although integrated membership in the UCCW may have been problematic for some, national representatives saw glimmers of hope. Nationally, United Council of Church Women membership had been integrated since the 1940s, and the group pushed for the same in local UCCW chapters. When Myrta Ross of the national UCCW, which was renamed United Church Women (UCW) in 1950, visited South Carolina in April 1951 she observed local councils meetings and concluded: "Very hopeful in South Carolina. Indeed thrilling in spots. Many needs which we have an opportunity to help, met."[119] Although Ross reported that the Spartanburg council was integrated, the Sumter council was struggling with the idea of doing so.

Black women were more visible as members and officers in the South Carolina council of UCW by the 1950s. Inez B. Bacoats, whose husband was president of Benedict College, was a member of the South Carolina UCW.[120] Anna D. Reuben, a graduate of Fisk University who had earned a doctorate from Columbia University in 1955, was the first black woman to hold an official position in the South Carolina UCW when she was elected secretary in 1952.[121] Reuben was also a former secretary of the South Carolina NAACP and chairperson of the executive board of the Sumter colored branch of the YWCA.[122] In 1955 a second black woman, Mayme S. Gordon of Dillon, South Carolina, was unanimously elected secretary of the South Carolina UCW. However, there was no substantial integration in the state UCW until the 1960s.

This fear of integration prompted state UCW members to suggest that "local Negroes should be urged to organize a council" in 1951. No records indicate that such a segregated branch was formed, yet despite the anxiety surrounding integrated meetings the organization clearly assumed a more proactive role in making racial changes as the *Brown* decision loomed. Indeed, the state council took steps to prepare its members for whatever changes might occur when the Court's decision was handed down. In 1951 Dabbs issued a letter to local councils announcing a meeting with Esther Stamats of the national UCW. Although the outcome of the meeting is unclear, Dabbs urged white women to attend to discuss the "big implications of which we are a part" and "the genius of leadership in such an adventure toward a New World." The end of the letter reveals the state council's commitment to racial change as Dabbs further encouraged churchwomen: "Please come—it is a great door open."[123]

In 1953, the state arm of UCW called upon church women to investigate conditions in South Carolina public schools using a pamphlet called "A Check List for Your Local Schools." Published by the SRC, the checklist suggested conducting a statistical and comparative study of black and white schools in the state by asking questions such as "What is the average salary of white and Negro teachers with comparable training and experience? What is the current operating expenditure per white and Negro pupil? How do white and Negro school buildings compare in age, appearance, type of construction, toilet facilities, lighting, ventilation, heating, auditoriums, gymnasiums, athletic stadiums, cafeterias, and libraries?"[124] By conducting such an exercise, the state council, clearly more progressive than local councils, forced white women to confront inferior conditions in South Carolina's black schools.

Caroline Lee Gillespie, chair of the Christian Social Relations Committee of the South Carolina UCW, stressed the seriousness with which the organization regarded the school desegregation case. Members of the state council felt that Christians should be informed and prepared to give guidance should

Brown order school integration.[125] Gillespie further asserted that southern church women were "nearing the threshold of an historic moment in the history of our nation and indeed of the world. Regardless of the decision of the Supreme Court, Christian people will have to be acquainted with the moral and spiritual issues which are at stake."[126]

Despite white southerners' responses to the Supreme Court decision, once it had been issued, Edith Dabbs immediately sent a letter to Governor James F. Byrnes expressing the position of United Church Women of South Carolina: "Both on a national level and statewise, we have always maintained that enforced segregation had no place in Christian activity and constituted a very real threat to our Democracy."[127] State political leaders were clearly dedicated to maintaining segregation in South Carolina. Thus, when church women looked to them to foster change, they did so in vain.

Dabbs also recognized the unique role the UCW could play in facilitating racial change throughout the state: "United Church Women come from practically every Protestant denomination in South Carolina and are the mothers and teachers, the home makers of our state."[128] Looking with faith to black and white South Carolinians to accept racial progress, Dabbs ended her letter to the governor by highlighting their morality and integrity: "Carolinians are not a hating people. Our citizens can be counted on, after a little shouting and letting off steam, to settle down to adjustment. As we work together to build a new and finer way of life for all our people, we shall realize that for the first time in history we need no longer cringe in apology before any other group. We are free at last . . . and free to build a shining model of Christian Democracy before the world."[129]

Although general white consensus against the *Brown* decision limited the activism of some white women's organizations in South Carolina, others chose to stand as an example of racial change. A gathering of southern church women in June 1954 in Atlanta reinforced these mandates. Attendees included chairpersons of Christian social relations committees and presidents of state councils of UCW throughout the South. Although it is not clear if any black women attended, conference attendees adopted a resolution that affirmed their belief in "human brotherhood and the inclusiveness of Christian fellowship and a Christian society in which segregation is no longer a burden upon the human spirit."[130]

At the two-day conference, leaders pointed out such specific problems as the amount of time necessary for whites to adjust to the fact that the Supreme Court decision called for immediate desegregation. Attendees studied strategies, techniques, and organizational procedures to be put in operation immediately in each state. Many of these women most likely struggled to overcome their upbringing in conservative, racially segregated communities. As historian Shannon Frystak has argued about activist women in Louisiana, "seeing that *Brown* was enforced became the ultimate test of one's courage and faith." Church women in South Carolina understood that they had to steel themselves for the battle ahead.[131]

Church women also wondered about the plight of black teachers who might find themselves unemployed after the decision. They did not consider that some black parents might want improved conditions in black schools rather than forced enrollment of black children in previously all-white schools. Conference attendees openly criticized southern ministers who failed to support the Supreme Court decision. Indeed, to them it was imperative to encourage clergy members to take a positive Christian stand on such issues and help Christian women find solutions to the "bitter climate of opinion" in their states. Finally, they adopted a statement that affirmed their acceptance of the Court's decision.[132]

After attending this conference, South Carolina UCW members reaffirmed their commitment to work for racial justice in South Carolina. They supported the Supreme Court decision because it gave them an opportunity to translate Christian belief into democratic ideals. Caroline Gillespie replayed these sentiments from the Atlanta conference: "We came from seventeen states, represented many denominations, and faced multiple problems. But one question and one purpose drew us close together: How shall I sing the Lord's song? Our days of working and thinking together helped to answer that burning question. We learned that while the problem may vary in degrees in different states, all of us face similar situations. New courage is found in the knowledge that one is not alone."[133] Members of local UCW chapters struggled among themselves and with their communities to determine what "singing the Lord's song" might mean locally.[134] South Carolina church women realized that they were not alone in combating the injustices of racial and social discrimination. Although they were ambivalent about what shape their activism and the risks involved would assume, church women realized that Christian doctrine mandated that they do something to bring about more harmonious race relations.

The national organization of United Church Women urged local branches to assume the lead in implementing racial change in their communities. It was not enough for a church woman to "fold her hands and pray for a peaceful conclusion to the whole matter." The national UCW prescribed specific actions such as "speaking up when race is mentioned to let people

know where you stand," "know[ing] the facts so that you can answer prejudice and opposition with irrefutable truths," and "try[ing] to arrange for
conversation between Negro and white citizens for better understanding
of the problems involved and ways and means of meeting them."[135] The
national body also urged local chapters to study facts about segregation
in their community, in schools, housing, churches, and public facilities. It
advocated cooperation with other community agencies and creation of a
concrete plan of action in accordance with Christian principles to aid community changes and challenges.[136] Registering its concern about growing
threats to teachers in southern states who were members of the NAACP,
the national UCW perceived charges of Communism as a very real threat
to American civil liberties as well as to the multifaceted activism of United
Church Women. According to one church woman, "If our Board of Education could decide that teachers could not be members of the NAACP, the
time might also come when teachers would not be permitted to join United
Church Women."[137]

In South Carolina, some members of UCW grappled with the implications of the *Brown* decision. In 1955 they met at St. Paul's Lutheran Church
in Columbia to promote public discussion about this issue throughout the
state. This effort was led by UCW member Priscilla Shaw, the mayor of Sumter.[138] The biracial panel at the meeting was titled "Our Schools, the Supreme
Court, and United Church Women" and included Horatia Nelson, president
of the Columbia Women's Council; Lincoln Jenkins, an African American
attorney; and James McBride Dabbs, UCW president Edith Mitchell Dabbs's
husband and a critic of southern racial injustice. Mayor Shaw emphasized
women's critical role in spearheading the changes that were facing South
Carolina as a result of the *Brown* decision: "Women have a tremendous responsibility to exert leadership in matters moral and spiritual." She paired
this responsibility with women's leadership roles as wives and mothers but
also underlined this by pointing out that their influence had been rendered
"quietly and without fanfare," thus underscoring the importance of their activism while being mindful of the racial climate in which they operated. Nelson reinforced black women activists' determination to procure first-class
citizenship and harkened back to the sacrifices of African American soldiers
when she asserted, "It is just as impossible to explain to a child why he is
barred from simple social privileges and public institutions as to convince a
soldier who has fought for and risked his life for his country, that he should
be subjected to the indignities of second class citizenship upon his return to
America."[139]

Throughout South Carolina there were those who saw UCW as the catalyst for racial change. Among those who recognized the group's important role in racial activism was Father Maurice V. Shean of the Catholic Oratory in Rock Hill, South Carolina. Shean was also the secretary of the Rock Hill Council for Human Relations in 1954.[140] Although he was not present at the meeting in Columbia, he suggested through his secretary, Mrs. Joseph Bonetti, that United Church Women urge Governor Timmerman to appoint a biracial council of women to study desegregation in the state. In addition to considering this suggestion, participants addressed concerns about desegregation in South Carolina by organizing themselves into discussion groups with such titles as "What Can You Do?" or "What Is the Church's Responsibility and Place?" The groups queried how they might translate their findings into local communities, concluding that it was necessary to get blacks and whites to meet together for discussion, which would enable a better understanding of problems that existed between the races.[141]

Those in attendance understood how difficult it had been to organize such a meeting. Grace T. Kennedy of Bennettsville, secretary of the UCW's Department of Christian Social Relations, lamented that whites in her community had refused to meet with blacks for discussions of any kind. Moreover, five UCW members in attendance requested not to receive further information about desegregation, claiming they were "unprepared for it at present."[142]

The national council encouraged South Carolina church women to help facilitate desegregation and racial understanding. In November 1956 it sent Esther C. Stamats, director of the Department of Christian Social Relations, to lead a workshop for United Church Women of Columbia on "Human Relations." The workshop was to offer tactics on dealing with racial issues. Organized into small groups, the participants asked "What holds us back?" and "What next steps can you take in your community?" They outlined such obstacles as breakdowns in communication, fear of reprisals, pressures to conform, and threats to freedom. The minutes for the workshop reveal the anxiety some women felt. The secretary reported that "attendance was very poor" but affirmed that of those who did attend, "everyone was exceedingly interested."[143]

The national council also pressured United Church Women in South Carolina to take the obvious step toward integration by welcoming African American women into their organization. In January 1957, when Mrs. David Baker, editor of *The Church Woman*, spoke to the Columbia organization about her experiences with a team of Christian women who had traveled abroad, she emphasized the "interdenominational, interracial, and inter-color composition" of its teams with church women around the world.[144]

The national UCW continued to push local chapters to work for better racial and social conditions throughout the nation. At the Eighth National Assembly of United Church Women in 1958 in Denver, whose theme was "Christianity and Freedom," members affirmed that although many tensions remained, there had been significant progress in race relations. However, they encouraged Christian women who were committed to change in their communities to act as a guiding conscience. The national UCW supported southern church women's work toward the elimination of discrimination in housing, public schools, health and recreational facilities, transportation, and public accommodations. It also urged women to support efforts in their local communities to establish interracial councils to work on community programs, in addition to recommending that the president of the United States call a White House conference on integration as soon as possible. The national UCW suggested that women be a positive Christian influence by working with people in the community and using church facilities to foster better communication between the races.[145] Finally, for their national assembly, the UCW extended an invitation to Arthur B. Spingarn, national president of the NAACP, requesting that it send a "fraternal delegate" to represent the organization.[146]

Conclusion

As the Supreme Court's *Brown v. Board of Education* decision ordered school desegregation, reactions varied throughout the South. For whites, the decision evoked emotions that ranged from outright hostility to withdrawal of support from those who had urged racial change in the state. Some blacks also withheld their support when they were faced with economic reprisals and outright violence from the white establishment. This did not stop the activism of black and white women's organizations, however. Although at this point instances of interracial interaction were limited, some black and white women were able to reach across the racial divide to effect change throughout the state, and some local groups like the Greenville YWCA became more assertive on racial issues.

By the end of the 1950s, the goals of black and white women often diverged. For black women and their organizations, equal educational and political access were still primary goals. However, such activism was not without risk. Some black women lost their jobs and very nearly their lives for challenging racial inequality. White women and their organizations, on the other hand, increasingly withdrew from overt racial activism after the *Brown* decision. Their retreat, however, did not stem the tide of racial change in South Carolina.

4

"Strength and Faith to Stand Together"

Civil Rights Activism and South Carolina YWCAs

May we pray that we be given strength and faith to stand together, though
our degrees of beliefs may differ.

VIRGINIA PROUTY, EXECUTIVE DIRECTOR OF THE CHARLESTON YWCA, 1963

In 1963, the National Board of the YWCA issued an "Urgent Memo on Civil
Rights" that outlined new policies and goals for YWCAs throughout the
country. These included supporting civil rights legislation, sponsoring the
1963 March on Washington, and accelerating the desegregation of community YWCAs. In Charleston, South Carolina, white members of the local
YWCA vigorously objected to these goals and because of them disaffiliated
from the national YWCA. Although she did not support desegregation,
Virginia Prouty, executive director of the Charleston YWCA, invoked the
Christianity upon which the YWCA was founded and urged members in
the local and national organization to "pray" for "strength and faith" as they
were caught in the middle of this controversy. As desegregation increasingly
became a reality, South Carolinians questioned how they would deal with a
society where separation of the races was no longer the law and local activists
were increasing efforts for full citizenship.

As in previous years, black and white women's organizations throughout the state responded to these issues in various ways. Black women and
their organizations continued to focus on obtaining voting rights for African Americans and access to better schools for their children. Some white

women, on the other hand, increasingly turned away from controversial racial activism after the *Brown* decision. These concerns reflected changing times as South Carolinians reexamined what had always been traditional and familiar as both groups of women dealt with the reality of desegregation.

Black and white women's organizations like the YWCA also recognized the dawning of a new era and responded to burgeoning changes in South Carolina. The Greenville YWCA, for example, highlighted education, employment, leisure, and racial integration among its programs and services for the 1960s. All of these had long been issues of concern to black and white activists in Greenville. For black and white women, Christian idealism remained the foundation for the YWCA's work and its members. It served as a touchstone for women's activism throughout the 1950s and 1960s by highlighting the religious imperative to facilitate racial and social change.[1] This was evident in the Greenville YWCA's meetings. In December 1969, when the meeting between the two local branches was called to order, the president of the board, invoking Christianity and perhaps the significance of its integrated membership, proclaimed the meeting "a special occasion due to its being Christ's birthday and also due to that fact that the Birnie Street Committee and the Board was [sic] meeting together."[2] Such Christian mandates were imbedded in the Greenville YWCA's activities in the early 1960s when they positioned civic training as part of the YWCA's program, emphasizing it as being just as important as religious and moral training. Moreover, the Greenville YWCA formed a public affairs committee that met regularly to study good citizenship and urge voter registration, issues that would assume an increasingly prominent role on the YWCAs civil rights agenda throughout the 1960s.

South Carolina was a state where, since the end of Reconstruction, politicians had often stooped to race-baiting and urged that social stability be placed above all other priorities to ensure that the lines between race and class were clearly drawn. But many women understood that racism impeded political, economic, and educational progress statewide. In 1958, women's groups like the YWCA had issued a statement appealing to political candidates to "deal with the race issue in a dignified manner."[3] YWCA members worked to change the political system by initiating efforts along with such women's organizations as the United Church Women, the American Association of University Women, and the League of Women Voters. Members urged state and local political candidates to honestly assess the issues facing South Carolinians regardless of race and to "raise the level of the campaign by discussing issues and not resorting to demagoguery."[4]

The Greenville YWCA and the Changing Racial Order

Although many southern YWCAs questioned how they should react to the changing racial order and thus define their relationship with the national YWCA, the Greenville YWCA solidified its position, asserting that their YWCA had no "family skeletons." That is, they largely agreed with the national body's position on racial inclusiveness and its involvement in the civil rights movement. Indeed, in many respects the Greenville YWCA was integrated. According to a 1960 YWCA Administrative Building Fund Campaign report, the board of directors and all association committees and councils were integrated. Black and white members attended regional and national meetings together. However, they continued to meet in separate facilities, and the housing, residence, camping, and public food service provided by the YWCA remained segregated.[5]

Moreover, the Greenville YWCA was not without its dissenting membership. Soon after African American women and girls were offered membership in 1949, three white members withdrew and three others resigned from the board of directors. Later, older members and other former leaders often chose to continue to pay dues and retain their membership but failed to attend all-association meetings, most likely because they did not want to be personally involved with "controversial" aspects of YWCA activism. Some women may not have wanted it to be known that they were members of an organization that openly supported civil rights initiatives or could not imagine working with black women as equals. On the other hand, newer members of the organization and the board had worked interracially through other organizations and thus brought this experience and an added impetus to the Greenville YWCA's racial activism.

But interracial activism did not preclude black women's desire to work independently of white oversight to enact changes and develop leaders within their communities. The Greenville YWCA, for its part, supported and encouraged black women's autonomy within the organization. In 1961 they proposed building a new facility for the predominantly black Birnie Street YWCA. In the February 1961 "Survey, Analysis, and Plan of Fund-Raising for YWCA of Greenville," they argued that a new facility would provide a "usable center for many Negro activities." White women recognized the spatial limitations of the current facility and posited that the building would provide "space and facilities for a really vigorous and significant YWCA program for Negro girls and women, such as is physically impossible in the present five-room bungalow." In its fund-raising campaign the Greenville YWCA pointed out the relative lack of wealth of its board of directors and the city's black community.[6]

The Birnie Street YWCA was a space where black education and community activism flourished. Because integrated membership often meant white paternalism and unequal membership for African American women, Birnie Street members stressed that a separate YWCA made them feel more secure and provided them with more opportunities for leadership and growth. It also allowed them to provide services directly to their community.[7] Some local African Americans, however, objected to a separate YWCA. In 1962 the Greenville Interdenominational Ministerial Alliance opposed the construction of a separate YWCA, claiming that it would "perpetuate segregation." Rev. C. Hayes, alliance president and pastor of Allen Temple African Methodist Episcopal Church in Greenville, asserted, "The proposed branch of the YWCA building that is to be built on Birnie Street is a black mark on Christianity." Hayes also commented, "While it is understood among the ministers that our position may not prevent the building of a segregated YWCA in Greenville (for there are those in our community who have a vested interest and who are sustained by the institution of segregation), we the Interdenominational Ministerial Alliance would want it to be known that we defy the promotion of segregation in any form."[8] Hayes pointed out those African Americans whose businesses or community interests benefited from segregation, but he turned to Christian convictions to support its dismantling.

However, black women saw a benefit in both perspectives. For them, a separate organization did not preclude interracial activism. They wanted "opportunities for wider experiences and for recognition." Thus, they acknowledged the benefits of interracial activism through participation in the Greenville YWCA, as well as the opportunities a separate branch provided to showcase black women's skills as community leaders.[9]

While the Greenville YWCA worked to implement national policies in South Carolina, its leaders acknowledged in a 1960 report that they had to tread lightly. Indeed, many whites in Greenville resisted desegregation, although their efforts were increasingly futile. Aware that change would need to occur slowly, YWCA members took steps to ensure that national policies were not highlighted in local newspapers. Although the board was integrated, its membership took care to keep pictures of integrated YWCA activities out of local papers. When all-association YWCA activities were reported, no attention was called to the fact that they were integrated.[10]

As the Greenville YWCA kept tabs on racial developments in the county, it supported two lawsuits (to open airport and library facilities to all citizens) and organized sit-ins at lunch counters throughout the city. YWCA members were incensed when city officials closed the public library in March 1960 after students from the predominantly African American Sterling High School attempted to desegregate its facilities. In September of the same year, Mrs. John F. Chandler, president of the Greenville YWCA, protested to Kenneth Cass, mayor of Greenville: "In this rapidly changing era when education assumes increasing importance, to deny citizens the use of books in our opinion is not only deplorable, but also a disaster." Chandler requested that "the City Council as a corporate body take appropriate action to open the library to all citizens without delay."[11] The library was reopened by the end of the month on a nondiscriminatory basis.[12]

The Greenville YWCA noted that local and state policy persisted in its attempts to maintain segregation at all costs. But members also acknowledged that its city was in a more favorable position than many other southern communities to accommodate racial changes. Not only did it have relatively few African Americans in its population, but it also had a biracial committee that had quietly worked to desegregate Greenville.[13] Thus, the groups recognized their role in improving racial conditions in Greenville and posited that the YWCA's activism was accepted because the organization maintained separate facilities for black and white women. Indeed, the YWCA was one of the few places where blacks and whites could meet to discuss racial issues, and it was most likely the only place in the white community with integrated dining facilities.

The Greenville YWCA believed it was in a controversial yet important position to advance racial progress, characterizing its work as "quiet and progressive" and its approach as a "conscious effort not to precipitate a crisis," noting additionally that it had "hazards as well as opportunities for moral leadership." It further asserted that in "unobtrusive, unspectacular, and moderate ways" the YWCA had offered "Christian leadership in Greenville to advances in the development of interracial relations."[14] Thus, the organization worked carefully to change race relations in Greenville and South Carolina while remaining mindful of the difficult racial climate in which it worked.

Although racial restrictions on the black and white branches of the Greenville YWCA had been lifted, black and white members did not stop using their respective facilities. For the black and white women in leadership positions in the YWCA, racial integration was relatively easy; many had established contacts across racial lines as a result of their early activism. Like many women involved in racial work, they shared a middle-class status and perspective. However, this was not the case for the general YWCA membership.[15]

Because of local social mores, the general membership of the Greenville YWCA, unlike its integrated leadership, had few opportunities to interact in the 1960s.[16] Yet, there was some movement in that direction. African American members began to participate in classes and programs, including swimming classes, at the white YWCA. Integrated activities seemed to work best among young people as the YWCA successfully cooperated with an interracial religious youth council.[17]

Black women's autonomy within the YWCA was dependent upon maintaining separate facilities, however. The Birnie Street YWCA (formerly the North Calhoun Street YWCA) created programs to support the African American community, such as an enrichment program for low-income mothers and periodic programs on sexual morality. As the 1960s came to a close, the Greenville YWCA supported Birnie Street teen programs on race relations and courses on black heritage. They also worked with the Greenville Council of Church Women by writing letters to local newspapers supporting juvenile correction studies.[18] Black and white YWCA members contributed to the empowering nature of this environment by maintaining separate facilities until the 1980s.

The Charleston YWCA and the Limits of Interracial Cooperation

Unlike the Greenville YWCA, the Charleston YWCA's limited efforts for interracial cooperation evaporated in the 1960s as the national YWCA pushed its civil rights initiatives. When the sit-ins began in the early 1960s, the national YWCA was one of the first organizations to publicly lend its support by offering funds and legal aid, by endorsing the 1963 March on Washington, by urging local branches—especially those in the South—to end racism and segregation within their organizations, and by participating in the National Women's Committee for Civil Rights, which met with President John F. Kennedy in July 1963 to discuss ways to solve social problems.[19] The Coming Street YWCA had been a branch of the central George Street YWCA since the 1920s, but when the YWCA's National Board began to encourage local associations to integrate, the central YWCA regarded this move as an encroachment upon their local autonomy. The Charleston YWCA immediately opposed the program because it required local chapters to support civil rights legislation and because they claimed the National Board spoke for all local associations without their consent or representation.[20] Some white members could not imagine the YWCA as an organization determined to challenge and destroy systematic segregation and discrimination.

The National Board did not take action against the Charleston YWCA for disapproving of the program, however. Ruth Lois Hill, the YWCA's southern regional director, claimed that there was correspondence between the Charleston YWCA and the national office but recognized that the national contributed only material and ideas to the local association, not financial assistance.[21] The National Board further acknowledged that "local groups have a certain amount of self-determination."[22] That is, local YWCAs were autonomous, and the National Board did not possess the power to force them to comply with their policies.[23]

The Charleston YWCA did, however, take modest steps to bring its city closer to national ideals. In October 1963, a month after they disapproved the civil rights directive from the National Board, the association members added an African American to their executive committee. They also formed a six-member biracial committee consisting of three members from the Coming Street branch's committee on administration and three members from the board of directors. Virginia Prouty, Charleston YWCA executive director, stated that the biracial committee's role was to "meet with the president and executive director to determine what steps need to be taken by both groups to make for more meaningful relations in the YWCA and in the community." According to Prouty, "Relationships between national and the local YWCA have been and continue to be excellent. At no time has there been any thought of disaffiliation."[24] However, the events that followed indicate that there had been some discussion about disaffiliation from the national YWCA.

Rather than desegregate, the Charleston YWCA sought to circumvent the national's directive by creating new but separate YWCA facilities. In a letter to the National Board, Prouty and Mrs. Bonum S. Wilson, president of the Charleston YWCA, made the Charleston position very clear: for more than ten years the YWCA had been working and planning for new facilities for the branch and central YWCAs.[25] They had anticipated breaking ground for this in the fall of 1963 but concluded that "the present civil rights situation, together with the directives from the National Board, will more than likely halt this badly needed construction."[26] But by the fall of 1964, the Coming Street YWCA had its new building.[27]

The letter also focused on the services they provided to the black and white communities in Charleston. It reported that integration in the Charleston YWCA occurred mainly among its leadership, as most black and white women interacted with each other only in committee and board meetings and leadership training sessions. Wilson and Prouty also argued that they had accomplished much by helping eradicate school dropouts and illegitimacy and by creating adult education and citizenship programs. The Charleston YWCA clearly saw itself fostering better race relations within the confines of a segregated society. Wilson expressed this sentiment in 1963 to Mrs. Archie D. Marvel, president of the National Board: "Within the bounds of the mores of this community the YWCA had helped to set the pace for understanding and communication."[28] The Charleston YWCA prided itself on having kept the lines of communication open with the branch YWCA and saw only progress in its relations yet to come. But, black women had grown tired of white women counseling them to be patient and faithful as they waited for racial justice. Unfortunately, the Charleston YWCA found it too distressing to consider complying with the national YWCA's civil rights agenda and asserted, "Under the circumstances, we feel that we cannot and must not promote further integration at this time."[29]

Hence the formation of a biracial committee then did not succeed in changing the segregated policies of the Charleston YWCA. Prouty declared that "the Charleston YWCA will not be altered by the pro-integration policy of the YWCA's National Board." The committee had been formed merely to bring black and white leaders together to "further understanding between branches."[30] According to Prouty, the biracial committee would help avoid disaffiliation or dissolution of either branch by allowing each group to discuss ways to remain segregated and autonomous of the national YWCA. The Charleston YWCA's reaction to the memo was indicative of racial tensions in the city. Prouty described black and white Charlestonians as "very tense and on a razor's edge" in a telephone conversation with Florence Harris, correlator of the YWCA's southern region. Prouty was further emotionally traumatized by local events, most notably the demonstrations led by blacks to dismantle segregation in the city.

Black members were further upset with the executive committee of the Charleston YWCA. Anna DeWees Kelly, executive director of the Coming Street YWCA, contacted Prouty and voiced her opposition to the Charleston YWCA's stand to Edith M. Lerrigo, general secretary of the National Board. Because there were no black members on the executive committee, their opinions were not represented in the Charleston YWCA's letter, which underscored their long history of racial exclusion and subordination within the local YWCA.[31]

The National Board dealt with the Charleston YWCA very carefully. It was clearly aware of the fragile nature of race relations in its southern associations. However, it urged the Charleston group to make a decision on integration that fell in line with the new philosophy of the National Board. Edith Lerrigo hoped that local branches would comply with national policy. She was confident in the Charleston YWCA's ability to align itself with YWCAs across the country as they worked to make their organizations more inclusive. "I feel sure that we can count upon the leaders of the Charleston Association to make their decisions within the frame of the Christian task of the YWCA." Lerrigo urged the Charleston YWCA to carefully consider its decision and recognized that because it was not financially supported by the national YWCA, it did indeed function as an autonomous entity. Although she left the issue of compliance with national policy up to the leaders and representatives of the Charleston YWCA, Lerrigo urged that this decision could best be made by representatives from the central and branch YWCAs, thus subtly urging interracial cooperation.[32]

Because the Charleston YWCA received funds from conservative organizations like the United Fund, they were concerned about any actions that might alienate contributors. The United Fund (later the United Way) often threatened to cut off financial support to organizations for what it considered radical social activism. This was clearly the case when the executive director of the Charleston United Fund told Florence Harris that he was "critical and astonished" that the National Board would support anything as "questionable" as the March on Washington. He also informed her that the Charleston YWCA had used appropriate methods for "building relationships" but that supporting any radical activities would "undo in Charleston all that had been previously done in improving communications between the two races."[33] The national YWCA had underestimated how angry some white Charlestonians were about its support of the civil rights movement. When the national YWCA's memo appeared in Charleston's News and Courier, Prouty expected to be overwhelmed with phone calls. She only received a phone call from a woman who exclaimed, "I will never donate to the YWCA again!"[34]

The integrated activism that had existed in the Greenville YWCA was not reflected in local YWCAs in most other parts of South Carolina. In Charleston, even at the leadership level, perpetual tension existed between the branch and the central YWCA. However, many black members tried to foster better and integrated efforts with the central YWCA. After the National Board passed its resolution changing its purpose and policies in April 1964, the newly formed biracial committee met in December 1964 to interpret the meaning of the resolution for members and new board members.[35] Some white members subtly proposed listing courses in the central YWCA's bulletin, but they wanted to make it clear that they were being taught at the black branch. Another member proposed a new building if there were to be integrated classes. The apprehension among some white members was palpable. When Phyllis Shaffer mentioned the course proposal, member Eleanor Craighill declared that she did not believe in interracial mixing. In March 1965, after the National Board sent a letter to the Charleston YWCA urging compliance with the Civil Rights Act of 1964 and a directive from the Civil Rights Commission, Prouty and two program staff members resigned.[36]

Because of the touted "Christian" purpose of the YWCA, black members, though aware of the racial dynamics of the South and South Carolina, were surprised by white members' negative reaction to the changing purpose of the YWCA's mission. And many white members were upset by the National Board's support of what were considered controversial topics in Charleston in the 1960s. Black members, however, were adamant about keeping a YWCA in the city and pushed the association to adopt the national's directives. Mrs. F. Perry Metz, the administration committee chair, urged discussion among its members. Another black member, Emily Fielding, pointed out small steps toward integration in one YWCA class and moved that the Charleston YWCA's administration committee be in accordance with the Civil Rights Commission's request for racial inclusiveness, particularly because it was also in compliance with the purpose and philosophy of the YWCA.[37]

Even as they did this, black women maintained contact with officials on the National Board and discussed their findings in their own meetings. In April 1965, Mrs. Metz met with Hattie Droll, part of the field staff for the southern region of the YWCA. When she reported to the Coming Street YWCA, Metz discussed the importance of a "closer union" of the central and branch YWCAs in Charleston, urging that they "work toward creating a feeling of one association."[38]

Black women interpreted compliance with national YWCA policy differently from white women. For blacks, compliance meant increased resources and community participation in a program that ensured racial inclusiveness. For white women, compliance almost certainly meant a loss in financial resources from the white community, especially since they functioned autonomously from the national organization.[39]

Throughout the 1960s, black women, and some white women, worked to maintain a collaborative relationship between the members of the central and the Coming Street YWCAs, while continuing to push for integration and better facilities for African Americans. In September 1965, Mrs. Singleton of the Coming Street YWCA gave a report from the pool committee stating that it was not possible to build a pool in the black areas of Charleston and proposed instead that blacks be allowed to use the central YWCA's swimming pool. Nonetheless, Phyllis Shaffer elaborated on the committee's findings, concluding that she did not see any reason why blacks should not have their own pool. Although a few white members favored integrating their pool, most immediately rejected the idea. This clearly demonstrated that, for white and black members alike, the basic tenets of the YWCA were subject to interpretation.[40] Many white members adhered to the mores of a racist, segregated society. They struggled with and often won the battle to use their interpretation of Christian activism to support injustice.

Black women understood the YWCA both nationally and locally as a racially inclusive organization. The National Board stressed this same understanding. According to Dorothy I. Height, director of the Office of Racial Justice of the National Board, "As women and girls of goodwill, it is easy to talk among ourselves and to justify token integration. But the times demand that we give leadership to becoming a truly open Association in an open society. Our Christian Purpose impels us to eradicate the vestiges of racism within Associations themselves."[41]

The national YWCA's support of civil rights activism threatened white members of the Charleston YWCA as they were confronted with desegregation. Nancy Hawk, president of the board of directors in Charleston, wrote the National Board claiming that charter members of the YWCA were displeased with changes in the national YWCA's policy. In 1966 the Charleston YWCA sent an integrated group to the national regional conference in Atlanta. According to Hawk, instead of discussing the "Guides to Participation" for local YWCA's association with the national YWCA, "the delegation discovered that the Conference was set up to influence their thinking and that the summary of each discussion group, as well as the final summary, embodied actually the feeling of the National Staff and the representatives rather than that of the regional participants."[42]

White YWCA members also saw the change in the National Board's policy as a "forerunner of eventual elimination of Christianity as the core of the YWCA and the transformation of this important international association into a congress of women dedicated to economic and social reform." Some black women, like Anna DeWees Kelly, quickly tired of white women's vacillation and outright refusal to integrate the Charleston YWCA and sought other opportunities. She resigned from the Coming Street YWCA in April 1966.[43]

Meanwhile, at its annual membership meeting in May 1966, the Charleston YWCA held its first discussion on withdrawal from the YWCA of the U.S.A. A motion to disaffiliate was defeated by 103 votes by members from the Coming Street YWCA. White YWCA members offered as their reasons for withdrawing from the national YWCA objections to proposed changes in the wording of the YWCA statement of purpose, which would delete the words "Committed by our Faith as Christians," and objections to national's stands on such issues as halting bombings in Vietnam, seating Red China in the United Nations, guaranteeing a minimum wage for all persons, abolishing capital punishment, and of course full integration of the organization.[44]

Nancy Hawk and charter members of the YWCA were distressed at the prospect of severing ties with the national YWCA but also argued that they had built a strong organization with little contact with the National Board. Thus, they felt they had little to lose from disaffiliation and posited that they would have more to offer the community if they "stress[ed] our Christian commitment."[45]

Some white women disagreed with the policies of the national YWCA but urged that the Charleston association maintain affiliation. Judith Wragg Chase argued that "You don't stop a head of buffalo by stepping aside," thus urging continued affiliation. Another member, Laura Martinez, called the disaffiliation move "a race issue," blatantly pointing out some white members' fear of racial integration and their reluctance to cultivate more equitable working relationships with black women.[46]

For black women in Charleston, fighting racism and other social injustices assumed a central position as part of the YWCA's Christian movement. After the central branch discussed disaffiliation from the National Board, hostilities between black and white members clearly reflected how differently the two groups perceived the YWCA as a community institution. In March 1967, Nancy Hawk met with Coming Street YWCA members to learn of their plans for the future, since they had chosen to remain affiliated with the National Board and were intent upon "blocking disaffiliation efforts." In Hawk's estimation, black women should have voted for disaffiliation and then applied for a charter, which would have allowed both groups to remain autonomous. She also felt that racially separate organizations were best in order for the Charleston YWCA to retain its Christian commitment. While Hawk admitted that the Charleston YWCA was open to everyone, the board felt that the purpose of the organization must "contain a Christian commitment if the organization is going to continue Christian." For Hawk, integration and national involvement in local affairs negated the effectiveness of the Charleston YWCA as a Christian organization. She further asserted: "It seems to our board that there is a strong movement in this country to water down Christian beliefs until they are acceptable to anyone, thereby making them more popular. We feel it is time an organization of Christians reiterated those precepts of their faith which make it unique without regard to its popularity. We think the crises of our modern world need a stronger, not a weaker, Christian commitment."[47]

Christianity for many white members of the Charleston YWCA meant local autonomy, white leadership, and adherence to southern mores like segregation. White YWCA members believed that they would best serve their community if they were "free to make decisions [themselves]" and allowed to retain their "traditional" and racially exclusive definition of Christianity.[48] Black women, however, did not perceive the YWCA's Christian purpose in quite the same way. For them, affiliation and abiding by national rules meant an expanded definition of its Christian purpose and was important because the YWCA's agenda was closely linked to the civil rights changes they themselves were pursuing in Charleston. Finally, they wanted to keep a YWCA branch operating in Charleston.[49] In a move that affected both black and white YWCA members, the overwhelming majority of the board of directors favored the break. With few exceptions, those who had opposed disaffiliation were members of the Coming Street branch.

Some white members of the Charleston YWCA did not see the break in quite the same terms and even hinted at Communist infiltration of the organization. Mrs. R. L. Kerr argued that the national YWCA had changed from a Christian organization into a "secular, socially conscious one." Mrs. Harry Lindstedt attacked the "socialist" stand the YWCA had taken "on many issues" and declared that the organization had "made pronouncements in areas best left to the experts."[50] Mrs. Maxwell Anderson insisted that a "Christian organization should stay out of politics."[51]

Black women, who had long fought against racism in the YWCA, wanted the organization to remain in Charleston as a fountainhead of Christian activism and democracy. In March 1967, when the Charleston YWCA failed once again to obtain the two-thirds majority necessary for disaffiliation, it was due to the determination of its black members. The vote, which represented the second attempt to break ties with the national YWCA, was held during the Charleston YWCA's annual membership meeting. In response to the vote, Nancy Hawk commented, "The proposal is defeated for now. I can't say at this point what may take place in the future."[52] She had underestimated the resoluteness of black members, who quite likely feared that disaffiliation from the national YWCA might very well mean the end of important programs upon which their community depended.

After the March meeting, white YWCA members lobbied their membership and increased their base of support. In May 1967, at a meeting held in the College of Charleston gymnasium, a final vote of 538 to 102 affirmed the Charleston YWCA's withdrawal from the National Board of the YWCA of U.S.A. This marked the end of a sixty-one-year affiliation with the National Board. Both the George Street and Coming Street YWCAs were disaffiliated by the vote.[53]

Not all white members of the Charleston YWCA supported disaffiliation and remained committed to what historian Nancy Marie Robertson called "a vision of Christian sisterhood."[54] Some white women also made not-so-subtle references to the Civil War in their opposition. After the final vote, Mrs. George C. B. Tolleson immediately stood and announced that she was withdrawing her membership from the central branch and retaining her membership at the Coming Street branch. Remarking on the decision to sever ties with the national YWCA, Tolleson quipped, "I presume the next step for this organization is to secede from the union!"[55]

After the vote, black women wasted little time in creating a new YWCA for the Charleston area. In June 1967 the Coming Street YWCA held its first meeting to initiate plans to reorganize a community YWCA for the Charleston area.[56] They also had to sever their ties with the central branch. The Coming Street branch, according to Nancy Hawk, was still a part of the central branch and only eligible for discontinuation by an act of the board of directors, the branch committee on administration, and a vote of the entire membership.[57] As a branch of the YWCA of Charleston, its black members were expected to uphold their responsibilities until they wrote a formal letter requesting disaffiliation. However, black women were determined to adhere to the mandates of the national YWCA and recognized the central YWCA's failure to do so. When they questioned the central YWCA about whether or not it was still operating under the national YWCA's constitution, they discovered that white members were operating under their own constitution, having deleted all references to the national body.[58]

African American women were adamant about retaining a local YWCA in the Charleston community and asserting their disaffiliation from the central YWCA. Most black members refused to support continued affiliation because white members made it clear that their presence was not wanted. That is, they had never been considered equal partners in the Charleston YWCA. One member, Mrs. Singleton, reported that she and other members had had "past unfriendly experiences" at the central YWCA. She further declared that she saw no advantage of remaining a "Branch to Central whose membership and leaders have always shown they did not accept us." Furthermore, although the Coming Street branch was supposed to have a representative on the board of directors, no one from the branch had been elected to serve, making it clear that white members desired neither black members' input nor their presence.[59]

The National Board provided black women with an opportunity to exercise autonomy by assisting the Coming Street branch in becoming a provisional YWCA, the first step to becoming a community YWCA. Local attorneys, several of them civil rights activists, assisted the Coming Street branch in reorganizing and securing deeds to property from the George Street YWCA.[60] Black members named their newly formed organization the YWCA of Greater Charleston, Inc. Executive Director Christine Osborn Jackson declared to Charlestonians that the chapter was the "only real Young Women's Christian Association in this area." While African American women were aware of the social mores in Charleston, they had a greater duty to pursue racial change for the city's black community in particular. They recognized that in order for the Charleston YWCA to be useful in this capacity, it had to remain affiliated with the National Board. The new organization received a charter from the state and applied for a national charter, which it received on February 2, 1970.[61]

This saga did not end with warm feelings between black and white members of the YWCA or between white members and the national YWCA. The George Street YWCA knew that the national YWCA had a copyright on the "Y" name, yet it continued to use it. They argued that they had been using the name since 1903, four years before the national YWCA was established. Conversely, the national YWCA posited that its predecessors, the International Board of Young Women's Christian Associations and the American Committee of Young Women's Christian Associations, had used the YWCA name since 1881. The George Street YWCA's position was ultimately untenable. In 1959 they had signed a contract agreeing to cease using the name and the "Y" symbol if they ever disaffiliated from the National Board.[62]

In 1970 the YWCA's National Board sued the George Street YWCA and requested that it discontinue use of the YWCA name and symbol. In 1971 the trial was conducted in federal court, with Judge Solomon Blatt Jr., the grandson of Jewish Russian immigrants and the son of a segregationist, presiding.[63] He decided in favor of the National Board and informed George Street YWCA members that after June 30, 1972, it could use any combination of the words "young, women, Christian and association" as long as "young" or the letter "Y" was not first in sequence.[64] The George Street YWCA appealed the ruling to the Fourth District Court in Virginia, but to no avail. In 1972 the George Street YWCA became the Christian Family Y, a name it retained until it closed in 2004.[65]

Conclusion

The dissolution of the George Street YWCA and the Coming Street YWCA into separate entities resulted in a different outcome than had occurred with the Greenville YWCA. Although those in leadership positions in both associations met to discuss YWCA programs and policies, Charleston's basic membership never came together in integrated programs or used common facilities. The Coming Street YWCA sought to include all Charlestonians in its programs, particularly after it became the YWCA of Greater Charleston. And indeed, it was able to retain a few white members who had objected to the George Street YWCA's resistance to integration. However, societal mores were slow to erode, and most of the Coming Street YWCA's functions and facilities benefited only African Americans, because many white women could not imagine themselves in a predominantly black facility or in an equal working relationship with black YWCA members. Each association demonstrated a different interpretation of the YWCA's Christian purpose. For George Street members it meant racial improvements while maintaining segregation within its YWCA. For the Coming Street YWCA, it meant including all Charlestonians in its programs and ensuring that its mandates supporting Christian activism and democracy were in line with those of the national YWCA.

Unlike black women's efforts for change, which became increasingly aggressive as the political and social environment changed, many white women and their organizations learned to tread the fine line between racial activism and local conservatism in the tumultuous 1960s. The Greenville YWCA carefully adhered to the mandates of its national branch yet worked quietly to integrate the organization and its facilities so as not to upset accepted racial practices. Rather than accept the mandates of the national YWCA for racial inclusiveness, the Charleston YWCA chose disaffiliation.

5

"Become Active in This Service to the Community"

The Possibilities and Limitations of Racial Change and Interracial Activism in South Carolina

As civil rights efforts gained increasing importance in the South, they converged with other, more radical forms of activism such as the Black Power movement in the late 1960s. According to historian Numan Bartley, "the civil rights victories of the mid-1960s achieved the original aims of the movement," that is, the dismantling of legalized segregation and disfranchisement. But at the same time, as black leaders such as Martin Luther King Jr. saw it, this did little to improve the situation of poor African Americans.[1] Consequently, during the late 1960s the civil rights movement maintained its momentum as its participants continued to fight for voting rights and against school desegregation and poverty.

As the 1960s progressed, black women not only pushed for the full integration of formerly segregated organizations like the YWCA and greater inclusion and interracial activism in organizations like United Church Women but also pursued with increased tenacity important civil rights issues such as voting rights. The drive for voting rights in particular, which had engaged South Carolina blacks since the 1940s, became a formal project for civil rights organizations. As the number of voting-rights cases in southern states increased under Attorney General Robert Kennedy, the Kennedy administration encouraged the creation of projects to help blacks register to vote.

The Voter Education Project (VEP) was formed in 1962 in reaction to many African Americans' frustration over their lack of such basic skills as reading and writing, which were required for voter registration. Philanthropic organizations provided funds for the VEP, which were administered by the Southern Regional Council. These funds were channeled to direct-action organizations such as the Southern Christian Leadership Conference and the Student Nonviolent Coordinating Committee, which allowed grassroots organizations to teach African Americans elementary skills to pass registration tests and provided moral support when they went to vote.[2] As part of a national effort that included church and local organizations throughout the South, the VEP was designed to reach ninety thousand potential voters over its first twelve months.

Women's Voting Rights Activism in the 1960s

Black women such as Septima Clark and Modjeska Simkins and white women like Alice Norwood Spearman, all of whom had fought for African American voting rights in the 1940s and 1950s, intensified their efforts in the 1960s, particularly before the passage of the Voting Rights Act in 1965. Clark's voting-rights activism had begun in the 1950s at the Highlander Folk School. According to sociologist Bernice McNair Barnett, without Clark's successes in citizenship education, the Voting Rights Act of 1965 would have been meaningless, because African Americans throughout the South had been virtually eliminated from the body politic.[3] In 1957, Highlander established citizenship schools on the South Carolina and Georgia Sea Islands to teach such fundamental elements as citizenship responsibility, reading, writing, and voter registration. The courses were taught by local African Americans like Clark and her cousin Bernice Robinson.[4]

Born in Charleston in 1898, Septima Poinsette Clark was the daughter of a former slave and a mother who had been born "free issue" in Haiti, where she had been taught to read and write. A graduate of the Avery Normal Institute in Charleston, Septima spent many years teaching in the public schools of South Carolina, but it was while studying at Avery that she began her racial activism. For example, in 1919, after joining the NAACP, she collected more than ten thousand signatures on a petition to have black teachers hired by the Charleston County School District after Senator Benjamin "Pitchfork" Tillman declared that African Americans would be unable to procure so many signatures. By 1920 there were black teachers in black public schools. The following year, black principals were installed.[5] In 1929, after the death of her husband, Nerie Clark, she settled in Columbia, where she remained until 1947. It was there that she began her work in citizenship education.[6]

Clark was first introduced to Highlander in 1952. She had learned of the school from Anna DeWees Kelly, another black Charlestonian and fellow Avery graduate. Born in 1913, Kelly sought a place where blacks and whites could meet together to discuss the racial, social, and economic problems plaguing the South. She found it at Highlander, which she attended on a scholarship in 1953.[7] The following year, Kelly and Clark both attended Highlander.[8] Clark was particularly dedicated to her work in the citizenship schools and was later appointed educational director. She recalled that her grassroots activism was a "great part of me." Because she had seen the devastating effects of racism and poverty firsthand on South Carolina's Sea Islands when she was a young teacher, Clark swore that the "remaining years of my workable life will be promoting citizenship programs somewhere somehow. I'll work wherever I'm needed and wanted."[9] Her work was not limited to Johns Island, however. Because curbing illiteracy went hand-in-hand with teaching blacks about political empowerment, she often traveled to small communities throughout South Carolina to talk about registering to vote.[10] In doing so, Clark inculcated African Americans with the fervor of civil rights activism along with a belief in their entitlement to first-class citizenship.[11]

As director of education at Highlander, Clark was not only instrumental in establishing a citizenship school on the South Carolina Sea Islands but also worked for the Southern Christian Leadership Conference (SCLC).[12] Founded in 1957, the SCLC took over the citizenship school in 1961 and renamed it the Citizenship Education Program.[13] Clark's experience at Highlander had prepared her to assist blacks on the Sea Islands as they found their political voice.[14] It also later informed her sense of racial justice as she supported and advised black women who were involved in the 1969 Charleston hospital strike for equal pay and improved working conditions at the Medical University of South Carolina.[15] Clark's cousin Bernice Robinson continued teaching at the citizenship school and became a consultant for teacher-training workshops all over the South, in addition to working on voter registration in Mississippi. In 1972 she became the first African American woman to run for the South Carolina House of Representatives.[16]

Support of the VEP and the quest for full citizenship for African Americans were not limited to Highlander or to black women. Many organizations embraced the cause. In South Carolina, Alice Norwood Spearman, through her position as executive director of the South Carolina Council on Human

Relations, worked tirelessly to recruit white and black women to promote black registration and voting. She sent letters to heads of such organizations as the State Council of Farm Women urging them to attend the second Conference on Registration and Voting in 1961 at the Penn Center on St. Helena's Island in Beaufort County. In her letter to Mrs. Marion McLester, president of that group, Spearman, aware of deeply entrenched racism in South Carolina's rural areas, especially requested her attendance and expertise to examine such difficulties as black illiteracy and white economic control, which severely limited voting and registration in those areas.[17] Spearman was adept at targeting black and white women heads of organizations or women in community outreach organizations. In a letter to Sarah Z. Daniels, a home demonstration agent and later president of United Church Women, Spearman urged her to attend the meeting and asserted that "because of your work as a home demonstration agent and your keen interest in building first class citizenship, we feel that you are admirably equipped to analyze and discuss the road blocks in the way of registration and voting which obstruct Negroes in small towns and rural areas."[18]

The workshop on voter registration, the theme of which was "Register today . . . so you can vote for a better tomorrow," was held April 1–3, 1961, in Frogmore, South Carolina. It was designed to organize individuals from small rural towns where few African Americans had registered or where registration was difficult generally. The workshop, organized by Spearman and Courtney Siceloff, director of the Penn Community Center on St. Helena's Island, also reached out to organizations involved in voter registration in South Carolina like the SCCHR, the NAACP, the Palmetto Voters League, the Congress of Racial Equality (CORE), and the SCLC, among others.[19] And it involved African American students from Howard University and Claflin College in addition to students from Cornell University and the American Friends Service Committee. The combined efforts of this and other such meetings resulted in the South Carolina Voter Education Project in 1965.[20]

Black women like Modjeska Simkins also continued their activism through local organizations in addition to speaking out against a myriad of civil rights offenses in the 1960s and beyond. Simkins used the all-black Richland County Citizens' Committee (RCCC) as a vehicle to promote change in South Carolina's political system. The RCCC was formed under the auspices of the South Carolina Citizens' Committee, which had been founded in 1944 and had supported numerous civil rights causes over the years. The group received its charter in 1956 and adopted as its motto "Leading the effort toward keen community awareness in non-partisan political action in Richland County."[21] Simkins had been assigned by the RCCC to produce written communications for the organization. She was the public relations director and an official correspondent for the organization in addition to writing its charter.[22]

Simkins was well suited to the various tasks within the organization as a result of more than twenty years' involvement in many civic organizations. As a correspondent for the RCCC, she enlisted a direct, almost brutal style in her messages to various political officials and African American constituents in Columbia. One of the more vocal members of the organization, Simkins was not afraid to attack white supremacy by calling attention to racial discrimination throughout the county.[23]

Simkins's activism did not stop at chastising white political candidates and allying white and black women. She also targeted African Americans whom she considered to be complacent about the changes taking place in South Carolina. In 1965, after President Lyndon B. Johnson signed the Voting Rights Act, Simkins urged African Americans to go to the polls on June 15 to vote and to transport others when they went. To those who hesitated, she instructed: "Don't worry about spending a little gas money on the full freedom fight. What we do may mean the great difference between joy and sadness for us on June 16, the day after."[24]

Simkins continued to expand her campaign for causes that were important not only to African Americans but to all dispossessed people. She sought to diversify the ranks of political officials at the local and state level. Once African Americans had regained the right to vote, Simkins grasped the opportunity to run for political office. In 1966 she ran for the Columbia City Council and the South Carolina House of Representatives. She was again plagued by the threat of Communist affiliations when Governor Robert McNair demanded that Simkins, a former Republican, either disprove her association with historian Herbert Aptheker, a noted Communist, or leave the Democratic Party.[25] In her classic self-assertive way, Simkins informed South Carolina Democratic leaders that if they found her membership untenable, "they will have to move because I intend to stay."[26] She subsequently lost the election. Simkins also continued speaking out against racial discrimination at Fort Jackson, the U.S. Army base in Columbia. Under the auspices of the RCCC, she drew attention to the South Carolina National Guard's failure to fully integrate its troops.[27]

Simkins was also a proponent of black self-determination, and like many African Americans she supported the Black Power movement. To this end, she and Septima Clark joined Blacks United for Action (BUA), founded in 1968 as a grassroots organization to procure the economic, social, cultural, and political security of black Carolinians. BUA members proposed establishing a federal credit union and cooperatives and created the Denmark Vesey Institute and the Summer Cultural Arts Program for Youth to educate the black community and provide African Americans with a sense of racial pride.[28]

The most pressing issue for black women like Simkins, however, remained African American political access. She was a member of the United Citizens Party (UCP), which was formed in South Carolina in 1969 by disgruntled black Democrats because the state party refused to nominate them for public offices and failed to adequately address their social and political concerns.[29] In 1970, South Carolina's failure to fully implement desegregation plans and the overall deceleration of civil rights activism prompted African Americans to support thirty-five-year-old black Columbia attorney Thomas Broadwater for governor.[30] In 1971, activist Victoria DeLee, the UCP's vice president as well as the founder and president of the Dorchester County branch of the NAACP, represented the party when she ran for Congress.[31]

Simkins was adamant that black votes in South Carolina not be taken for granted by either political party. She asserted, "We must labor for the time when no political party in South Carolina can say they have the black vote tied up the way the Democrats do now." She was further determined to ensure that blacks and whites understood that they had to vote for the candidate who best represented their concerns rather than a political party in order to effect greater change in South Carolina.[32] Simkins was later named the UCP's "Honorary Lifetime President."[33] She maintained an active civil rights agenda, which included women's and environmental rights, until her death in 1992.[34]

Black Political Activism in South Carolina after the Voting Rights Act

Unfortunately, there were still problems implementing voter registration in some parts of South Carolina. After the enactment of the Voting Rights Act, African American leaders complained about white officials who intentionally slowed the voter-registration process in such counties as Allendale, Barnwell, Charleston, Clarendon, Dorchester, Jasper, and Orangeburg, which had a large black population. Federal observers were later sent to Clarendon and Dorchester Counties.[35] Voting rights held great significance for

African Americans in South Carolina and throughout the South. Not only did it result in improved services in African American communities, but the ballot also gave those who acquired it a sense of pride. But federal acts could not change hearts, and the struggle for equality and justice continued. Many African Americans depended on whites for employment and credit, and the fear of retaliation kept many of them from exercising their right to register and vote.[36]

Although the voter-registration drives directed by CORE, the VEP, the SCLC, and the NAACP were notable in 1965, they were not able to eliminate the long-term effects of deeply entrenched racism in South Carolina.[37] Indeed, the Voting Rights Act made only a dent in South Carolina's political establishment. South Carolina politicians challenged the act, claiming it was unconstitutional and would result in placing illiterate African Americans on juries. They overlooked the fact that many whites were only slightly more literate. According to Rev. J. Herbert Nelson of Orangeburg, the state president of the NAACP, "We have had illiterate whites on juries for 300 years and nobody said anything about it."[38] But despite politicians' efforts, many blacks registered to vote the summer after the Voting Rights Act was passed. By September 1965, another seven thousand African Americans registered to vote.

However, because many blacks lacked basic education, they still faced obstacles in gaining access to the polls. Their efforts were also hindered by the fact that registration offices were often closed during hours when most blacks could leave work to register, since many blacks in South Carolina were agricultural workers.[39] According to Rev. I. DeQuincey Newman of Columbia, a field secretary for the NAACP, "More registration days and longer hours would practically serve all our problems. In most rural counties, there hasn't necessarily been a conscious effort to prevent Negroes from registering but it is an economic fact of life that they can't."[40] Thus it was not only education that limited African American registration; economic necessity also demanded that blacks work to sustain themselves and their families.

Armed with the long-overdue right to vote, black voters registered in South Carolina. Their numbers grew from 58,000 in 1965 to 220,000 by 1970. African Americans voted Democratic and actively participated in Democratic Party matters.[41] By 1970, according to South Carolina historian Walter Edgar, their "representation at the state convention was virtually proportional to their numbers in the total population." South Carolina's political developments did not stop there. In 1968, Democrats elected twelve black South Carolinians to their delegation to the national party convention. And by 1970, with support from the UCP, Herbert U. Fielding of Charleston County and James L. Felder and I. S. Leevy Johnson of Richland County became the first African Americans to serve in the South Carolina House of Representatives since Reconstruction.[42]

As African Americans exercised their newly won right to vote, whites began to accept desegregation throughout the state, although slowly in the public schools. It was not until the 1960s that public schools began to desegregate. However, black admittance to formerly all-white schools often meant no more than token African American representation. In fact, it was not until 1963, as a result of *Brown v. School District 20 of Charleston County*, which ruled that racial differences should not be a factor in school placement, that formerly all-white public schools in the county were desegregated.[43]

As desegregation in public schools spread throughout the state, South Carolina whites responded by creating private schools with private funds or applying for tuition grants from the general assembly. The tuition grant program had been created as a "safety valve" against desegregation in the state's public schools.[44] John H. Whalen, a Columbia newsman and avowed segregationist, is an example of some whites' refusal to allow their children to attend school with African Americans. In 1964, after Columbia schools admitted twenty-two African Americans, Whalen not only applied for tuition grants for his two sons but also drove them forty-five miles daily to the private Wade Hampton Academy in Orangeburg. Whalen's application was denied when the board of trustees of Richland County School District One voted unanimously to stand by its previous decision not to participate in South Carolina's tuition grant program.[45]

Despite Whalen's support for continued segregation, there were some heartening developments. In Rock Hill, Maggie S. Bailey, an African American who taught in neighboring Chester County, became one of nine candidates for two seats in a special election for the Rock Hill school board.[46] Furman University, in Greenville, despite having differences over desegregation policy with the white State Baptist Convention (which contributed to the school's financial support), received its first African American students in January 1965, becoming the first private college in South Carolina to desegregate.[47]

The Challenge of Interracial Activism in United Church Women

The national headquarters of women's religious organizations like United Church Women urged their local chapters to facilitate racial change in southern communities. UCW in South Carolina was the second major women's organization to confront directives for integration from its national body. At a 1962 national meeting in Columbus, Ohio, the national board of directors issued a "Christian Social Relations Resolution" that encouraged individual church women and local and state UCW councils to "build a climate of opinion in which no person can be subjected to the kind of cruel, retaliatory tactics now being used; and to strive to destroy as rapidly as possible the pattern of segregation."[48] This would prove difficult in South Carolina, as the UCW, in the midst of controversies and inconsistencies, became increasingly silent and reserved in its activism in the 1960s.

In the 1950s, under Edith Dabbs's presidency, the state UCW was still, at least tenuously, an interracial organization. This was not the case in local branches, although the Greenville branch had participated in integrated activities as early as the 1940s.[49] Dabbs, by this point, had become a resident of Charleston, where she faced scathing attacks from the local *News and Courier* for her activism.[50] Other white members of the organization faced ostracism, or even violence, for their activism. As a result, in the 1960s the leadership of UCW of South Carolina adopted a defensive position, no longer overtly promoting itself as an integrated organization and refusing to support the growth of the SCCHR and its position on interracial cooperation and racial change. For several years, many members of the SCCHR had not been invited to the UCW's annual meeting. Notices were sent only to members of the board of directors, who were presumably all white, and to other white members. This alienated many of the black members of the organization. Previously, members of the two organizations had worked together, particularly because UCW was an interracial, all-female organization and the SCCHR's membership, though predominantly male, was headed by a woman and integrated.[51]

Alice Norwood Spearman, executive director of the SCCHR and a member of UCW (she became its chairman of program concerns in 1969),[52] chastised UCW for yielding to white pressure and ignoring their by-laws mandating interracial cooperation and racial understanding. In her estimation, "No one has the right, not even an officer, to set aside the provision in our by-laws that [an] annual membership meeting be held." However, despite the decision of the board of the organization, she urged as many women as possible to attend a meeting to be held at St. John's Episcopal Church in Columbia to discuss the changes taking place in a joint meeting with the SCCHR.

Spearman also called for black women's cooperation in this matter. In a confidential letter to Sarah Z. Daniels, a black member and officer of UCW of South Carolina, Spearman asked her to bring other black women who might be interested in the agenda of the SCCHR. With such a request, Spearman hoped to return UCW to its former usefulness as an integrated organization. She was adamant about maintaining organizations such as the UCW, which was able, at least up to a point, to function interracially.[53] Clearly, many UCW members were only marginally concerned about the struggles some South Carolinians faced daily, but not all were apathetic. Indeed, many urged that any Christian woman from South Carolina should be willing to put "cause above personal prestige" and thus continue their work for racial change in the state.[54]

United Church Women of South Carolina became even more hesitant to take the lead in improving race relations as the national branch stepped up its racial activism by instituting a program titled "Assignment: *Race*." As a precursor to "Assignment: *Race*," UCW officials submitted reports from around the country on local councils approached for workshops for racism programs. For South Carolina, they received a report only from Columbia. Nationally, UCW had received a three-year grant for $66,000 from the Field Foundation, which allowed it to establish "Assignment: *Race*" at its ninth national assembly in Miami Beach in 1961. The program was designed to launch a nationwide, interdenominational attack on racial discrimination in churches, housing, schools, and places of employment. The UCW used money from the Field Foundation to recruit and train women to work for improved race relations in their communities. The program had a three-pronged goal: full participation for all without racial distinctions in local churches and denominations, in the council of church women, and in the community, where women were to focus on areas where racial tensions were the highest and needs were the most pressing.[55] "Assignment: *Race*," which lasted from 1961 to 1964, was directed nationally by Carrie E. Meares of Fountain Inn, South Carolina, a former YWCA director and a 1919 graduate of Winthrop College.[56]

Before the 1960s, local councils in South Carolina, unlike the national organization, did not aggressively pursue integrated membership or projects on race relations and civil liberties. In a 1975 interview, Edith Dabbs recalled that the UCW was considered a "scandalous" organization given its "liberal" leanings and that "even harder than that [was] getting white women to be willing to have Negroes come into their membership on equal footing."[57]

According to summaries of reports from state and local UCW councils between 1957 and 1959, South Carolina had numerous councils, yet in 1957 and 1958 only two were involved in economic and industrial relations. None were involved in race relations and civil liberties. As of 1959, only one council was involved in race relations and civil liberties.[58] Although strong and visible racial activism from UCW Columbia women was slow in coming, the organization expressed awareness of racial inequalities and social issues in South Carolina when other local chapters and white women's organizations were reluctant—even afraid—to do so.

UCW of South Carolina's failure to pursue racial matters in the 1960s is evident in reports from UCW regional meetings. Whereas other councils around the country were concerned with racial matters among a slew of other concerns, the South Carolina council shifted its interests to the predominantly African American migrants in Charleston and throughout the state. The organization's migrant committee took on new importance, particularly after record-breaking rains in June 1962, which were disastrous for Charleston County farmers, migrant workers, and local farm laborers, many of whom were black. Under the auspices of UCW of South Carolina, Rev. Vernon F. Frazier led a crash feeding program for these individuals. Charleston's branch gave approximately $400 worth of food to migrants unable to work in the area and started a drive to secure clothing and other supplies for migrants.[59]

After President Lyndon Johnson announced his nationwide War on Poverty in 1964, business, civic, and religious organizations sought to form coalitions to attack problems that pervaded the nation.[60] In response, the national UCW formed the Women's Inter-Organizational Committee.[61] Renamed Women in Community Service (WICS) in that same year, the group was affiliated with the Women's Job Corps and recruited young people—young women in particular—to work for its anti-poverty program. A joint effort by United Church Women, the National Council of Catholic Women, the National Council of Jewish Women, and the National Council of Negro Women in cooperation with the National Board of the YWCA, WICS volunteers combated racism, poverty, illiteracy, unemployment, and malnutrition.[62]

Because new federal laws protected African Americans from legal discrimination, the trajectory of the civil rights movement turned to economic issues such as poverty that had a disproportionate impact on blacks. In accordance with this, in 1965 the national UCW formed a three-year program with the theme "People, Poverty, and Plenty." Because local UCW branches sometimes found fighting poverty less controversial than fighting for civil rights, they followed suit as chapters of WICS formed in South Carolina. UCW Columbia and the SCCHR assisted these efforts by cosponsoring

Project Head Start programs in twenty-five counties in South Carolina. This allowed the UCW to engage in racial activism without direct references to race. A War on Poverty program, Project Head Start operated for eight weeks during the summer and educated children from disadvantaged homes who were entering first grade in the next academic year. WICS members were also concerned about young women from poor families throughout the state. In Charleston, at the WICS organizational meeting, women discussed ways to improve impoverished young women's situations. Mrs. Paul Pfeutze of the WICS national headquarters in Washington, D.C., addressed the women and outlined the ways in which participation in the Job Corps program uplifted young women.[63]

WICS gave black women an opportunity to facilitate change in South Carolina and provided evidence of limited ecumenicalism.[64] After an organizational meeting in 1965, Mrs. Calvin R. Greene was installed as project director of WICS in Charleston. Greene, a librarian at Charles A. Brown High School in Charleston, graduated from South Carolina State University and received a master's degree in library science from Indiana University. Trained to help the less fortunate, she had also been a Job Corps volunteer and a social welfare worker for the predominantly African American St. Catherine's Auxiliary of the Blessed Sacrament Roman Catholic Church in Charleston. Other women installed as assistant directors of WICS in Charleston were members of the local Council of Jewish Women, the Council of Negro Women, and UCW.[65]

In addition to participation in WICS, UCW Columbia worked to alleviate poverty throughout the state in other ways. In 1966 it held a worship service with the theme "Poverty and Affluence." This was later restructured as a study course and a yearly worship event. It was also in 1966 that United Church Women severed its ties with the National Council of Churches and changed its name to Church Women United (CWU).[66] In 1967, Latitia Anderson of the Division of General Studies at the University of South Carolina and head of the South Carolina Head Start Program, spoke to CWU Columbia members about how the philosophy of the "Poverty and Affluence" programs could be used to help people statewide. Recognizing the impact that CWU could have on this kind of activism, Anderson urged members to "become active in this service to the community."[67]

Although CWU's efforts improved living and health conditions among poor black migrant workers, they were not pioneers in assisting them and their families. Black women and their organizations had been doing this since the early decades of the twentieth century. They had ongoing projects to bring health and social change to African Americans on South Carolina's Sea Islands. For example, when Septima Clark was a young teacher on Johns Island in the 1920s, she was instrumental in securing funds from the Gamma Xi Omega chapter of Alpha Kappa Alpha Sorority to help blacks obtain ring-worm treatment and diphtheria immunization. She also enlisted the support of a white women's Presbyterian group and white Charlestonian Mrs. Ashley Halsey, who then used her influence to improve the island's water system, help families upgrade their diets, and convince landowners to inspect tenant homes.[68]

By the end of the 1960s and into the early 1970s, CWU councils in South Carolina retreated from a liberal position on race relations to focus almost solely on more conservative issues such as migrant poverty. In 1968, CWU Columbia member Mrs. F. E. Reinartz suggested taking a trip to Charleston for a "Go-See" tour of migrant camps.[69] Because many of the migrant camps were on the Charleston Sea Islands, CWU Charleston was especially concerned about the conditions and care of migrant children. As many of the migrants in the South Carolina Lowcountry were African American and Latino, it is possible that CWU found it easier to help them because it enabled them to align themselves with national movements focusing on economics and poverty without subjecting themselves to any suspicion for racial activism. Indeed, their effort served only to improve living and health conditions; it did not threaten the status quo by calling for equality or full citizenship. To this end, church women developed day-care activities and provided clothes and health kits for families through their May Fellowship Day offering. They sponsored African American minister Willis Goodwin as a chaplain in the migrant camps as part of Rural Mission Inc. on Johns Island.[70] CWU Charleston also helped secure funds from the Office of Economic Opportunity in the mid-1960s to create the South Carolina Commission for Farm Workers to help expand services available to migrant workers.

In addition to their efforts to aid migrant workers, CWU continued working to end illiteracy in South Carolina, recognizing that having basic reading skills meant increased access to better employment opportunities. At their annual meeting in 1969 they adopted a resolution to "commit our energies and talents, and to focus our efforts on the elimination of hunger and illiteracy and on meeting these needs for job training and placement and adequate housing."[71] CWU participated in South Carolina's Adult Basic Education (ABE) program in the late 1960s and 1970s. ABE was designed to "eliminate the inability of adults in need of basic education to read and write English." According to the 1960 Census, 23 million Americans over twenty-five years of age had completed less than eight years of schooling.[72] Although the committee of women who submitted this resolution was predominantly white, blacks most often spearheaded adult education programs. With the help of Alice Leppert of CWU's national staff and program specialists in adult basic education, black members like Ada Campbell and Johnette Edwards, who was later appointed to South Carolina's Commission on the Status of Women, held workshops for Charleston volunteers under the leadership of adult education professors from the University of South Carolina. Septima Clark was co-chair of the local unit of basic education volunteers in Charleston and helped to plan workshops on Johns Island in cooperation with local and state adult education leaders.[73] In Columbia, church women supported the Greater Columbia Literacy Council, which trained volunteers to help those who could not read.[74]

While the Voter Education Project of the 1960s educated and prepared African Americans for the benefits of citizenship, ABE raised the education level of adults and helped them become better-informed voters.[75] It further encouraged all segments of the community to work together to provide increased social and economic opportunities for poor blacks and others.[76] This variation of community-based improvement had long been a part of black women's and many white women's activist agendas.

By the 1960s, then, due to the increasing focus on literacy and voting-rights issues in the national CWU, black women carved out more space for their activism and a larger presence in some local CWU councils because these were concerns that were of particular importance in their communities. For some, integration had never been a problem. CWU in Aiken, for example, had always been integrated. Others admitted to their struggle for a fully inclusive membership. In 1967 a member from Columbia admitted that her council had been "playing at being a part of the national group for many years" and that only the Spartanburg and Aiken councils had been fully integrated from the beginning.[77]

In some cases, black members of CWU were in the majority. In Orangeburg County, where there was a large population of educated African Americans and two institutions of higher learning, there existed a predominantly black CWU chapter that increasingly sought to work with women from other races and denominations. In 1965 the predominantly African American St. Paul's Episcopal Church sponsored a community forum titled "Knowing the Time" that local African American church women in Orangeburg used to create an organization through which women of all faiths could convene to discuss social problems. Other community church women responded overwhelmingly to these efforts, and they too were later invited to attend the community forums. They would eventually form Church Women United in Orangeburg in 1965.

Although the Aiken and Orangeburg chapters of CWU provide examples of the possibilities of integrated racial activism, black members were not visible in the Columbia chapter until the 1960s and became more so in the 1970s.[78] Some black women's names appear in the minutes along with their church affiliations, making it clear that CWU Columbia was at least marginally integrated by the late 1960s. Although there were not many black women members of the organization, one black woman stands out as an active member. Myrtle Ruff Witherspoon was born in 1898 in Newberry County to Silas and Hattie Caughman Ruff. A product of the Newberry County Public Schools, she was a graduate of the Normal division of South Carolina State College. Witherspoon's name does not appear in CWU Columbia records until 1967, yet it is clear that she used her involvement to promote changes for African Americans in Columbia and throughout Richland County. She was most active in South Carolina's Office of Economic Opportunity and served on a similar committee in CWU Columbia, requesting donations and volunteers from among its members. She assumed a more prominent position in CWU Columbia in the early 1970s and served as its president in 1970 and 1971.[79]

Black women also assumed leadership positions in CWU South Carolina. In 1971, Waltena Josie, a retired staff member from South Carolina State College, the organizer and first leader of CWU Orangeburg, was elected president of CWU South Carolina and selected as a member of the National Board of Managers. Josie's faith transformed into activism from the time she was an undergraduate at South Carolina State College. She was also an active member of the Episcopal Church and a former high school teacher.[80]

Although it is not clear what their relationship was to CWU before the 1960s, both Witherspoon and Josie augmented CWU racial activism with their educational and organizational skills. Becoming leaders in the organization, they actively involved themselves in CWU programs that served African American communities. Integrated membership in CWU by the 1960s also illustrates how far white women members had come as they adopted its national mandates for integrated councils and its agenda for combating racial injustice.

Church Women United in South Carolina, Columbia, and Orangeburg made small steps toward racial and social improvements in South Carolina despite deep-seated racial attitudes that limited any activism deemed controversial. As was the case with the national CWU, in the 1940s religion proved a powerful incentive for encouraging women to examine their own communities as they realized that Christianity was incompatible with undemocratic practices. Unlike members of the Charleston YWCA, however, CWU members agreed on how their Christian faith should be used to serve black and white South Carolinians. The *Brown v. Board of Education* Supreme Court case in the 1950s was an important watershed for CWU Columbia and CWU South Carolina, as members further acknowledged racial problems in South Carolina and throughout the South. Although some members shied away from overt racial activism after the *Brown* decision, others pushed the organization to live up to the example of the national CWU, which called for church women to fight racial and social injustices.

Church Women United in Columbia and South Carolina also struggled with black women's participation, although they supported separate but equal efforts on black women's behalf. Yet some branches, like CWU in Aiken, had proudly maintained integrated membership since the 1950s. In Orangeburg, black church women extended the services of the women's organizations of their churches and created a predominantly African American branch of Church Women United that welcomed members of all races and denominations. By the late 1960s, black women were token members of CWU South Carolina and CWU Columbia, and at least two women, Myrtle Witherspoon and Waltena Josie, also held leadership positions, attesting not only to their assertiveness but also to the growth in consciousness of white members since earlier decades.[81]

Church Women United of Columbia also made overtures to women of other faiths in the late 1960s. In 1967, one of the council's projects was a "Living Room Dialogue" in which twelve women from Protestant and Catholic denominations met monthly in each other's homes to dispel myths and confusion between the churches. In this same year they also passed a motion to invite three Jewish women to attend a CWU luncheon as its guests, although it does not appear that they ever became members. However, in 1968 they noted the official affiliation of the Roman Catholic and Greek Orthodox Churches with the organization.[82] On the whole, unfortunately, the ecumenicalism that had occurred nationwide was considerably less extensive in South Carolina.

Even with such limited developments in Church Women United's membership, black and white women largely continued to work separately for racial and social change. It is possible that some white women believed it was right to support such social causes as adult basic education and alleviating poverty among blacks and migrant workers in the South Carolina Lowcountry, but not civil rights for African Americans. They might have also assumed that once the federal government passed crucial civil rights legislation ending legalized segregation and discrimination, CWU's work for racial justice was done.[83] But they did understand, at the very least, that women's belief in socially active Christianity resulted in much-needed improvements for blacks throughout South Carolina. Despite tremendous obstacles to interracial activism, CWU branches throughout the state implemented small but important steps toward racial and social justice in South Carolina.

Conclusion

Throughout the 1960s, black women and some white women continued to promote African American voting rights in South Carolina. Their activism, aided by the Voter Education Project and later the passage of the Voting Rights Act, involved teaching blacks the responsibility of full citizenship and helping them to acquire the necessary basic skills to register to vote. African American women were further encouraged by the changing racial climate to not only increase the number of black political officials but to also run for office themselves. As the 1960s came to a close, however, they still found their political access limited and the South Carolina Democratic Party unresponsive to their most pressing concerns. African American women recalled black exclusion from the state Democratic Party in the 1940s and again formed a third political organization to address the needs of all South Carolinians.

Although United Church Women of South Carolina had functioned nominally as an integrated organization, increased local pressures after the *Brown* decision forced white members to deemphasize their interracial activism and to instead focus on the endemic poverty among South Carolina's migrant workers. Black women, on the other hand, carved out a space for leadership opportunities even within these limitations and, in cooperation with other ecumenical groups, continued their ongoing pursuit for racial, educational, and economic parity.

Epilogue

In the 1940s, 1950s, and 1960s, black and white women worked individually and through various organizations for racial and social change in South Carolina, although they often disagreed on the form it should assume. In the 1940s, blacks and some whites used the rhetoric of the war years to promote racial activism. At the same time, white women and their organizations attempted to foster racial understanding between the races. This often meant discussing racial problems or attempting to solve them through such organizations as the Commission on Interracial Cooperation, the YWCA, and United Church Women while at the same time maintaining segregation. But their efforts to maintain the status quo revealed an awareness of how pervasive racism was in the Palmetto State, and even these efforts led to some improvements for African Americans in South Carolina.

Black women's goals in the 1940s included obtaining equal pay for teachers and voting rights. Black women used the resources of such organizations as the NAACP, the South Carolina Federation of Colored Women's Clubs, and the Progressive Democratic Party not only to fight for full citizenship but also to secure support from other middle-class black women.

This decade also revealed increasing activism among white women and their organizations. Although members of the YWCA and United Church Women did not actively welcome black women, they began seriously questioning racial inequalities in South Carolina. Others bravely sought membership in integrated, mixed-gender organizations like the CIC and the Southern Regional Council, where they gained greater knowledge about racial conditions throughout the state and the South.

Because they were unable to join some white women's groups, black women were often forced to form and maintain predominantly African American organizations through which they promoted their activism. This attests to their quest for autonomy and agency against great odds to bring about changes most relevant to their communities. They skillfully used racial exclusion to their advantage to work for changes and opportunities denied South Carolina's African American population.

After World War II and amid discussions surrounding *Brown v. Board of Education*, blacks and whites in South Carolina supported racial and social activism in various ways. For African Americans, the years before *Brown* were highlighted by victory with *Elmore v. Rice,* in which Judge J. Waties Waring declared that blacks could not be excluded from South Carolina's Democratic primary. Black women found themselves involved in this case as individuals and as members of organizations like the South Carolina Federation of Colored Women's Clubs and the Columbia Women's Council, which worked to further include African Americans in the political process. Individual black and white women were also able to form tenuous alliances for interracial activism. Some African American women recognized that working across racial lines was the most expedient way to bring about much-needed changes in black communities. And often, white women were committed to activism that improved African American lives but did not transgress racial norms. There were, however, black and white women who formed strong personal and professional relationships and were uncompromising in their racial activism. Modjeska Simkins and Alice Norwood Spearman Wright are examples of activists who were stalwart in their zeal for equitable opportunity and access for all South Carolinians. Spearman was particularly unyielding in her dedication to racial equality for black Carolinians. Even though her activism was not without its risks, she was able to enact a great deal of change through her participation in the South Carolina Council on Human Relations and through her association with like-minded whites.

Under the auspices of religiously based organizations like United Church Women and the YWCA, white women began to pay more attention to racial injustices in South Carolina after World War II. Indeed, within such organizations, religion often was the driving force for political activism. Although YWCAs in South Carolina were still primarily interested in promoting improvements in segregated facilities and fostering better race relations, not racial equality, the intensity of this activism varied in different parts of the state. The Greenville and Columbia YWCAs were more outspoken about racial injustice in their cities. The Charleston YWCA, which had always been hesitant to address racial issues, experienced increased tensions in the community and between black and white YWCA members after Elizabeth Waring's speech to the Coming Street YWCA in 1950. United Church Women in South Carolina and Columbia had, by this point at least, begun to pay more attention to racial injustices throughout the state and were encouraged by its national body to combat them. But even as they attempted to do this, many of the members shied away from racial activism, not only because they feared reprisals but also because they were unprepared to deal with the ramifications of desegregation in their communities.

When *Brown v. Board of Education* was decided by the U.S. Supreme Court on May 17, 1954, blacks and whites in South Carolina understood that change in the racial status quo was inevitable. However, they interpreted the *Brown* decision in different ways. Some blacks resisted the decision and membership in organizations like the NAACP because they feared economic reprisals. However, most African Americans welcomed the decision as a catalyst to further activism. Black women and their organizations in particular used the decision and the momentum of the civil rights movement to continue to push for access to equal educational opportunities and voting rights. White women, on the other hand, withdrew their support for racial changes after the Supreme Court decision and instead turned to less controversial activism like addressing the poverty of migrant workers in the South Carolina Lowcountry. This resistance to racial activism reached a climax in the 1960s, when United Church Women decided not to hold integrated meetings any longer.

Although many religious organizations in South Carolina saw it as a Christian duty to promote racial and social change, during the 1960s black and white members displayed different understandings of Christian activism. For some white women in the Charleston YWCA, their understanding of Christianity directed them to support racial improvements, not to embrace the national YWCA's civil rights agenda, which included integrating local branches. Instead, they chose disaffiliation. But black women saw their Christian duty differently and not only supported the national agenda but also pushed the Charleston YWCA to integrate its membership.

Even by the 1960s, black and white women, with the exception of a few individual leaders, failed to achieve truly interracial activism. Among organizations like the YWCA and United Church Women that were integrated nationally, this occurred only to a limited extent in South Carolina by the end of the decade. Unfortunately, it was difficult for most white South Carolina women to imagine black women as their equals and to work within integrated organizations, even as they supported improvements for African Americans around the state. South Carolina was unique in this regard as local YWCAs and UCW branches in other parts of the country had long since integrated their memberships. Still, white women's efforts, though limited, were courageous because they often supported racial and social change in the face of a hostile environment.

By the 1970s, some white women and their organizations focused increasingly on combating poverty in South Carolina because it did not call direct attention to race. Such activism was considered less controversial even as it directly assisted African Americans and other impoverished groups. But more outspoken white women like Alice Spearman Wright continued to rely on their interracial women's network to advance racial and sexual equality throughout South Carolina. Likewise, black women like Modjeska Simkins and Septima Clark understood that despite the passage of important civil rights legislation, much remained to be done to improve the quality of African American lives. Although they later included women's rights and environmental issues on their activist agendas, they remained committed to such important issues as voting rights and equal educational access in subsequent decades.

Notes

Abbreviations

ARC Avery Research Center for African American History and Culture, College of Charleston, South Carolina

GCAHUMC General Commission on Archives and History of the United Methodist Church, Drew University, Madison, New Jersey

JDL James B. Duke Library, Furman University, Greenville, South Carolina

LPASC Louise Pettus Archives and Special Collections, Winthrop University, Rock Hill, South Carolina

SCCHRP South Carolina Council on Human Relations Papers

SCHS South Carolina Historical Society, Charleston

SCL South Caroliniana Library, University of South Carolina, Columbia

SCPC South Carolina Political Collections, University of South Carolina, Columbia

SCR South Carolina Room, Greenville County Library, South Carolina

SCSUHC South Carolina State University Historical Collection, Miller F. Whitaker Library, Orangeburg, South Carolina

SHC Southern Historical Collection, Wilson Library, University of North Carolina at Chapel Hill

SSC Sophia Smith Collection, Smith College, Northampton, Massachusetts

Introduction

1. This is not to disregard African American agency and autonomy after Emancipation. Black South Carolinians attempted and oftentimes succeeded in renting or purchasing land, finding relatives, and generally reconstructing and living their lives apart from whites.

2. Newby, "South Carolina and the Desegregation Issue," 3, 4, 5; Hemmingway, "Prelude to Change," 212.

3. Lau, *Democracy Rising*, 12.

4. Edgar, *South Carolina*, 513.

5. Ibid., 486, 515.

6. After retiring, she married Marion A. Wright in 1970. Wright served as president of the Southern Regional Council from 1952 to 1958.

7. Lynn, *Progressive Women*, 8, 9.

8. Edgar, *South Carolina*, 515–16; "Democrats Serve Notice Primary Private Affair," *Aiken (S.C.) Standard and Review,* May 31, 1946; "Carolina County Gives Vote Parity," *New York Times,* June 13, 1948, 54. South Carolina was also one of only two states that did not allow absentee voting for its women and men in uniform.

9. "South Carolina, the Extremist," *Lighthouse and Informer* (Columbia, S.C.), May 25, 1947, 8; Quint, *Profile in Black and White,* 5.

10. Jones-Branch, "'To Speak When and Where I Can,'" 218.

11. Edgar, *South Carolina*, 522; Lander, *History of South Carolina,* 244.

12. J. W. White, "The White Citizens' Councils," 261–62.

13. Ibid., 270.

14. Cox, "'Integration with [Relative] Dignity,'" 274–75; Synnott, "Desegregation in South Carolina," 53.

15. Edgar, *South Carolina*, 545.

16. The following works address the critical role of women in racial activism in South Carolina: Edgar, *South Carolina;* Synnott, "Alice Norwood Spearman Wright"; Myers, *Black, White and Olive Drab;* Grose, *South Carolina at the Brink;* W. B. Moore and Burton, *Toward the Meeting of the Waters;* Lau, *Democracy Rising;* Baker, *Paradoxes of Desegregation;* Johnson, *Southern Ladies, New Women;* and Charron, *Freedom's Teacher.*

17. West and Blumberg, "Reconstructing Social Protest from a Feminist Perspective," 22.

18. Barnett, "Invisible Southern Black Women Leaders," 176–77; Gore, *Radicalism at the Crossroads,* 6–7.

19. See Erskine, "'This Fellowship without Barriers of Race.'" The Memphis chapter of United Church Women had been integrated since its inception. See Little, *You Must Be from the North,* 53–56.

Chapter 1. "The Lord Requires Justice of Us"

1. "The Lord Requires Justice of Us," *Southern Frontier,* April 1943, 2.

2. Lau, *Democracy Rising*, 132; "Teachers' Pay Fight Taken to S.C. Senate," *Atlanta Daily World,* February 23, 1941, 1; "Palmetto Teachers Group Organizes," *Chicago Defender,* December 9, 1939, 6.

3. Brown, "Civil Rights Activism in Charleston," 22.

4. Jones, "'Loyal Women of Palmetto,'" 52.

5. D. G. White, *Too Heavy a Load*, 23, 27, 66. See also Johnson, *Southern Ladies, New Women;* and Rouse, "Out of the Shadow of Tuskegee." Also by Rouse, *Lugenia Burns Hope,* 5.

6. The NACW was founded in Washington, D.C., in 1896.

7. Chappell, *Inside Agitators,* 34–35.

8. Rouse, *Lugenia Burns Hope,* 107.

9. Jones, "'Loyal Women of Palmetto,'" 41; Jones-Branch, "'To Speak When and Where I Can,'" 214; Johnson, *Southern Ladies, New Women,* 9.

10. Johnson, *Southern Ladies, New Women,* 13, 92; Minutes of Meeting of the State Interracial Committee of South Carolina, November 19, 1925, and Annual Meeting, South Carolina Committee on Interracial Cooperation, March 15, 1941, Commission on Interracial Cooperation, reel 53, series 7: 191.

11. Collier-Thomas, *Jesus, Jobs, and Justice,* 326.

12. *National Negro Digest, Special South Carolina Educational Number* 4, no. 3 (1940): 28; "S.C. Club Women to Hold Big Meet," *Chicago Defender,* June 11, 1927, 5; "S.C. Women to Raise Funds for Girls' Home," *Chicago Defender,* May 28, 1927, 5; "Girls' School Is Requested of South Carolina Solons," *Atlanta Daily World,* February 17, 1943, 1; Fields, *Lemon Swamp and Other Places,* 197; Johnson, *Southern Ladies, New Women,* 278.

13. Newby, *Black Carolinians,* 252; Johnson, *Southern Ladies, New Women,* 182, 185; "Federated Clubs: State Federation of South Carolina Issues Calendar," *Chicago Defender,* March 4, 1944, 15.

14. Sitkoff, "African American Militancy," 71.

15. Janken, *White,* 249–50.

16. Skinner, "Sibling Institutions, Similar Experiences," 2, 3; Sitkoff, "African American Militancy," 74.

17. Newby, *Black Carolinians,* 276; Sitkoff, "African American Militancy," 71.

18. Newby, *Black Carolinians,* 276.

19. Sumter NAACP Minutes, April 12, 1942, 1, 2, Sumter NAACP Records, SCL; Roefs, "Leading the Civil Rights Vanguard," 472; Richards, "The Eminent Lieutenant McKaine," 14.

20. "Sumter Teachers Set Mass Meeting in Salary Fight: Attorney Boulware, Mrs. Simkins to Open Campaign September 27," *Atlanta Daily World,* September 19, 1942, 6; Tushnet, *NAACP Legal Strategy,* 87.

21. Modjeska M. Simkins, "Negro Teachers Called to Arms," *Atlanta Daily World,* May 8, 1943, 2.

22. Ibid.

23. Ibid.

24. Chappell, *A Stone of Hope,* 64–65.

25. "Equal Pay Lawyers in Charleston," *Lighthouse and Informer,* February 6, 1944, 1; "Teachers' Suit For Equal Salaries Filed," *Palmetto Leader,* Columbia, South Carolina,

November 13, 1943, 1; "Sumter Teachers Set Mass Meeting in Salary Fight," *Atlanta Daily World*, September 19, 1942, 6; "Seek Equal Pay in S.C. Schools," *Chicago Defender*, November 20, 1943, 7; "Harold R. Boulware, Lawyer; Was a Pioneer in Civil Rights," *New York Times*, January 30, 1983, 26.

26. Baker, *Paradoxes of Desegregation*, 54–55; Charron, *Freedom's Teacher*, 163–65.

27. *A Monthly Summary of Events and Trends in Race Relations*, April 1943, 7.

28. Edgar, *South Carolina,* 515.

29. Baker, *Paradoxes of Desegregation*, 54–55.

30. Roefs, "Leading the Civil Rights Vanguard," 473; "Teachers' Victory Tips Off Fireworks," *Atlanta Daily World*, April 7, 1944, 2. Duvall later married Tuskegee Airman Nathaniel C. Stewart Sr.

31. Terry, "J. Waties Waring," 16. The plaintiff was Albert N. Thompson, a black teacher at Columbia's Booker T. Washington High School. Yarbrough, *A Passion for Justice*, 44.

32. "New Reign of Terror Charged to S.C. Klan," *Atlanta Daily World*, February 25, 1940, 1; "Hoodlums Are Blamed after Racial Riots," *The State* (Columbia, S.C.). The date of the paper is unknown, but the *Atlanta Daily World* confirms that the race riots occurred in 1942. See "Propaganda Is Blamed in S.C. Riots," *Atlanta Daily World*, August 20, 1942, 2.

33. *A Monthly Summary of Events and Trends in Race Relations*, December 1943, 8–9; "Florence Prisoner Whipped, Chained for Letter Newspaper Published," *Atlanta Daily World*, October 29, 1943, 1.

34. "Abolition of Discriminations Sought: South Carolina Citizens Seek to End Discriminations," *Carolina Tribune* (Raleigh), April 5, 1941.

35. "Advancement Group Holds Session Here," *The State*, June 19, 1941.

36. Simon, "Race Relations," 241; "State NAACP Conference in Columbia: Interesting Program Planned," *Palmetto Leader* (Columbia), June 7, 1941, 1.

37. Simon, "Race Relations," 242; "Negroes Barred from Voting in South Carolina," September 13, 1940, Papers of the NAACP, The Voting Rights Campaign, 1916–1940, part 4, reel 10.

38. Wendell Berge to Thurgood Marshall, July 11, 1942, Papers of the NAACP, The Voting Rights Campaign, 1916–1940, part 4, reel 10; *Gaffney (S.C.) Ledger*, February 28, 1942; "School Board Fires Teacher for Trying to Register, Vote," *Atlanta Daily World*, June 26, 1942, 1; "Negroes Barred from Voting in S. Carolina," *New York Amsterdam News*, September 28, 1940, 16; John McCray, "The Need for Changing," *Atlanta Daily World*, June 28, 1942, 5; "Court Hears S.C. Voting Rights Case," *Chicago Defender*, February 28, 1942, 9; "Whites Facing Trial; Denied 4 Vote Rights," *Chicago Defender*, March 7, 1942, 4; "Mrs. Gaffney to Speak July 12th in Georgetown," *Atlanta Daily World*, July 11, 1942, 3; "3 Indicted in S.C. Vote Case by U.S. Jury," *Chicago Defender*, December 6, 1941, 4.

39. "Enthusiastic Crowds Hear Marshall Talk of 'Primary' Issue," *Atlanta Daily World*, June 30, 1942.

40. "S.C. Democrats Draw Up Rules for White Control of Party," *Charleston News and Courier*, May, 20, 1949, 1.

41. Roefs, "Impact of the 1940s Civil Rights Activism," 158.

42. "Senator Olin D. Johnston Dead; South Carolina Democrat, 68," *New York Times*, April 19, 1965, 29; Farmer, "Memories and Forebodings," 242.

43. *A Monthly Summary of Events and Trends in Race Relations*, April 1944, 15.

44. "Whites Reply to S.C. Resolution," *Atlanta Daily World*, March 16, 1944, 1.

45. Ibid.; Hoffman, "Genesis of the Modern Movement," 351.

46. "Challenged Gov. Johnston to Debate White Supremacy," *Arkansas State Press* (Little Rock), May 12, 1944, 1; "Request for Debate with Governor Olin D. Johnston," 1944, *Modjeska Monteith Simkins: In Her Own Words*, Digital Collections, SCPC, http://www.sc.edu/library/digital/collections/simkins.html.

47. "Request for Debate with Governor Olin D. Johnston," 1944, Simkins Papers.

48. "Challenge S.C. Governor to Debate on 'Supremacy' Issue: Olin Johnston Fails to Reply to Columbian," *Atlanta Daily World*, May 12, 1944, 1.

49. This was done after several South Carolina whites called attention to the exclusive and discriminatory nature of the organization's original name. For more information, see Lau, *Democracy Rising*, 136; and "Democratic Party Drops Colored Tag," *Atlanta Daily World*, April 28, 1944, 5.

50. Frederickson, *The Dixiecrat Revolt*, 45. The newspaper, originally named the *Charleston Lighthouse,* was established in early 1939 to replace the more conservative *Palmetto Leader*. It became the *Lighthouse and Informer* in 1940 after McCray moved the paper to Columbia and merged it with the Sumter *People's Informer.* Roefs, "Leading the Civil Rights Vanguard," 468–69; "Democratic Convention Scenes in Chicago," *Chicago Defender*, July 29, 1944, 18. McKaine also ran against Johnston for the U.S. Senate in 1944.

51. Edgar, *South Carolina*, 519; *A Monthly Summary of Events and Trends in Race Relations*, December 1943, 10; ibid., April 1944, 7; ibid., June 1945, 320, 349; ibid., May 1943; Drago, *Initiative, Paternalism* and *Race Relations,* 238; John H. McCray, "Progressive Demos Prepare for Nat'l Confab Contest," *Atlanta Daily World*, July 7, 1944, 2; The PDP supported Truman's civil rights plank in 1948. See "Progressive Democrats Endorse Harry S. Truman," *Florence (S.C.) Morning News*, May 14, 1948, 1; and "S.C. Negro Party to Elect National Convention Delegates," *Charleston News and Courier*, May 25, 1948, 6.

52. Crawford, "African American Women," 121.

53. Mrs. Bessie House to John H. McCray, February 19, 1945, reel 10, John Henry McCray Papers, SCL.

54. Sarah Z. Daniels to John H. McCray, March 14, 1945, reel 7, and October 6, 1945, reel 14, ibid.; Lau, *Democracy Rising*, 196.

55. Sarah Z. Daniels to John H. McCray, October 6, 1945, reel 14, McCray Papers, SCL.

56. "Dr. Weston Honored for Work in Adult Education and Citizenship," *The Pal-

mettoan, April 1963, 11. Weston also earned a master's degree and pursued a Ph.D. at Columbia University. "Prominent Leader Entertained Here," *New York Amsterdam News,* September 6, 1947, 8; see also "Ballots Only Hope Mrs. Weston Says," *Lighthouse and Informer,* July 6, 1947, 1.

57. "Dr. Weston Honored for Work in Adult Education and Citizenship," *The Palmettoan,* April 1963, 11. A Jewish couple, Gennie Seideman and her husband, Jules, a Columbia merchant, were involved in the PDP and gave the organization a biracial image. Most of the funds for the PDP came from African Americans, but its first independent contribution of five dollars came from an unnamed white widow in Richland County. The Seidemans were apparently the organization's best fund-raisers. They managed to obtain donations from anonymous white backers, presumably members of Columbia's small Jewish community. Gennie Seideman also wrote South Carolina governor Strom Thurmond in 1947 protesting the Willie Earle lynching in Greenville. She further expressed concerns about her safety as a person of Jewish ancestry in a racially intolerant country and asserted that "lynching and race killing can be halted if the full force of our government is turned against such crime" and "that even white Protestant Americans will not be safe if this [racial violence] is not checked." Gennie Seideman to Governor Strom Thurmond, February 17, 1947, box 47, folder 636, J. Strom Thurmond Papers, Clemson University Libraries—Special Collections. See also Egerton, *Speak Now against the Day,* 228; C. Webb, *Fight against Fear,* 148; Gravely, "Civil Right Not to Be Lynched," 104; and Richards, "Osceola E. McKaine," 168, 194. The Willie Earle lynching was the last recorded in South Carolina. See Garris, "Decline of Lynching in South Carolina," 2, 63.

58. Blumberg, "White Mothers as Civil Rights Activists," 168.

59. "Democrats Ask Full Participation in South," *Atlanta Daily World,* October 18, 1945, 1; "Program Conference of National Council of Negro Democrats, Eastern Region, October 15–16, 1945," reel 14, McCray Papers, SCL.

60. Minutes of State Committee Meeting, Progressive Democratic Party, January 1946, Annie Bell Weston Vertical File, SCL. In the 1960s, Weston was also president of the Weston Women Citizens League. See Dr. Annie B. Weston to Mrs. T. B. Stackhouse, December 6, 1965, box 1, folder 4, Eunice Temple Ford Stackhouse Papers, SCL.

61. Minutes of State Committee Meeting, Progressive Democratic Party, January 1946, and "Program—1946 Biennial Convention of the Progressive Democratic Party of South Carolina, Columbia, SC, May 22, 1946," Annie Bell Weston Vertical File, SCL; W. D. Workman Jr., "Poll Tax on State's Women Could Net over $500,000," *Charleston News and Courier,* August 15, 1958, 10B: 8; Sullivan, *Days of Hope,* 107. The poll tax was instituted in South Carolina in 1895. See Bunche, *Political Status of the Negro,* 328 and 363.

62. "Colonial Dames Honor Mrs. T. B. Stackhouse," *South Carolina Club Woman* 24, no. 2 (Summer 1969): 14–15, box 1, folder 2, Stackhouse Papers, SCL.

63. "Eunice Temple Ford Stackhouse," box 1, folder 10, Stackhouse Papers, SCL.

64. Ibid. She was also an honorary member of the South Carolina Federation of Col-

ored Women's Clubs. See "World Who's Who Lists Mrs. Stackhouse," *The World Who's Who of Women* (Cambridge, England: Melrose Press, 1973), box 1, folder 4, Stackhouse Papers, SCL; Synnott, "Crusaders and Clubwomen," 53.

65. "South Carolina White Democrats Ask Negro Participation in Primary," *Southern Frontier*, June 1942, 2.

66. Sullivan, *Days of Hope*, 146.

67. "South Carolina SRC Group to Assist Negro Voters," *Southern Frontier*, December 1945, 4.

68. *Southern Frontier*, South Carolina Issue, April 1940, 2.

69. Mrs. Jessie D. Ames to Mrs. Una Roberts Lawrence, Mission Study Editor of the The Home Mission Board of the Southern Baptist Convention, December 13, 1929, Commission on Interracial Cooperation, reel 53, series 7: 216. Davis was also chairperson of the South Carolina Council of the Association of Southern Women for the Prevention of Lynching. See Hall, *Revolt against Chivalry*, 174, 183, 195, 204–5.

70. Shankman, "The South Carolina Council for the Common Good" (paper presented at the South Carolina Historical Association Annual Meeting, April 1982), 2, LPASC.

71. Ibid., 1.

72. Minutes—Women's Council for the Common Good, box 24, folder 212, Mary E. Frayser Papers, LPASC; Shankman, "The South Carolina Council for the Common Good," 2; "To: The Members of the Executive Committee of the Council for the Common Good from Christine S. Gee, President," May 21, 1943, box 3, folder 9, Laura Smith Ebaugh Collection, JDL.

73. Shankman, "The South Carolina Council for the Common Good," 7; "Annual Meeting of the S.C. Women's Council for the Common Good," November 4, 1944, and Laura Smith Ebaugh to Mrs. T. B. Stackhouse, April 18, 1945, box 3, folder 9, Ebaugh Collection, JDL.

74. "Annual Meeting, South Carolina Committee on Interracial Cooperation," March 15 and 27, 1941, and 1942, Commission on Interracial Cooperation Papers, reel 53, series 7: 191; "South Carolina Has Third Conference, Definite Aims Adopted," *Southern Frontier*, February 1940, 1. Paul was president of SCFCWC in 1946. That year, she sought ways to help improve the homes of rural black families, many of which were in squalid condition. After a survey was taken by a representative of the Central Board of Education in New York, Paul wrote requesting funds for her project. In 1952 she founded a rural "demonstration home" in Kingstree, South Carolina, where four or five black women lived to learn modern home-management techniques they could then use to improve their own homes. Appointed in 1930, Paul served as the supervisor of the black home demonstration agents for twenty-eight years. "Founds Unique House; Retires as Supervisor," *Chicago Defender*, January 23, 1960, 14; "S.C. Demonstration House Speeds Rural Home Improvement Program," *Chicago Defender*, December 5, 1953, 3; "South Carolina Finds New Way to Better Homes," *Atlanta Daily World*, October 21, 1956, 5; Harris, "Grace under Pressure," 213; Harris, "A Ray of Hope for Libera-

tion," 193; "Biographical Sketch: Marion Baxter Paul," *The Palmettoan*, April 1963, 19. Paul was also a Jeanes teacher. See McClure, *Jeanes Teachers;* and Fairclough, *A Class of Their Own.*

75. "Richland Interracial Committee to Meet Tuesday, March 30th," *Palmetto Leader*, March 27, 1943, 1; "Annual Meeting South Carolina Committee of Southern Commission on Interracial Cooperation," *Palmetto Leader*, April 3, 1943, 1.

76. Interview with Modjeska Simkins, November 15, 1974, Interview G-0056-1, Southern Oral History Program Collection (#4007), SHC. See also "Interracial Comm. Hold Annual Meet," *Atlanta Daily World*, March 31, 1944, 3.

77. Hall, *Revolt against Chivalry*, 59, 66. The ASWPL was founded in 1930. See Dudley, "A History of the Association of Southern Women," 1.

78. "Lynching Number One, 1942, Women Protest—Editor Gloats," *Southern Frontier*, February 1942, 4.

79. Hall, *Revolt against Chivalry*, 257.

80. Julie R. Reynolds to Mrs. George E. Davis, January 19, 1941, Commission on Interracial Cooperation Papers, reel 53, series 7:192.

81. Collier-Thomas, *Jesus, Jobs, and Justice*, 328.

82. "Methodist Women of South Declare for Equal Race Opportunities," *Southern Frontier*, March 1943, 1; "White and Negro Church Women Join Hands," *Southern Frontier*, September 1943, 2.

83. "Greer Interracial Assemblage," *Palmetto Leader*, February 6, 1943, 1.

84. "The Lord Requires Justice of Us," *Southern Frontier*, April 1943, 2.

85. "Methodist Women of South Declare for Equal Race Opportunities," *Southern Frontier*, March 1943, 1; "White and Negro Women Join Hands," *Southern Frontier*, September 1943, 2; Mary V. Barnes of the Women's Missionary Society, South Carolina Conference, the Methodist Episcopal Church South, to Jessie Daniel Ames, May 12, 1940, and Jessie Daniel Ames to Mrs. J. M. Barnes, June 18, 1940, South Carolina Records, Association of Southern Women for the Prevention of Lynching, reel 7.

86. Minutes, January 11, 1944, Church Women United of South Carolina Records, LPASC; Rock Hill, South Carolina, Chapter of the AAUW, Minutes, November 11, 1943, AAUW Papers, LPASC; *Southern Frontier*, South Carolina Issue, April 1940.

87. Calkins, *Follow Those Women*, 58; "Women Advance New Church Unity," *New York Times*, October 13, 1949, 30; Hartmann, *The Other Feminists*, 96. The NCC was founded in 1950 and replaced the Federal Council of Churches.

88. Calkins, *Follow Those Women*, 65; Hartmann, *The Other Feminists*, 97; Collier-Thomas, *Jesus, Jobs, and Justice*, 367. Some sources say that UCCW membership reached as high as ten to fifty million women in twenty-five hundred local councils by 1966. See Wiggins, "United Church Women," 4. Wiggins argues that this number might be incorrect, since membership numbers are difficult to obtain.

89. "New Race Problems," *The Church Woman*, February 1943, 35, 1222-3-3:06, GCAHUMC.

90. Hartmann, *The Other Feminists*, 97; Findlay, *Church People in the Struggle*, 49.

91. Galeone, "The Role of Church Women United," 2.

92. Minutes, January 11, January 21, 1944, box 1, folder 2, Church Women United of Columbia Records, LPASC.

93. In 1956 a recommendation was adopted changing the name from the Christian Conference for Negro Women to the Interdenominational Christian Conference at Benedict College. A recommendation was adopted in 1968 that the conference be discontinued because of changing times that made segregated conferences unnecessary. See Quattlebaum, *Women of the Church Synod of South Carolina Presbyterian Church.*

94. Giddings, *When and Where I Enter,* 172.

95. Collier-Thomas, *Jesus, Jobs, and Justice,* 310.

96. Minutes, January 11, January 21, March 21, 1944, box 1, folder 2, Church Women United of Columbia Records, LPASC; Woloch, *Women and the American Experience,* 324; "Juvenile Delinquency in Wartime," *The Church Woman,* June 1944, 27, and "Race Relations," *The Church Woman,* June 1944, 23, 1222-3-3:08, GCAHUMC.

97. "Opportunity Awaits You at the Opportunity School," Columbia Army Air Base, January 2–March 27, 1947, box 1, folder 6, Alice Norwood Spearman Wright Papers, SCL.

98. Tolbert, *South Carolina's Distinguished Women,* 113; "Memorandum, re: Dr. Wil Lou Gray's Approaching 80th Birthday, August 29," August 22, 1963, box 16, folder 1270, Wil Lou Gray Papers, SCL.

99. Ogden, "The Making of a Southern Progressive," 88–89; Laura Smith Ebaugh, State Chairman of Public Affairs, YWCA, to SCYWCA Public Affairs Chairman and Executive Directors, March 28, 1952, box 9, folder 8, Ebaugh Collection, JDL; J. M. Dabbs to Miss Wil Lou Gray, October 18, 1950, box 9, folder 708, Gray Papers, SCL.

100. The first opportunity school was established in 1921 as a boarding school. Sessions typically lasted a month, with students ranging from those who could not read to college graduates working on special projects. The admission fee was one dollar. The school for African Americans at Seneca Junior College in Seneca, South Carolina, offered essentially the same curriculum as the white opportunity school. Blacks could also attend opportunity schools at Voorhees Technical School and Benedict College. See Lander, *History of South Carolina,* 137; Gray, Gray, and Tilton, *The Opportunity Schools of South Carolina,* 16–17. Seneca Junior College was the first school for African Americans in Clemson. Students came from "the back country hills of Blue Ridge, South Carolina and Georgia." From L. K. McMillan, *Negro Higher Education,* 23; Ogden, "Wil Lou Gray and the Politics of Progress," 160; see also "Penal Expert Talks on Ignorance and Crime," *Chicago Defender,* April 27, 1940, 8; "Dixie Adult Schools Making Progress," *Chicago Defender,* February 28, 1931, A1; and Closing Exercises, Opportunity School, Voorhees Jr. College–Denmark, S.C., July 24, 1936, box 4, folder 214, Gray Papers, SCL.

101. Interview with Modjeska Simkins by Jacquelyn Hall, July 28–31, 1976, Southern Oral History Program Collection, SHC.

102. Egerton, *Speak Now against the Day,* 426.

103. M. S. Sims, *The YWCA,* 25.

104. "The YWCA and Interracial Practices," *Southern Frontier*, April 1944, 2.

105. Weisenfeld, *African American Women*, 197; Robertson, *Christian Sisterhood*, 160.

106. "The YWCA and Interracial Practices," *Southern Frontier*, April 1944, 2.

107. Collier-Thomas, *Jesus, Jobs, and Justice*, 376; Lynn, *Progressive Women*, 41.

108. Rouse, *Lugenia Burns Hope*, 100.

109. Rossinow, *The Politics of Authenticity*, 110–11.

110. For more information see Rauschenbusch, *Christianity and the Social Crisis*; Spain, *How Women Saved the City*, 65; Lynn, *Progressive Women*, 45.

111. Knotts, *Fellowship of Love*, 40.

112. Taylor, "'On the Edge of Tomorrow,'" 7, 8, 9.

113. Babcock, "Contribution of the National Student YMCA and YWCA," 373–74.

114. Interview with Modjeska Simkins, November 15, 1974, Interview G-00560-1. Southern Oral History Program Collection (#4007), SHC.

115. Report of the President, 1944–1945, box 1, folder 3, Winthrop Student YWCA Papers, LPASC.

116. Correspondence from Mary E. Frayser, Faculty Advisor, Interracial Relations Committee, Winthrop College YWCA, October 21, 1941, box 10, folder 306, SCCHRP, SCL. A student YWCA at South Carolina State University shared many of the same concerns, but it appears that its members did not work with the Winthrop YWCA or attend the interracial conference in 1941. See Annual Report of the Young Women's Christian Association of State A & M College, September 1946–May 1947, SCSUHC. See also Mack, *Parlor Ladies and Ebony Drudges*, 59; Johnson, *Southern Ladies, New Women*, 9, 13, 76, 92.

117. Madden, "'In the Thick of the Fray,'" iv.

118. Rossinow, *The Politics of Authenticity*, 111.

119. Mary E. Frayser to Elizabeth Stinson, October 25, 1940, box 5, folder 32, Winthrop Student YWCA Papers, LPASC.

120. The following books were selected as references for white students: *Brown America*, by Edwin R. Embree; *The Negro in American Civilization*, by Charles S. Johnson; *Facing Facts in South Carolina*, by H. C. Brearley and Mabel Montgomery; *South Problems of South Carolina*, by G. Croft Williams; and *The Negro in South Carolina*, by Marguerite Talbot.

121. Interracial Study at Winthrop College, November 27, 1940, box 5, folder 32, Winthrop Student YWCA Papers, LPASC; Inter-Collegiate Meeting on Interracial Relations, October 15, 1941, box 4, folder 11, Ebaugh Collection, JDL.

122. "An Interracial Relations State Inter-Collegiate Forum," Winthrop College, November 1, 1941, box 4, folder 11, Ebaugh Collection, JDL.

123. Reports of the Findings Committees of the First and Second South Carolina Inter-Collegiate Institute of Interracial Relations Held at Winthrop College, Rock Hill, South Carolina, January 11, 1941, and November 1, 1941, box 1, folder 3, Winthrop Student YWCA Papers, LPASC.

124. Report of the Findings Committee of the First South Carolina Inter-Collegiate

Institute on Interracial Relations Held at Winthrop College, Rock Hill, South Carolina, January 11, 1941, and Report of the President of the YWCA, 1941–1942, box 1, folder 3, Winthrop Student YWCA Papers, LPASC.

125. Records Relating to the Interracial Institute at Winthrop College, 1939–1942, box 5, folder 32, Winthrop Student YWCA Papers, LPASC.

126. Egerton, *Speak Now against the Day*, 239; Findlay, *Church People in the Struggle*, 5; Jelks, *Benjamin Elijah Mays*, 2, 4, 88. Mays received his doctorate on December 17, 1935.

127. Mays, *Born to Rebel*, 252; "Benjamin Mays Was Driven to Greatness," *Atlanta Daily World*, February 22, 1987, 2.

128. YWCA President's Report, 1944–1945, box 5, folder 3, Winthrop Student YWCA Papers, LPASC. Friendship Junior College was founded in 1891 as Friendship Institute. It became the Friendship Normal and Industrial College in 1906 and a junior college in 1931. See E. L. Hercules, "Friendship Jr. College in Plea for Aid," *Chicago Defender*, December 17, 1938, 4.

129. Part of her expenses were paid by the Winthrop YWCA. YWCA President's Report, 1944–1945, box 1, folder 1, Winthrop Student YWCA Papers, LPASC.

130. Clayton, "College Interracialism in the South," 267; Robertson, *Christian Sisterhood*, 98.

131. Collier-Thomas, *Jesus, Jobs, and Justice*, 382; Weisenfeld, *African American Women*, 191; Robertson, *Christian Sisterhood*, 164; "Protestants, YWCA Drop Race Segregation Policy," *Chicago Defender*, March 16, 1946; "Racial Equality in Y.W.C.A. Urged," *New York Times*, March 6, 1946, 22. Dr. Benjamin Mays was the keynote speaker. See "Dr. Mays to Be Guest Speaker at YWCA Centennial Dinner June 27," *Chicago Defender*, June 25, 1955, 15; Lynn, *Progressive Women*, 49; "YWCA Delegates Find Welcome at Atlantic City's Swank Hotels," *Chicago Defender*, March 16, 1946, 4; "YWCA Votes to Drop Color Lines," *New York Amsterdam News*, March 9, 1946, 1.

132. Mrs. W. B. Nichols, Acting General Secretary, YWCA, to Dr. J. M. McCain, President, Agnes Scott College, April 10, 1946, box 2, folder 17, Winthrop Student YWCA Papers, LPASC.

133. Babcock, "Contribution of the National Student YMCA and YWCA," 375.

134. President's Report, Winthrop YWCA, 1946–1947, May 17, 1947, box 1, folder 3, List of YWCA and WCA Officers, 1902–1962, box 1, folder 2, Winthrop Student YWCA Papers, LPASC; Babcock, "Contribution of the National Student YMCA and YWCA," 375; Rossinow, *The Politics of Authenticity*, 91.

135. Erskine, "'This Fellowship without Barriers of Race,'" 2.

136. Robert P. Stockton, "Local YWCA Loses Right to Use Name," *Charleston News and Courier*, November 4, 1971, 1-A.

137. Gilmore, *Gender and Jim Crow*, 192.

138. Roydhouse, "Bridging Chasms," 275.

139. Minute Book, 1954–1967, entries for 1955, YWCA of Greater Charleston Records, South Carolina.

140. Belle Ingles, Visitation Report, Charleston, South Carolina, October 16–19, 1944, National Board of the YWCA of the USA Records, Series IV, A, reel 213.2, SSC.

141. Ibid.

142. Davis was formerly the secretary of the national YWCA. A graduate of Sam Houston College in Austin, Davis, an African American, joined the national staff during World War II as director of its United Service Organizations division. See "Miss Mamie E. Davis Named to Highest YWCA Office," *Atlanta Daily World*, April 26, 1940, 1; "Mamie E. Davis Dies at 70; Former Y.W.C.A. Executive," *New York Times*, November 25, 1975, 40; and "Woman Named Secretary of Nat'l Y.W.C.A.," *Chicago Defender*, April 27, 1940, 10.

143. Mamie E. Davis, Evaluation Report, Coming Street Branch YWCA, November 14, 1946, National Board of the YWCA of the USA Records, Series IV, A, reel 213.2; Erskine, "'This Fellowship without Barriers of Race,'" 80.

144. Erskine, "'This Fellowship without Barriers of Race,'" 50.

145. Report of YWCA Study Committee, March 1970, box 2, folder 37, Columbia YWCA Records, SCL.

146. Monthly Report of the General Secretary to the Board of Directors of the YWCA, February 1940, box 3, folder 74, Columbia YWCA Records, SCL.

147. Monthly Report of the General Secretary to the Board of Directors of the YWCA, May 13, 1943, box 3, folder 74, Columbia YWCA Records, SCL.

148. Minutes, March 9, 1944, June 1944, box 3, folder 74, Columbia YWCA Records, SCL.

149. Minutes, October 1944, box 3, folder 74, Columbia YWCA Records, SCL.

150. Ingraham, a Quaker and a Brooklyn, New York, native, was president of the National Board from 1940 to 1946. She also founded the United Service Organizations, for which she was awarded the Medal for Merit in 1946 from President Harry S. Truman. She was the first woman to win the award. See "Mary S. Ingraham Is Dead at 94; Helped Guide Creation of City U," *New York Times*, April 20, 1981, 10.

151. YWCA Board Meeting, January 1945, box 3, folder 87, Columbia YWCA Records, SCL; M. S. Sims, *The YWCA*, 83.

152. YWCA Board Meeting, May 1945, box 3, folder 87, Columbia YWCA Records, SCL; Erskine, "'This Fellowship without Barriers of Race,'" 51; Robertson, *Christian Sisterhood*, 171; Trolander, *Professionalism and Social Change*, 22–24; Carson, *Settlement Folk*, 183–84.

153. YWCA Board Meeting, June 1945, September 13, 1945, box 3, folder 87, Columbia YWCA Records, SCL; Erskine, "'This Fellowship without Barriers of Race,'" 50.

154. Hendricks, *Gender, Race, and Politics*, 131; Materson, *For the Freedom of Her Race*, 15.

Chapter 2. "The Negro Only Wanted a Chance to Live"

1. Frederickson, "'As a Man, I Am Interested in States' Rights,'" 268; Clark, *Echo in My Soul*, 95.

2. Charleston Metropolitan Council of Negro Women to Mrs. J. Waties Waring, January 30, 1950, box 1, folder 1, Johnette Edwards Papers, LPASC.

3. Edgar, *South Carolina,* 515.

4. Lander, *History of South Carolina,* 169, 195.

5. Affidavit, George Elmore, State of South Carolina, County of Richland, August 13, 1946, Papers of the NAACP, The Voting Rights Campaign, 1916–1950, part 4, reel 10.

6. Woods Aba-Mecha, "Black Woman Activist," 205.

7. "S.C. Vote Ban Appeal to Be Heard Nov. 18," *Atlanta Daily World,* November 4, 1947, 1; "Courts Define the Right to Vote," *New South,* February 1949, 2.

8. "Circuit Court Affirms Waring's Ruling against S.C. White Primary System," *Atlanta Daily World,* January 3, 1948, 5; "Negro Enrollment Order by Court," *Charleston News and Courier,* July 9, 1949, 1.

9. Grose, *South Carolina at the Brink,* 36; Sullivan, *Days of Hope,* 145; interview with Modjeska Simkins, May 11, 1990, Interview A-0356, Southern Oral History Program Collection (#4007), SHC; Hemmingway, "Prelude to Change," 223.

10. "Birmingham Hosts Rights Conference," *Atlanta Daily World,* April 19, 1962, 1; "Educators in South Nix Region Plan," *Chicago Defender,* July 9, 1949, 26.

11. "Photo Standalone 1—no Title (Modjeska Simkins)," *Atlanta Daily World,* August 12, 1937, 1; interview with Modjeska Simkins by Jacquelyn Hall, July 28–31, 1976, reel 1, 35, Simkins Papers, SCPC; "Postgraduate Seminar for S.C. Medicos," *Chicago Defender,* January 18, 1941, 12.

12. "Mrs. Simkins to Speak for Darlington NAACP," *Atlanta Daily World,* November 9, 1944, 4; "Speaking Engagement in Cheraw, South Carolina," May, 20, 1944, *Modjeska Monteith Simkins: In Her Own Words,* SCPC. After serving for seventeen years, she was not reelected secretary of the state conference in 1957. See Lau, *Democracy Rising,* 211.

13. Alice Stovall, Secretary to Thurgood Marshall, to Mrs. A. W. Simkins, April 13, 1949, Papers of the NAACP, The Voting Rights Campaign, 1916–1950, part 4, reel 9.

14. Woods Aba-Mecha, "Black Woman Activist," 207; "South Carolina Urges Drive for Vote," October 14, 1948, Papers of the NAACP, The Voting Rights Campaign, 1916–1950, part 4, reel 11; Cohodas, *Strom Thurmond,* 102.

15. Quint, *Profile in Black and White,* 5.

16. "The White Primary," *New South,* June–July 1948, 15; "Richland Party Books Open to Negro Electors," *Charleston News and Courier,* June 11, 1949, 1:2; "Democrats in 2 Counties Drop Oath," *Charleston News and Courier,* June, 17, 1948, 1:1; "Negro Vote Split in South Carolina," *New York Times,* June 28, 1948, 12; "Effect of New Waring Order Is Not Clear," *Charleston News and Courier,* July 9, 1948; "S.C. Negroes Being Urged to Enroll on Party Books," *Charleston News and Courier,* July 10, 1948, 1; "All-White Status of S.C. Party Thing of Past," *Charleston News and Courier,* July 18, 1948, 8:5–6.

17. Frederickson, *The Dixiecrat Revolt,* 112–13.

18. Carl Lawrence. "Southern Negro Demos Demand Seats: Democrats in Fight over Seats and Civil Rights," *New York Amsterdam News,* July 10, 1948, 1, City Edition.

19. "Progressive Democrats Choose National Delegates to Fight for State Seats: 'REG-ULARS' SEEK OVER AS HEAT DEVELOPS," *Atlanta Daily World*, June 3, 1948, 3.

20. Ibid. Mrs. Bessie E. Tapps from Summerville was the other delegate. Josephine Wood from Gaffney was selected as an alternate at large.

21. Emory O. Jackson. "S.C. Lily-Whites Favored over Negro Demos at Phila.," *Atlanta Daily World*, July 14, 1948, 3; Frederickson, *The Dixiecrat Revolt*, 127–28.

22. Quint, *Profile in Black and White*, 5, 6.

23. C. B. Motley to Miss Karen, RE: *Brown v. Baskin* case, April 7, 1949, Papers of the NAACP, The Voting Rights Campaign, 1916–1950, part 4, reel 9; Edgar, *South Carolina*, 519; Quint, *Profile in Black and White*, 7; "Citizens Go to Polls in Quietness Tuesday," *Atlanta Daily World*, August 13, 1948, 5.

24. Divorce was so uncommon at this time that South Carolina did not have any laws on the subject. Governor Benjamin "Pitchfork" Tillman's proposal to legalize divorce in South Carolina was rejected at the 1895 convention. Governor Strom Thurmond signed a divorce bill into law in 1949. See Egerton, *Speak Now against the Day*, 407; Edgar, *South Carolina*, 445; Frederickson, "'As a Man, I Am Interested in States' Rights,'" 267; "South Carolina Votes for Divorce: Majority Endorses Amendment," *Florence Morning News*, November 3, 1848, 1.

25. Southern, "'Beyond Jim Crow Liberalism,'" 217; Henry Beckett, "The North Must Interfere—But Use Tact," *New York Post*, November 2, 1948.

26. Olson, *Freedom's Daughters*, 217; Yarbrough, *A Passion for Justice*, 53.

27. Egerton, *Speak Now against the Day*, 408.

28. Ibid., 362; "Ex-GI Buddies Backing Isaac Woodard in Damage Suit," *Chicago Defender*, November 22, 1947, 3; Nora Holt, "Blinding of Issac Woodard American Hero: Story How SC Cops Gouged Out His Eyes," *New York Amsterdam News*, August 17, 1946, 9.

29. Egerton, *Speak Now against the Day*, 408.

30. Southern, "'Beyond Jim Crow Liberalism,'" 210.

31. Frederickson, "'As a Man, I Am Interested in States' Rights,'" 267, 268; "Widow of Judge Waring Dies," *New York Amsterdam News*, November 9, 1968, 6; Shattuck, *Episcopalians and Race*, 61.

32. Shattuck, *Episcopalians and Race*, 61; Lancia, "Giving the South the Shock Treatment," 59. Waring left Westover at nineteen to marry. She never graduated from the institution (ibid., 12).

33. Southern, "'Beyond Jim Crow Liberalism,'" 215.

34. Waring had been suggested by Rose Huggins, executive director of the Coming Street YWCA. Huggins, a Greenville native and a former elementary school teacher, was a graduate of St. Augustine College in Raleigh, North Carolina, and the Atlanta University School of Social Work. See Charron, *Freedom's Teacher*, 193; and "Photo Standalone 1—no Title (Rose Huggins)," *Atlanta Daily World*, March 20, 1949, 1.

35. Frederickson, "'As a Man, I Am Interested in States' Rights,'" 268; Clark, *Echo in My Soul*, 95.

36. "White Supremacists Assailed by U.S. Judge Waring's Wife," January 16, 1950. Although the name of the newspaper is not clear, I think this might be from the *Lighthouse and Informer*. Papers of the NAACP, The Voting Rights Campaign, 1916–1950, part 4, reel 11.

37. "Equality Speech Still Hot Issue in S. Carolina: Klan Promises to Answer Mrs. Waring at Another Time," *Atlanta Daily World*, January 19, 1950, 1; "Impeachment of Judge Waring Sought in S.C.," *Atlanta Daily World*, February 8, 1950, 1; "Mrs. Waring Sets D.C. on Ear: Wife of U.S. Judge Scares Race Bigots," *Chicago Defender*, February 18, 1950, 1. Thurmond might have said "beneath comment." See, Cohodas, *Strom Thurmond*, 221.

38. Thurgood Marshall to Mrs. J. Waties Waring, January 23, 1950, Papers of the NAACP, The Voting Rights Campaign, 1916–1950, part 4, reel 11.

39. Clark, *Echo in My Soul*, 95; see also Charron, *Freedom's Teacher*, 194–208.

40. Clark, *Echo in My Soul*, 97.

41. Ibid., 97–98.

42. Ibid., 98.

43. Both blacks and whites attended Mrs. Waring's speech. "Equality Speech Still Hot Issue in S. Carolina: Klan Promises to Answer Mrs. Waring at Another Time," *Atlanta Daily World*, January 19, 1950, 1.

44. Walter White to John McCray, January 24, 1950, Papers of the NAACP, The Voting Rights Campaign, 1916–1950, part 4, reel 11.

45. Terry, "J. Waties Waring," 158.

46. Charleston Metropolitan Council of Negro Women to Mrs. J. Waties Waring, January 30, 1950, box 1, folder 1, Edwards Papers, LPASC.

47. Yarbrough, *A Passion for Justice*, 111; Charron, *Freedom's Teacher*, 203; Brown, "Civil Rights Activism in Charleston," 259–64; "The American Negro in College, 1942–1943," *The Crisis*, August 1943, 234, 237. Veal's thesis is titled "Children Who Cannot Read: A Study of Their Home Environment." The Veals divorced in 1960s. See "Mrs. Veale [*sic*] Gets Divorce Decree," *New York Amsterdam News*, July 23, 1960, 13.

48. Elizabeth Waring to Ruby Cornwell, October 21, 1955, Ruby Cornwell Papers, ARC.

49. Reed Blaine, "Staid Old South Shocked," *Uniontown (Pa.) Morning Herald*, March 23, 1950, 4.

50. "Judge Waities Waring to Retire from Post," *Chicago Defender*, February 2, 1952, 4; Yarbrough, *A Passion for Justice*, 21.

51. "Photo Standalone 14—no Title (Testimonial dinner honoring Judge J. Waties Waring)," *Chicago Defender*, December 4, 1954, 3.

52. Synnott, "Feminists or Maternalists?" Marion A. Wright was president of the Southern Regional Council from 1952 to 1958. See Synnott, "Crusaders and Clubwomen," 55.

53. "Mrs. J. W. Waring, Widow of Judge: Survivor of Ordeal after Segregation Ruling Dies," *New York Times*, November 1, 1968, 47; "Widow of Judge Waring Dies," *New York Amsterdam News*, November 9, 1968, 6; Lancia, "Giving the South the Shock Treatment," 73.

54. "Federated Clubs: State Federation of South Carolina Issues Calendar," *Chicago Defender*, March 4, 1944, 15.

55. "Federation Women Launch Vote Drive," *Atlanta Daily World*, May 11, 1946, 4; "14th Annual Meeting of Federation of Womens Club Is Scheduled," *Atlanta Daily World*, July 17, 1947, 7.

56. Ethelyn Murray Parker to John H. McCray, September 27, 1947, reel 14, McCray Papers, SCL; "Dr. Samuel Higgins Installs Charleston Council Women," *Atlanta Daily World*, July 16, 1953, 4.

57. Parker to McCray, September 27, 1947.

58. National Association of Colored Women Convention, Minutes, Reports, and Greetings, 1950, South Carolina Federation of Colored Women's Clubs to National Association of Colored Women's Clubs, reel 12, Records of the National Association of Colored Women's Clubs, 1895–1992, part 1.

59. "Women's Council Push Registration," *Lighthouse and Informer*, April 2, 1949, 4.

60. "Woman Leader Hits Adults, Churches," *Lighthouse and Informer*, May 11, 1947, 3. Charlotte Hawkins Brown founded the Palmer Memorial Institute for African Americans in Guilford County, North Carolina. She led this school for fifty years. See Wadelington and Knapp, *Charlotte Hawkins Brown.*

61. Hazel O. Reese to John H. McCray, January 7, 1947, and McCray to Reese, January 10, 1947, reel 14, McCray Papers, SCL.

62. "Women Fail to Use Political Power Says Secretary of Progressive Democratic Party," 1947, reel 14, McCray Papers, SCL.

63. Woods Aba-Mecha, "Black Woman Activist," 204.

64. Minutes, November 23, 1947, Sumter NAACP Records, SCL.

65. Minutes, July 25, 1948, ibid.

66. Woods Aba-Mecha, "Black Woman Activist," 12.

67. "Women's Council Meets Monday," *Lighthouse and Informer*, April 23, 1949, 1. Mrs. Nelson was also a member of the South Carolina Federation of Colored Women's Clubs. See "Mrs. Steward, Key Speaker for S.C. Federation," *Atlanta Daily World*, April 27, 1949, 2. Mrs. Nelson's husband, Guerney/Gurney, was a psychology professor and dean at Benedict College. See "S.C. Has Worst Race Baiters," *Chicago Defender*, January 29, 1944, 10; Elizabeth Galbreath, "Typovision," *Chicago Defender*, April 19, 1941, 16; Morris, *Origins of the Civil Rights Movement*, 53, 90.

68. "Clement Speaks for Women's Council on Voting Sunday," *Lighthouse and Informer*, October 24, 1948, 2; "A Political Action Mass Meeting," November 24, 1949, box 2, folder 39, Simkins Papers, SCPC; Spears, *One in the Spirit*, 136, 138–39. The Christian Action Council, founded in 1933, used religion or religious beliefs to help black and white South Carolinians discuss and resolve racial and social problems. Collins was executive director from 1948 to 1950.

69. Woods Aba-Mecha, "Black Woman Activist," 350–52; General Report-Columbia Women's Council Political Action Rally, Benedict College Chapel, Friday Evening, April 21, 1950, box 2, folder 39, Simkins Papers, SCPC. On the first day of the Seventy-seventh Congress, January 3, 1941, Mitchell, along with six other congressmen, introduced six anti-lynching bills. "Six Anti-lynching Bills Introduced in Congress," *Southern Frontier*, February 1941, 1.

70. Woods Aba-Mecha, "Black Woman Activist," 353.

71. "Mrs. Tilly Reports Action on SRC Separation Study," *New South*, December 1946, 15.

72. Minutes, May 2, 1947, November 7, 1947, and March 21, 1944, History of the Woman's Interdenominational Missionary Unions, South Carolina, 1915–1940, box 1, folders 1–2, Church Women United of Columbia Records, LPASC.

73. Minutes, November 15, 1946, box 1, folder 2, Church Women United of Columbia Records, LPASC.

74. "Southern Women Hold Conference on Human Rights," *A Monthly Summary of Events and Trends in Race Relations*, June 1947, 346. "Human rights" was often used as a euphemism for "civil rights."

75. "Southern Women Pledge Voting Help to Aides," *Lighthouse and Informer*, September 17, 1949, 1; Mjagkij, *Men and Women Adrift*, 161.

76. Goldfield, *Black, White, and Southern*, 51. "Church Women Open Conference Here Today: Mrs. Roosevelt to Address Meet This Evening," *Atlanta Daily World*, September 8, 1949, 1.

77. "Church Women Open Conference Here Today."

78. "Southern Church Women Draft Action Program," *New South*, September 1949, 2–3; Goldfield, *Black, White, and Southern*, 51; "Church Women Open Conference Here Today."

79. M. S. Sims, *The YWCA*, 83–84.

80. "The New Social Role of American Churches," *A Monthly Summary of Events and Trends in Race Relations*, December 1946, 140; Annual Report for 1929, box 1, folder 1, Greenville YWCA Records, SCL. See also "Southern Town Works on Plan to Aid Negroes," *New York Herald Tribune*, June 3, 1950; "What Greenville Is Doing about Community Problems," *Greenville American*, May 5, 1950, and May 19, 1950; "Negro Survey to Be Presented at Meeting May 29" and "Straw in the South Wind: Negroes Begin to Share Larger Civic Role," *Christian Science Monitor*, November 10, 1950, box 1, folder 28, Greenville YWCA Records, SCL; Erskine, "'This Fellowship without Barriers of Race,'" 30; Simpson, *The First Fifty Years*, 10.

81. Ladd, *Negro Political Leadership in the South*, 74.

82. Edgar, *South Carolina*, 459.

83. O'Neill, "Memory, History," 286.

84. Olive Walser, Visitation Report, Greenville, South Carolina, November 5–6, 1946, National Board of the YWCA of the USA Records, Series IV, A, reel 213.4, SSC; Laura Smith Ebaugh to Elizabeth Herring, National YWCA, November 18, 1950, box 9, folder 7, Ebaugh Collection, JDL; Simpson, *The First Fifty Years*, 44; Margaret Keith,

Chairman, Public Affairs Committee, Greenville YWCA, to Governor J. Strom Thurmond, May 5, 1947, box 47, folder 635, J. Strom Thurmond Papers, Special Collections, Clemson University Libraries, Clemson, South Carolina. Thurmond received similar letters from the Charleston YWCA, the Columbia Council of Church Women, and the Opportunity School of South Carolina. Lau, *Democracy Rising*, 156; "Trial of Earle Lynchers Underway at Greenville," *Lighthouse and Informer*, May 18, 1947, 1.

85. Belle Ingels, Visitation Report, Greenville, South Carolina, March 4, 1946, National Board of the YWCA of the USA Records, Series IV, A, reel 213.4, SSC; "The Greenville Plan," *New South*, July 1950, 8; Drake, "The Negro in Greenville," 239; O'Neill, "Memory, History," 287.

86. "Greenville, S.C., Phillis Wheatley Center, Greenville, S.C., 1918–1936," *Chicago Defender*, August 28, 1937, 17; see Carretta, *Phillis Wheatley.*

87. "Welfare Worker Visits City," *Chicago Defender*, September 21, 1918, 10; Lydia Dishman, "From Humble Beginnings: The Phyllis Wheatley Center," *Greenville Magazine*, July 2003, 62–63, Hattie Logan Duckett Biographical File, SCR; Hunter, *Nickel and a Prayer*, 135, 235, notes 21–22.

88. Huff, *Greenville,* 314; Dishman, "From Humble Beginnings," 62–63; "Hattie Logan Duckett, 1885–1956," Duckett Biographical File, SCR. Jesse Jackson, a native of Greenville, learned how to swim and play pool at the Phillis Wheatley Center. See E. Richard Walton. "Phillis Wheatley Elects New Board for Transition Phase," *Greenville News*, May 18, 2006, 1B, Phillis Wheatley Center File, SCR.

89. Belle Ingels,Visitation Report, Greenville, South Carolina, March 4, 1946, National Board of the YWCA of the USA Records, Series IV, A, reel 213.4, SSC.

90. Robertson, *Christian Sisterhood,* 166.

91. "Mrs. Duckett's Center Helped All Races," *Greenville Piedmont*, Friday, February 14, 1975, box 1, folder 19, Greenville YWCA Records, SCL; Lau, *Democracy Rising*, 90; "Program Submitted by Mrs. Hattie Duckett, Greenville County," Minutes, S.C. Commission on Interracial Cooperation, May 2, 1939, Commission on Interracial Cooperation, reel 53, series 7:192; Gordon, *Sketches of Negro Life,* 187; Interracial Committee of the Greenville County Council for Community Development, Minutes, February 7, 1938, box 2, folder 7, Interracial Cooperation, 1937–1939, Greenville County Council for Community Development Papers, JDL. The GCCCD was established in 1936 to coordinate the efforts of social welfare, educational, and recreational organizations and agencies in Greenville County. In the same year, the GCCCD received an $80,000 grant from the General Education Board of New York City to support its efforts, which were headquartered at Furman University. See GCCCD finding aid, JDL; Henderson, "Building Intelligent and Active Public Minds," 42; and Lau, *Democracy Rising*, 91–94. Many of the Interracial Committee's meetings were held at the Phillis Wheatley Center.

92. Judith Bainbridge, "Greenville Owes Debt to Hattie Duckett," *City People* (Greenville), March 14, 2001, 1, 16; "Hattie Logan Duckett, 1885–1956," Duckett Biographical File, SCR; "Interracial Comm. Hold Annual Meet," *Atlanta Daily World*, March 31,

1944, 3. Duckett and members of the Interracial Committee, most notably Laura Smith Ebaugh, a sociology professor at Furman, conducted a similar survey in the 1930s. See box 2, folder 7, Interracial Cooperation, Greenville County Council for Community Development Papers, JDL.

93. "Praise for Greenville's Big Idea," *New South*, July 1950, 6–7; Judith Bainbridge, "Greenville Owes Debt to Hattie Duckett," *City People*, March 14, 2001, 1, 16; "Hattie Logan Duckett, 1885–1956," Duckett Biographical File, SCR; Simpson, *The First Fifty Years*.

94. "Praise for Greenville's Big Idea," *New South*, July 1950, 7.

95. "SC City Forges Ahead on Job Equality Plan," *New York Amsterdam News*, November 25, 1950, 10, City Edition.

96. "Survey, Analysis, and Plan of Fund-Raising for YWCA of Greenville," February 1961, 74–75, Greenville YWCA Records, SCL.

97. "Praise for Greenville's Big Idea," *New South*, July 1950, 6; "SC City Forges Ahead on Job Equality Plan," *New York Amsterdam News*, November 25, 1950, 10.

98. Report of Local Visit by National Board Member, March 1949, Greenville, South Carolina, National Board of the YWCA of the USA Records, Series IV, A, reel 213.2, SSC; "SC City Forges Ahead on Job Equality Plan," *New York Amsterdam News*, November 25, 1950, 10.

99. "SC City Forges Ahead on Job Equality Plan," *New York Amsterdam News*, November 25, 1950, 10.

100. Public Affairs Committee Minutes, Greenville YWCA, June 4, 1953, and September 3, 1953, box 1, folder 18, Greenville YWCA Records, SCL.

101. Public Affairs Committee Minutes, Greenville YWCA, September 3, 1953, November 5, 1953, and December 3, 1953, box 1, folder 18, Greenville YWCA Records, SCL; Laura Smith Ebaugh to Mrs. F. I. Whitfield, Executive Director, Charleston YWCA, February 20, 1950, box 9, folder 7, Ebaugh Collection, JDL.

102. Annual Report of the Public Affairs Committee, Greenville YWCA, 1953, box 1, folder 12, Greenville YWCA Records, SCL.

103. Greene, *Our Separate Ways*, 109.

104. "Young Women's Christian Association 36th Annual Membership Meetings," February 9, 1950, box 3, folder 72, Columbia YWCA Papers, SCL.

105. Narrative Report for the Program Year, 1952–1953, to the National Board of the Young Women's Christian Association, box 3, folder 77, 11, Columbia YWCA Records, SCL. Eight years before, Phyllis Wheatley members stopped attending board meetings because they were never sent notices. Elizabeth C. Ledeen claimed this was not a deliberate policy; it just "happened." Black women were not invited to meetings until 1950–51. See Synnott, "Crusaders and Clubwomen," 65, 66; Joyner, "How Far We Have Come"; and Carter, "Civil Rights and Politics in South Carolina," 410, 424.

106. Kathleen Carpenter, Visitation Report, March 22–25, 1950, Charleston, South Carolina, National Board of the YWCA of the USA Records, Series IV, A, reel 213.2, SSC.

107. Pauline R. Schaedler, Visitation Report, March 30–31, April 1, 1950, Charleston,

South Carolina, National Board of the YWCA of the USA Records, Series IV, A, reel 213.2, SSC.

108. Minute Book, 1954–1967, entries for 1955, YWCA of Greater Charleston Records, GCAHUMC.

Chapter 3. "How Shall I Sing the Lord's Song?"

1. Kluger, *Simple Justice*, 4.
2. Edgar, *South Carolina*, 522; Lau, *Democracy Rising*, 197.
3. "Missiles Thrown at Home of Minister in S. Carolina," *Atlanta Daily World*, September 21, 1955, 2; Reverend J. A. DeLaine to Flutie Boyd, April 7, 1948, folder 2, J. A. DeLaine Papers, SCL.
4. Lau, *Democracy Rising*, 196, 199; James M. Hinton to Levi Pearson, March 12, 1948, J. A. Delaine Papers, Digital Collections, SCL, http://www.sc.edu/library/digital/collections/delaine.html; Reverend J. A. Delaine to Harold R. Boulware, March 6, 1948, folder 3, Delaine Papers, SCL. Sarah Z. Daniels had also led two attempts to get blacks registered to vote in Manning.
5. Byrnes, *All in One Lifetime*, 408, 412. Figg, an opponent of school desegregation, later served as the dean of the University of South Carolina Law School from 1959–70. See Edgar, *South Carolina Encyclopedia*, 322.
6. Edgar, *South Carolina*, 522; Arnold DeMille. "Wait Court Rule on SC School Bias," *New York Amsterdam News*, June 2, 1951, 1; Byrnes, *All in One Lifetime*, 408, 412.
7. Kluger, *Simple Justice*, 26.
8. Ibid., 23; "Negroes Will Seek to Enter White Schools," *Charleston News and Courier*, November 18, 1950: 1; Lau, "From the Periphery to the Center," 117.
9. Gona, *Dawn of Desegregation*, 108.
10. Kluger, *Simple Justice*, 24; Lau, *Democracy Rising*, 204.
11. Gona, *Dawn of Desegregation*, 115.
12. Burton, Burton, and Appleford, "Seeds in Unlikely Soil," 185–86.
13. Goldfield, *Black, White, and Southern*, 78, 87.
14. Edgar, *South Carolina*, 524.
15. Muse, *Ten Years of Prelude*, 70.
16. Edgar, *South Carolina*, 525; Quint, *Profile in Black and White*, 28.
17. Woods, *Black Struggle, Red Scare*, 49, 56.
18. Edgar, *South Carolina*, 527; Quint, *Profile in Black and White*, 38.
19. Woods Aba-Mecha, "Black Woman Activist," 236.
20. "Segregation Backed by Episcopal Women," *Charleston News and Courier*, October 7, 1955, 1-B, 3–4.
21. The South Carolina Republican Party differed from the Republican Party of the Reconstruction era. Its southern members broke away from the Democratic Party in the late 1930s because they objected to Roosevelt's New Deal programs, his plan to "pack" the Supreme Court, the purging of congressmen who opposed his policies, and

the small but increasing number of blacks in South Carolina who were registering as Democrats. "Mrs. Cornelia Dabney Tucker by Albertine Moore, 1944," box 1, folder 1, Cornelia Dabney Ramseur Tucker Papers, SCL; "Elephant in South Carolina," *Oakland (Calif.) Tribune*, October 24, 1939, editorial page; "South Carolina Has New G.O.P.," *Gastonia (N.C.) Daily Gazette*, December 1, 1938, 8; Edgar, *South Carolina*, 508, 509; Kittel, *Cornelia Dabney Tucker*, 35, 38. Tucker quit this position in 1943 and later left the Republican Party entirely to dedicate more time to her Australian ballot campaign. She succeeded in 1951. Tucker later opposed the 1962 Supreme Court decision against prayer in public schools. See "Ballot Campaign Will Be Pressed: Mrs. Tucker Quits Post as Publicity Director for the Republican Party," *Charleston News and Courier*, January 20, 1943, 12; Edgar, *South Carolina Encyclopedia*, 981; and W. D. Workman Jr., "Palmetto Profiles: Mrs. Cornelia Dabney Tucker," *South Carolina Magazine*, May 1948, 5.

22. "Russia's Cherished Aim," *Charleston News and Courier*, June 3, 1954, 4-A.

23. "Mrs. Tucker Renews Fight for Segregation In Schools," *Charleston News and Courier*, June 1, 1955, 5-A; "Mrs. Tucker Says Deprived of Vote," *Florence Morning News*, November 3, 1948, 1; "South Carolina Has a New Republican Party," *The Daily Inter Lake* (Kalispell, Mont.), November 30, 1938, 2; "South Carolina Has New G.O.P." and "Woman Usurps the S.C. House," *Gastonia (N.C.) Daily Gazette*, December 1, 1938, 8, and March 15, 1940, 2; Kittel, *Cornelia Dabney Tucker*, 45–62; "Senator to Hear Mrs. Tucker's Secret Vote Plea," *Charleston News and Courier*, January 8, 1946, 1; Woods, *Black Struggle, Red Scare*, 56.

24. The American Legion, a conservative veterans organization, was founded in 1919. See Pencak, *For God and Country*, 46.

25. "Desegregation Involves U.S. Security, Says Mrs. Tucker," *Charleston News and Courier*, June 16, 1955, 10-A; Kittel, *Cornelia Dabney Tucker*, 29–31, 80–81.

26. Western Union telegram from Senator Olin D. Johnston to Mrs. C. D. Tucker, July 14, 1955, box 1, folder 4, Tucker Papers, SCL.

27. "Petition Now Has about 400 Names," *Charleston News and Courier*, June 7, 1955, 9-B. Modjeska Simkins recalled that Tucker had been a member of the South Carolina Committee on Interracial Cooperation at one point but that she was a paternalist who supported vocational education only for black students. See interview with Modjeska Simkins by Jacquelyn Hall, November 15, 1974, Interview G-0056-1, Southern Oral History Program Collection, SHC.

28. "Mrs. Tucker Writes to Ike," *Charleston News and Courier*, June 29, 1955, 12-A; letter to the editor of the American National Research Report from Mrs. Cornelia Dabney Tucker, July 15, 1955, box 1, folder 6, Tucker Papers, SCL.

29. Woods, *Black Struggle, Red Scare*, 56.

30. "An Open Letter to Three Southern Governors," *New South*, July 1951, 1; "S.C. Schools Will Continue Segregation, Byrnes Says," *Charleston News and Courier*, January 25, 1951, 5-A.

31. Bartley, *The Rise of Massive Resistance*, 44–45; O'Neill, "To Endure, but Not Accept," 89; Byrnes, *All in One Lifetime*, 407.

32. "South Acts to Keep Pupil Segregation," *New York Times*, May 28, 1951, 16.

33. Edgar, *South Carolina*, 524; Woods, *Black Struggle, Red Scare*, 25.

34. Daniel, *Lost Revolutions*, 231.

35. Brown, "Civil Rights Activism," 78.

36. Woods Aba-Mecha, "Black Woman Activist," 238.

37. "Threatened South Carolina Leader Refuses to Leave," *Atlanta Daily World*, December 13, 1955, 2. And indeed, they did. In 1955, South Carolina NAACP president James M. Hinton called for a boycott statewide and against Coca-Cola in Orangeburg in particular because the company refused to deliver to African Americans merchants. "If Coca Cola is too good for delivery to Negro merchants here, it is too good for Negroes anywhere to drink," he commented. See "Touch Not, Says Orangeburg," *South Carolina Independent* (Columbia), October 15, 1955, 1; and J. W. White, "The White Citizens' Councils," 266.

38. Woods Aba-Mecha, "Black Woman Activist," 239; "South Carolina's Plot to Starve Negroes," *Jet Magazine*, October 20, 1955, 8–13; "Threatened South Carolina Leader Refuses to Leave," *Atlanta Daily World*, December 13, 1955, 2.

39. Loreice Hackney, President, Young Women's Civic League, to Dr. Channing Tobias, December 1, 1955, Papers of the NAACP, Part 8, reel 28, Reprisals, 1940–1955.

40. "Negro Woman Renounces the NAACP," *Charleston News and Courier*, September 14, 1955, 1-B.

41. "Ex-Member Denounces NAACP; Denies Coercion," *Palmetto Leader*, October 1, 1955, 1.

42. Interview with Strom Thurmond, July 20, 1978, Interview A-0334, Southern Oral History Program Collection (#4007), SHC; "Strom Thurmond of South Carolina," *Chicago Defender*, October 18, 1958, 10.

43. Woods, *Black Struggle, Red Scare*, 66; Badger, "From Defiance to Moderation," 10–11.

44. Edgar, *South Carolina*, 527–28.

45. "Thurmond Makes Comments on State's Racial Situation" and "Governor Says Segregation Is Will of People," *Charleston News and Courier*, September 15, 1955, 1-B; Edgar, *South Carolina*, 528.

46. W. F. Murphy, "The South Counterattacks," 380. This move was also supported by Cornelia Dabney Tucker, who, like many white Carolinians, considered the organization a Communist front. See "Pocketbook Attack against NAACP Sought, Mrs. Tucker Says State Should Not Provide Salaries," *Charleston News and Courier*, January 10, 1956, 10-A; "The Meek and the MIGHTY: The Bus Decision and Its Impact on the South," *Daily Defender*, December 13, 1956, 1; "Cornelia Dabney Tucker," in Edgar, *South Carolina Encyclopedia*, 981.

47. "NAACP Limited by South Carolina," *New York Times*, March 18, 1956, 87:4.

48. "Teachers in Appeal, Ask Supreme Court to Void South Carolina Law," *New York Times*, April 24, 1957, 33:1; "17 S. Carolina Teachers Protest NAACP Ban," *Chicago Defender*, May 11, 1957, 6.

49. Edgar, *South Carolina*, 528; Mrs. Andrew W. Simkins, "Action against College Called Unconstitutional," *Atlanta Daily World*, January 12, 1958, 4; "Timmerman Refuses to Clarify Allen Univ. De-Certification," *Atlanta Daily World*, January 5, 1958, 1; Quint, *Profile in Black and White*, 117–18.

50. Mrs. Andrew W. Simkins, "Action against College Called Unconstitutional," *Atlanta Daily World*, January 12, 1958, 4.

51. "Bill Would Ban Employees from the NAACP," *Charleston News and Courier*, August 26, 1955, 1-B.

52. Fraser, *Charleston!* 409; Clark, *Ready from Within*, 37.

53. Preskill, "Developmental Leadership of Septima Clark," 226; Crawford, Rouse, and Woods, *Women in the Civil Rights Movement*, 89; Charron, *Freedom's Teacher*, 242, Clark, *Echo in My Soul*, 112–15. It was not until 1976 that Governor James Edwards acknowledged that Clark had been terminated unjustly and was entitled to her pension.

54. "Teacher Challenges S.C. Law, Is Fired," *The Afro-American*, Baltimore, Maryland, June 1957; interview with Jessica Pearson Brown, *South Carolina Voices of the Civil Rights Movement, A Conference on the History of the Civil Rights Movement in South Carolina, 1940–1970*, November 5–6, 1982, Charleston Museum, 99–101.

55. Brown interview, 81. In 1949, Esau Jenkins founded the Progressive Club on Johns Island to provide African Americans with practical and political education. He formulated the idea for the first citizenship school on the island. See Carawan and Carawan, *Ain't You Got a Right?* 146.

56. Gona, *Dawn of Desegregation*, 154–55; "Minor Damage to Rev. DeLaine's Church," *South Carolina Independent*, October 15, 1955, 1; "S.C. Whites Burn Church to Chase Minister," *Jet Magazine*, October 20, 1955, 3–5; Badger, "From Defiance to Moderation," 10.

57. Interview with Modjeska Simkins by Jacquelyn Hall, July 28, 1976, 76, Southern Oral History Program Collection, SHC; "DeLaine Home Repeatedly Fired at, Mrs. DeLaine Prostrate in Columbia," Papers of the NAACP, Part 18: Special Subjects, 1940–1955, Series C: General Office Files, reel 33; "Pastor Guns Way Out of SC," *New York Amsterdam News*, October 22, 1955, 1; "Rev. DeLaine Speaker in Long Island," *New York Amsterdam News*, February 11, 1956, 22.

58. "DeLaine Home Repeatedly Fired at, Mrs. DeLaine Prostrate in Columbia," Papers of the NAACP, Part 18: Special Subjects, 1940–1955, reel 33.

59. "Segregation Group Confers in Secret," *New York Times*, December 30, 1955, 1.

60. "Dean Who Fought Bias Leaves Post: South Carolina U. Educator Reported Ousted after an Attack on Segregation," *New York Times*, November 24, 1955, 24:3.

61. Solomon, "Problem of Desegregation," 321.

62. "Dean Lays Ouster to Color Line Stand," *New York Times*, November 25, 1955, 19.

63. "Epidemic to Fear," editorial reprinted from the *Cheraw Chronicle* in *New South*, February 1957, 12.

64. "Defiance of Law Growing in South 3 Groups Report," *New York Times*, June 15, 1959, 1.

65. American Friends Service Committee, Inc., to the National Association for the Advancement of Colored People, December 13, 1955, Papers of the NAACP, Part 18: Special Subjects, 1940–1955, Series C: General Office Files, reel 33.

66. "Aiken Is Site of Bi-Racial YWCA Lunch," *Charleston News and Courier*, January 6, 1956, 1-B. The Aiken branch was founded in 1954 as South Carolina's first integrated YWCA. It closed in 1960 because of a loss of funds due most likely to local resistance to integration. See Lewis, "The Young Women's Christian Association's Multiracial Activism," 92; "Formation of Permanent YWCA for Aiken County to Be Discussed May 26," *Aiken Standard and Review*, May 21, 1954, 6; "Aiken County YWCA Will Close Program," *Aiken Standard and Review*, September 29, 1960, 1; and "Little Black Angel: Josie Hazel Earned Her Wings Long Ago as Teacher, Youth Worker, Volunteer," *Aiken Standard and Review*, January 8, 1982, 5A.

67. "Discretion Lacking," January 6, 1956, *Aiken Standard and Review*, 4.

68. Lander, *History of South Carolina,* 204; Tyson, "Dynamite and 'The Silent South,'" 277, 285. All of the contributors to *South Carolinians Speak* were white. John B. Morris, the rector of St. Barnabas Episcopal Church in Dillon, South Carolina, who compiled and published the booklet along with four other Protestant ministers, argued that if blacks were asked to contribute most white Carolinians would refuse to read the pamphlet. John B. Morris to Helen Christensen, April 13, 1957, box 1, John B. Morris Papers, SCL.

69. G. M. Bryan, *These Few Also Paid a Price,* 80–81.

70. Quint, *Profile in Black and White*, 172; Wright and Shankman, *Human Rights Odyssey*, 282; "Blames Politicians for Racial Violence in State," *Atlanta Daily World*, December 14, 1957, 1; "Bomb Home of Southern Moderate," *Daily Defender*, November 21, 1957, 3; Shattuck, *Episcopalians and Race*, 75.

71. *South Carolinians Speak* also contained contributions and calls for moderation from other women, such as Helen Burr Christensen, a civic leader in Beaufort, who urged that the "Negro must receive equal opportunities, but must realize that equality cannot be bestowed, it must be earned," and Julia Rees Reynolds of Sumter, who asserted that "the time is ripe for a more widespread Negro representation on school boards, city councils and juries and in the Legislature." Reynolds also called for admission to graduate and professional schools on the basis of "intellectual and moral qualifications." From "12 in South Offer Racial Solutions," *New York Times*, October 23, 1957, 25:1; "South Carolina Klansmen Freed," *Atlanta Daily World*, July 27, 1958, 6. The contributors were denounced by Governor George Bell Timmerman Jr. See Edgar, *South Carolina*, 528.

72. Robert P. Martin Jr.'s Confession, December 6, 1957, folder 1, Claudia Sanders Papers, SCL.

73. Mrs. James H. Sanders to Mr. Johnson, March 19, 1974, folder 1, Sanders Papers, SCL; Mrs. James H. Sanders to Reverend John B. Morris, October 29, 1957, box 1 (folders not numbered), Morris Papers, SCL.

74. Tyson, "Dynamite and 'The Silent South,'" 290–91; Foster, "We Cannot Be Still," 65, 68, 71.

75. Mrs. James H. Sanders to Mr. Johnson, March 19, 1974, Sanders Papers, SCL.

76. *South Carolina Council on Human Relations, 1934–1976*, finding aid, 1, SCL.

77. "Council Advocates Bi-Racial Amity," *Charleston News and Courier*, August 10, 1955, 1-B.

78. Alice Spearman to Esther Cole Franklin, February 18, 1955, box 34, folder 946, SCCHRP, SCL.

79. M. L. Bryan, *Proud Heritage,* 29.

80. South Carolina Division Southern Regional Council, Inc., Statement of Dues Return, February 1951, box 10, folder 736, Gray Papers, SCL; Biographical information, box 71, folder 3, and 1948 speech, box 72, folder 13, Harriet Porcher Stoney Simons Papers, 1916–1971, SCHS.

81. Synnott, "Alice Norwood Spearman Wright," 200.

82. Minutes, August 18, 1954, Meeting of the League of Women Voters Presidents of Southern States Held in Atlanta, Georgia, July 27–28, 1954, box 75, folder 16, Simons Papers, SCHS.

83. Daniel, *Lost Revolutions,* 231. However, Simons helped establish the Charleston Council on Human Relations in 1965. See Synnott, "Crusaders and Clubwomen," 64.

84. Interview with Alice Spearman Wright, WNSC-TV Channel 30, Rock Hill, South Carolina, July 3, 1981, in Chepesuik, Evans, and Morgan, *Women Leaders in South Carolina,* 41.

85. "Introducing Mrs. Eugene Spearman," *South Carolina Clubwoman,* January 1951, 5, box 1, folder 12, Spearman Wright Papers, SCL; Synnott, "Alice Norwood Spearman Wright," 188.

86. Synnott, "Alice Norwood Spearman Wright," 188.

87. Sylvia L. Hill, Director of Development, to Mrs. Alice Spearman, January 7, 1968, box 1, folder 20, Spearman Wright Papers, SCL; "Region III NCNW Holds Meet in Greenville, S.C," *Atlanta Daily World,* April 24, 1957, 2. She also attended the National Council of Negro Women's annual regional meeting in Daytona, Florida, in 1955, where she participated in a panel titled, "Education, the Arsenal of Democracy." See "Points of Historical Interest seen by Women of Regional Meet," *Atlanta Daily World,* May 4, 1955, 4.

88. Annual Regional Conference, Region III, National Council of Negro Women, Fuller Normal and Industrial School, Greenville, South Carolina, April 19–20, 1957, box 11, folder 348, SCCHRP, SCL.

89. Interview with Alice Spearman Wright, WNSC-TV Channel 30, Rock Hill, South Carolina, July 3, 1981 in Chepesuik, Evans, and Morgan, *Women Leaders in South Carolina,* 42.

90. "South Carolina Emergency Relief Administration," Memorandum, April 15, 1935, box 1, folder 4, and "Introducing Mrs. Eugene Spearman," *South Carolina Clubwoman,* January 1951, box 1, folder 12, Spearman Wright Papers, SCL.

91. Hayes, *South Carolina and the New Deal,* 65–66; Daniel, *Lost Revolutions,* 230.

92. Daniel, *Lost Revolutions,* 230; interview with Modjeska Simkins by Jacquelyn Hall, November 15, 1974, Interview G-0056-1, Southern Oral History Program Collection, SHC.

93. Interview with Modjeska Simkins by Jacquelyn Hall, July 28–31, 1976, 104, Southern Oral History Program Collection, SHC.

94. Hayes, *South Carolina and the New Deal*, 67.

95. Woods Aba-Mecha, "Black Woman Activist," 284; "Mrs. Simkins to Address Florence NAACP," *Lighthouse and Informer*, May 1, 1954, 1; Hall, *Revolt against Chivalry*, 102; Synnott, "Alice Norwood Spearman Wright," 188; Lynn, *Progressive Women*, 57.

96. Alice N. Spearman to Anna D. Kelly, April 15, 1955, box 11, folder 345, SCCHRP, SCL.

97. Interview with Anna DeWees Kelly by Edmund Drago, August 20, 1984, ARC.

98. Spearman to Hester S. Medlen, of the South Carolina Education Association, May 1, 1955, box 11, folder 345, SCCHRP, SCL. The Palmetto Education Association was the black teachers' organization.

99. "Facts in YWCA Facilities," February 1958, box 1, folder 5, SCCHRP, SCL.

100. Annual Report of the Public Affairs Committee, January 11, 1954, box 1, folder 18, Greenville YWCA Records, SCL; S. A. Murphy, *Breaking the Silence*, xv–xvi.

101. "Women's Group Act toward Public School Preservation," *Charleston News and Courier*, May 25, 1954, 6–8; Quint, *Profile in Black and White*, 99; Edgar, *South Carolina*, 527.

102. Howard G. McClain, "Preparedness Measure: South Carolina's School Amendment," *New South*, February 1953, 1–5; "Why the League of Women Voters Opposes the Constitutional Amendment to Remove State Responsibility for a System of Free Public Schools," box 75, folder 16, Simons Papers, SCHS; Quint, *Profile in Black and White*, 95.

103. Bagwell, *School Desegregation in the Carolinas*, 138–39; Edgar, *South Carolina*, 523.

104. "Statement Approved by the Board of Directors of Greenville YWCA, March 14, 1956," box 2, folder 33, Columbia YWCA Records, SCL.

105. Ibid.

106. Ibid.

107. "YWCA Facts—Program and Principles, Greenville, SC, 1958," box 1, folder 5, Greenville YWCA Records, SCL.

108. Ibid.

109. Ibid.; *Survey, Analysis, and Plan of Fund-Raising for YWCA of Greenville*, 79, 80, box 1, folder 7, Greenville YWCA Records, SCL.

110. United Fund of Greenville County Report of Capital Fund Committee Concerning Requests from YWCA and YMCA for Permission to Conduct Capital Fund Campaigns, April 3, 1958, box 1, folder 5, Greenville YWCA Records, SCL.

111. Ibid.

112. Ibid.

113. Virginia Prouty, Visitation Report, Charleston, South Carolina, November 18, 1955, National Board of the YWCA of the USA Records, Series IV, A, reel 273.3, SSC.

114. Hattie Droll, Visitation Report, Charleston, South Carolina, October 8–11, 1956, National Board of the YWCA of the USA Records, Series IV, A, reel 273.3, SSC.

115. Ibid.

116. Hattie Droll, Visitation Report, Charleston, South Carolina, November 16, 1957, National Board of the YWCA of the USA Records, Series IV, A, reel 273.3, SSC.

117. *The Church Woman*, April 1950, 36, 1222-3-3:14, GCAHUMC. UCCW's first president was Mrs. W. E. (Susie) Durant of Elliott, South Carolina. See *The Church Woman*, May 1950, 19, 1222-23:14, GCAHUMC.

118. "Through the Years with Church Women United in South Carolina," 9, 10, box 2, Edith M. Dabbs Papers, SCL. In subsequent years, UCCW, with some difficulty, moved its meetings to local churches. Dabbs recalled that while black churches were willing to accommodate the integrated group, most white churches, with the exception of the Lutheran and Episcopal churches, were less willing to do so. Many white pastors were reluctant to anger their congregations by supporting the meetings of such a liberal Christian organization. Dr. Kenneth Morris of Ebenezer Lutheran Church (Dabbs called it St. John's Episcopal Church in "Through the Years") was the first to allow UCCW to use its facilities, in 1951. According to Dabbs, of the thirty to forty women who attended the meeting approximately, six were black women. See also interview with Edith Mitchell Dabbs by Elizabeth Jacoway Burns, October 4, 1975, Interview G-0022, Southern Oral History Program Collection (#4007), SHC; Harvey, *Freedom's Coming*, 200.

119. "Report of Field Trip to South Carolina on Leadership Training Institutes, April 14–19, 1952, box 2, Dabbs Papers, SCL.

120. She was also a member of the National Association of Ministers Wives. See "National Ass'n of Ministers' Wives News," *Atlanta Daily World*, December 1, 1962, 4. Mrs. Bacoats left South Carolina for Virginia in 1973. See "Mrs. Bacoats Leaving the State," in *The South Carolina Church Woman*, June–July 1973, 6, box 6, folder 8, Church Women United in South Carolina Records, LPASC.

121. "Mrs. Reuben Secretary of Bi-Racial Group," *Lighthouse and Informer*, April 5, 1952, 4. Reuben was a former secretary of the South Carolina NAACP and chairperson of the executive board of the Sumter branch of the YWCA. She was also a member of the National Council of Negro Women. See "Points of Historical Interest Seen by Women of Regional Meet," *Atlanta Daily World*, May 4, 1955, 4. She was the resource consultant for a panel on "Education, the Arsenal of Democracy," which included Alice Norwood Spearman. In 1964 she served on the American Teachers Association Textbook Review Commission, which challenged negative portrayals or omissions of African Americans in the textbooks used in southern schools. See "Need for Proper Treatment of Minority in School Texts Cited," *Atlanta Daily World*, January 23, 1964, 2.

122. Unidentified newspaper clipping from 1952, Church Women United of Columbia Records, LPASC. See also "Mrs. Reuben Secretary of Bi-racial Group" *Lighthouse and Informer*, April 15, 1952, 4.

123. Edith M. Dabbs, Chairman, Public Relations, the South Carolina Council of Church Women, 1951, box 24, folder 637, SCCHRP, SCL.

124. "A Check List for your Local Schools," *New South*, September 1953, 1–8.

125. Caroline Lee Gillespie, Chairman, Christian Social Relations Committee,

United Church Women of South Carolina, January 30, 1954, box 24, folder 637, SC-CHRP, SCL.

126. Ibid.

127. Quint, *Profile in Black and White,* 170–71; "Southern Leaders Confer," *The Church Woman,* August–September 1954, 30–31, 1222-3-3:18, GCAHUMC; Open Letter to Governor James F. Byrnes from Mrs. Edith M. Dabbs, President, United Church Women of South Carolina, May 19, 1954, Southern Regional Council Papers, Series VIII, reel 196.

128. Dabbs to Byrnes, May 19, 1954.

129. Ibid.

130. "Southern Church Women 'Promote Christian Society,'" *New South,* August 1954, 6.

131. Frystak, *Our Minds on Freedom,* 77.

132. "Southern Leaders Confer," *The Church Woman,* August–September 1954, 30–31, 1222-3-3:18, GCAHUMC.

133. "Echos from the Atlanta Conference," *The Church Woman,* October 1954, 37, 1222-3-3:18, GCAHUMC.

134. United Church Women, Minutes of Meeting, March 6, 1956, box 24, folder 652c, SCCHRP, SCL.

135. "Segregation," *The Church Woman,* June–July 1955, 48, 1222-3-3:18, GCAHUMC.

136. "Workshop on Race Relations," *The Church Woman,* November 1955, 32–33, 1222-2-3-3:19, GCAHUMC.

137. "Coming to Grips with Segregation," *The Church Woman,* October 1955, 19, 1222-3-3:19, GCAHUMC.

138. Shaw was the first female mayor in South Carolina. Unidentified newspaper article, May 3, 1954, box 2, Dabbs Papers, SCL; "Bennettsville Club Meets This Week: Miss Shaw, Mayor of Sumter, Talks," *Florence Morning News,* October 15, 1954, 7-A.

139. "South Carolina Council of Church Women's 5th Annual Assembly," 1955, box 1, folder 18, Spearman Wright Papers, SCL.

140. Minutes, February 28 and May 5, 1954, box 1, folder 7, Rock Hill Council on Human Relations Records, LPASC.

141. United Church Women, Minutes of Meeting, March 6, 1956, box 24, folder 652c, SCCHRP, SCL.

142. Ibid.

143. Minutes, November 26, 1956, ibid. The national UCW referred to such meetings as "Race Relations" workshops. Church women in Columbia clearly changed the name to distract any attention away from activism deemed controversial and thus dangerous.

144. Minutes, January 3, 1957, ibid.

145. "United Church Women 8th National Assembly, October, 30, 1958," *New South,* December 1958, 14.

146. Mrs. W. (Dorothy) Murdoch MacLeod, General Director, United Church Women to Arthur B. Spingarn, President, NAACP, August 14, 1958, Papers of the NAACP, Part 24, Special Subjects, 1956–1965, Series B, Foreign Affairs, Leagues and Organizations, reel

32. Murdoch, a South Carolina native and a graduate of Winthrop College, was the guest speaker at the sixth annual meeting of UCW South Carolina in January 1955. See Minutes of the Sixth Annual Meeting of UCW of South Carolina, box 2, Dabbs Papers, SCL.

Chapter 4. "Strength and Faith to Stand Together"

1. Lynn, *Progressive Women*, 10.
2. Birnie Street Committee and Board Meeting, December 10, 1969, box 1, folder 2, Greenville YWCA Records, SCL.
3. Bagwell, *School Desegregation in the Carolinas*, 151; "Political Activity," *Southern School News*, June 1958, 15.
4. YWCA Administrative Building Fund Campaign (Study), 1960, 55, box 1, folder 6, Greenville YWCA Records, SCL; Sproat, "'Firm Flexibility,'" 171. Sproat argues that the idea that some were born to rule and others to be ruled became an important instrument of control during the "desegregation crisis."
5. YWCA Administrative Building Fund Campaign (Study), 1960, 55, box 1, folder 6, Greenville YWCA Records, SCL.
6. "Survey, Analysis, and Plan of Fund-Raising for YWCA of Greenville, February 1961," 53 and 61, box 1, folder 7, Greenville YWCA Records, SCL.
7. Robertson, *Christian Sisterhood*, 166.
8. "Separate White, Negro YWs Hit," *Greenville News*, March 14, 1962; "Pastors Hit 'Y' Policy," *Greenville Piedmont*, March 14, 1962, box 3, SCCHRP, SCL.
9. YWCA Administrative Building Fund Campaign, Study (1960), 75, box 1, folder 6, Greenville YWCA Records, SCL.
10. Ibid.
11. "7 Arrested in Greenville," *New York Times*, March 17, 1960, 37; Mrs. John F. Chandler, President, Greenville YWCA, to Honorable Kenneth Cass, Mayor, City of Greenville, September 15, 1960, box 1, folder 18, Greenville YWCA Records, SCL; "Close Library after 20 S.C. Pupils Use It," *Chicago Defender*, March 12, 1960, 11; "Open Library in Greenville," *New York Amsterdam News*, September 24, 1960, 36; "Sitdown in a Library," *New York Times*, July 17, 1960, 19.
12. O'Neill, "Memory, History," 290.
13. Ibid., 292.
14. Sosna, *In Search of the Silent South*, 74, 76, 88.
15. Erskine, "'This Fellowship without Barriers of Race,'" 46.
16. Ibid.
17. Greenville YWCA Program Report, 1965, box 1, folder 30, Greenville YWCA Records, SCL.
18. "Minutes—Birnie Street Committee and Board Meeting," December 10, 1969, box 1, folder 2, Greenville YWCA Records, SCL.
19. Lynn, *Progressive Women*, 145; "YWCA National Board Backs Sit-in Objective," *Chicago Defender*, April 23, 1960, 9; "YWCA Joins Struggle for Equal Rights," *Chicago Defender*, July 2, 1966, 8.

20. "No Action Planned against Local 'Y,'" *Charleston News and Courier,* October 2, 1963, 17-A.

21. "YWCA Announces 4 Regional Appointments to Nat. Staff," *Atlanta Daily World,* August 31, 1963, 6.

22. "No Action Planned against Local 'Y,'" *Charleston News and Courier,* October 2, 1963, 17-A.

23. Weisenfeld, *African American Women,* 192.

24. "'Y' Board to Add Negro," *Charleston News and Courier,* October 3, 1963, 1-B.

25. "A Building Program for the YWCA," *Charleston News and Courier,* March 25, 1962, 3-C.

26. Mrs. Bonum S. Wilson, President, YWCA, Charleston, South Carolina, to Mrs. Archie D. Marvel, President, National Board YWCA, August 14, 1963, box 28, folder 124, National Board of the YWCA of the USA Records, SSC; "YWCA Plans Changed Due to Deficit," *Charleston News and Courier,* January 30, 1963, 7-B; "Ground Broken: YWCA Starts 2 Buildings," *Charleston News and Courier,* November, 28, 1963, 1-B.

27. "YWCA Branch Opening Set Tomorrow," *Charleston News and Courier,* September 12, 1964, 1-B.

28. Barbara J. Stambaugh, "Charleston YWCA Refuses to Agree to Integration: National Board Policy Is Rejected in Letter," *Charleston News and Courier,* August 16, 1963, 1-B; Mrs. Bonum S. Wilson, President, YWCA, Charleston, South Carolina, to Mrs. Archie D. Marvel, President, National Board YWCA, August 14, 1963, box 28, folder 124, National Board of the YWCA of the USA Records, SSC.

29. Stambaugh, "Charleston YWCA Refuses to Agree to Integration: National Board Policy is Rejected in Letter," *Charleston News and Courier,* August 16, 1963, 1-B; Erskine, "'This Fellowship without Barriers of Race,'" 93; Weisenfeld, *African American Women,* 195.

30. "YWCA Hasn't Altered Race Policy," *Charleston News and Courier,* December 22, 1963, 14-A; Erskine, "'This Fellowship without Barriers of Race,'" 94–95.

31. Mary Jane Willet to Sallie N. Johnson, August 22, 1963, box 124, folder 10, National Board of the YWCA of the USA Records, SSC.

32. Ibid.

33. Ibid.; Trolander, *Professionalism and Social Change,* 132, 140, 193

34. Virginia Prouty to Ruth Hill, Correlator, Southern Region, October 3, 1963, box 124, folder 10, National Board of the YWCA of the USA Records, SSC.

35. "National YWCA Approves Full Integration Credo," *Atlanta Daily World,* April 28, 1964, 2; "National Confab Delegates from West Side Area to Report on Cleveland Meet," *Chicago Defender,* May 30, 1964, 7.

36. Committee on Administration Minutes, December 16, 1964, Minute Book, 1954–1967, YWCA of Greater Charleston Records, South Carolina; Dorothy Height, "A Woman's Word," *New York Amsterdam News,* April 24, 1965, 33.

37. Minutes, April 12, 1965, Minute Book, 1954–1967, YWCA of Greater Charleston Records, South Carolina.

38. Ibid.

39. Minutes, March 15, 1965, ibid.

40. Minutes, September 20, 1965, ibid.

41. Dorothy I. Height, "Black and White Decisions," *The YWCA Magazine,* February 1966, 2; Collier-Thomas, *Jesus, Jobs, and Justice,* 383.

42. Mrs. John C. Hawk, President, YWCA Board of Directors, Charleston, South Carolina, to the President, YWCA Board of Directors, June 1967, YWCA Greenville, box, 1 folder 20, Greenville YWCA Records, SCL; Erskine, "'This Fellowship without Barriers of Race,'" 97.

43. Interview with Anna DeWees Kelly by Edmund Drago, August 24, 1984, ARC; Mrs. Mildred B. Holloway, Personnel Consultant, National Board of the YWCA of the U.S.A., to Mrs. Anna DeWees Kelly, Branch Executive—YWCA, June 7, 1966, box 2, folder 19, "Age Meets Youth," *The Catholic Banner,* South Carolina, December 1968, 1, box 1, folder 1, James Middleton, Executive Director, Charleston County Economic Opportunity Commission, to Mrs. Anna D. Kelly, Project Director, Foster Grandparent Program, September 22, 1978, box 2, folder 16, all in Anna D. Kelly Papers, ARC. Kelly continued to work with the St. Catherine's Auxiliary of the Blessed Sacrament Church and the Catholic Charleston Deanery, where she served as the chairperson of the "International Committee." The St. Catherine's Auxiliary was an affiliate of the Charleston Deanery of the Diocesan Council of Catholic Women, which was an affiliate of the South Carolina Council of Catholic Women. See Minutes, 1964–1981, box 1, folder 4, and "Human Rights—The Challenge Is Now," Concerns, International, 1967–2006, box 1, folder 25, South Carolina Council of Catholic Women Papers, Diocese of Charleston Archives.

44. "Policies Attacked, YWCA Votes to Quite National Organization," *Charleston News and Courier,* May 20, 1966, 1-A; Mrs. John C. Hawk, President, YWCA Board of Directors, Charleston, South Carolina, to President, YWCA Board of Directors, St. Louis, Missouri, February 13, 1967, box 28, folder 1, National Board of the YWCA of the USA Papers, SSC.

45. Mrs. John C. Hawk, President, YWCA Board of Directors, Charleston, South Carolina, to President, YWCA Board of Directors, St. Louis, Missouri, February 13, 1967, box 28, folder 1, National Board of the YWCA of the USA Papers, box 28, folder 1, SSC.

46. "Policies Attacked, YWCA Votes to Quite National Organization," *Charleston News and Courier,* May 20, 1966, 2-A; "Miss Judith Wragg Weds Lieut. Chase, U.S.A., in July," *Atlanta Constitution,* June 21, 1931, 3K; "Fate of Museum on Slavery in Doubt," *New York Times,* July 6, 1987, 8; "Slave Mart Museum Keeps Black Man's History Alive," *Chicago Defender,* August 27, 1966, 24; "News Notes: Classroom and Campus," *New York Times,* July 26, 1964, E7.

47. "YWCA Meeting Set to Plan Break with National Assn.," *Charleston News and Courier,* March 6, 1967, 10-B.

48. Ibid.

49. Minutes, March 1967, YWCA of Greater Charleston Records, South Carolina.

50. "Policies Attacked, YWCA Votes to Quite National Organization," *Charleston News and Courier,* May 20, 1967, 1-A.

51. Ibid.

52. Joel M. Clemons, "YWCA Effort to Cut Ties with National Body Fails," *Charleston News and Courier,* March 18, 1967, 1-B.

53. The Charleston YWCA was not the only one to disaffiliate from the National Board. The Baton Rouge YWCA voted 18–8 to withdraw in June 1967. See "Baton Rouge YWCA Votes to Withdraw," *Charleston News and Courier,* June 26, 1967, box 1, folder 20, Greenville YWCA Records, SCL.

54. Robertson, *Christian Sisterhood,* 172.

55. "Policies Attacked, YWCA Votes to Quite National Organization," *Charleston News and Courier,* May 20, 1967, 1-A; Erskine, "'This Fellowship without Barriers of Race,'" 98.

56. Erskine, "'This Fellowship without Barriers of Race,'" 98; Committee on Administration Minutes, June 19, 1967, YWCA of Greater Charleston Records, South Carolina.

57. Committee on Administration Minutes, June 19, 1967, ibid.

58. Ibid.

59. Committee on Administration Minutes, February 19, 1968. The Summerville branch also decided to operate as an independent organization. Committee on Administration Minutes, March 18, 1968, YWCA of Greater Charleston Records, South Carolina.

60. Committee on Administration Minutes, June 17, September 16, 1968, January 20, March 17, 1969. Judith Chase was nominated chairman of the board of directors of the provisional YWCA of Greater Charleston. See Special Meeting, Organizing, Minutes, February 17, 1969, YWCA of Greater Charleston Records, South Carolina.

61. "New YWCA Called Only 'Real' YWCA," *Charleston News and Courier*, December 16, 1969, 5-A; Minutes, February 2, 1970, YWCA of Greater Charleston Records, GCAHUMC; Erskine, "'This Fellowship without Barriers of Race,'" 99.

62. "Injunction Sought against YWCA of Charleston," *Charleston News and Courier,* March 7, 1970.

63. C. Webb, *Fight against Fear,* 119.

64. "Injunction Sought against YWCA of Charleston," *Charleston News and Courier,* March 7, 1970.

65. Minutes, September 1971, November 1–3, 1971, YWCA of Greater Charleston Records, South Carolina. The organization changed its name to Charleston Family and Youth in 2003. Schuyler Kropf, "Financial Woes Close Doors at Charleston Family, Youth," *Charleston Post and Courier,* February 26, 2004, 1B.

Chapter 5. "Become Active in This Service to the Community"

1. Bartley, *The New South*, 341.

2. Aiken, *The Cotton Plantation South,* 188.

3. Barnett, "Invisible Southern Black Women Leaders," 169. Highlander, founded in 1932 by Myles Horton, was a regional model for progressive education and politics. It hosted blacks and whites who learned to work across the racial divide for justice and equality.

4. "The Citizenship Program Continues to Expand," *Highlander Reports,* October 1, 1960–September 30, 1961, box 32, folder 348, SCCHRP, SCL.

5. Clark, *Echo in My Soul,* 61.

6. McFadden, "Septima P. Clark," 88.

7. "Photo Standalone 5—no Title (Anna DeWees Kelly)," *Atlanta Daily World,* October 12, 1951, 5. In 1951, Kelly was director of the Coming Street YWCAs Y-Teen program; Anna DeWees Kelly, interview by Edmund Drago, August 24, 1984, ARC; Charron, *Freedom's Teacher,* 215; Clark, *Ready from Within,* 30; Inventory of the Anna D. Kelly Papers, 1930s–1999, ARC.

8. Clark, *Echo in My Soul,* 118; Charron, "We've Come a Long Way," 126; interview with Anna DeWees Kelly.

9. Septima Clark to Myles Horton, July 3, 1961, SCSUHC.

10. Interview with Septima Poinsette Clark, July 25, 1976, Interview G-0016, Southern Oral History Program Collection (#4007), SHC.

11. Charron, *Freedom's Teacher,* 217.

12. "Integrated Unit Views Mixing," *Chicago Defender,* July 30, 1955, 4.

13. Charron, *Freedom's Teacher,* 302; Septima Poinsette Clark, "The Movement . . . I Remember," 30, box 3, folder 18, and Part III, A Workshop for Volunteer Teachers in the Citizenship Educational Program of the Southern Christian Leadership Conference, 1965, 101, box 8, folder 4, Septima Poinsette Clark Collection, ARC.

14. McFadden, "Septima P. Clark," 90; "Thousands of Dixie Negroes Studying to Win Right to Vote," *Chicago Daily Defender,* March 25, 1963, 8; Charron, *Freedom's Teacher,* 2.

15. Interview with Mary Moultrie, July 28, 1982, Jean-Claude Bouffard Civil Rights Interviews, ARC.

16. McFadden, "Septima P. Clark," 178. In 1970, Robinson became the supervisor of Volunteers in Service to America (VISTA) for the South Carolina Commission for Farm Workers Inc. See biographical information, box 1, folder 1, Bernice V. Robinson Papers, ARC.

17. Alice N. Spearman to Mrs. Marion McLester, March 24, 1960, box 26, folder 683, SCCHRP, SCL.

18. Ibid.

19. "CORE's Vote Drive in S.C. Continues," *Chicago Defender,* October 16, 1965, 6.

20. Alice N. Spearman to Courtney Siceloff, March 23, 1960, and Elizabeth Siceloff to May F. Kennard, March 30, 1960, box 26, folder 683, SCCHRP, SCL; "S.C. Vote Drive Heads NAACP Summer Project," *Chicago Defender,* June 19, 1965, 35. The Penn Community Center, originally named the Penn Normal and Industrial School, was founded in 1862 by northern missionaries Laura Towne and Ellen Murray to educate African Americans living off the coast of South Carolina. Civil rights activists used its facilities because it permitted integrated groups to meet there. See interview with Elizabeth and Courtney Siceloff, July 8, 1985, Interview F-0039, Southern Oral History Program Collection (#4007), SHC; Edgar, *South Carolina,* 391; Edgar, *South Carolina Encyclopedia,* 711; and Dan Carter, "Civil Rights and Politics in South Carolina: The Perspective of

One Lifetime, 1940–2003," 410. In 1960 Siceloff was also president of the SCCHR. See Alice N. Spearman to SCCHR members, October 7, 1960, box 3, folder 4, Ebaugh Collection, JDL.

21. "Vote against Hate on February 25," n.d., box 3, folder 4, Simkins Papers, SCPC.

22. Woods Aba-Mecha, "Black Woman Activist," 366.

23. J. H. Moore, *Columbia and Richland County,* 425–26.

24. "Friends! Voters! Our Job Is Cut Out for Us!" box 2, folder 39, Simkins Papers, SCPC.

25. "Demos Demand Woman Disprove Marxist Link," *Big Spring (Tex.) Daily Herald,* April 15, 1966, 6-A; "Vote Simkins for South Carolina House of Representatives for Richland County," 1966, *Modjeska Monteith Simkins: In Her Own Words,* SCPC.

26. "Agitator Told to Leave Party," *Rocky Mount (N.C.) Evening Telegram,* April 15, 1966, 13.

27. Myers, *Black, White and Olive Drab,* 198–99.

28. Blacks United for Action Inc., box 12, folder 1, Septima Poinsette Clark Papers, ARC.

29. Bethea, "Alienation and Third Parties," 11.

30. Grose, *South Carolina at the Brink,* 287; "United Citizens Party Certified by State," *Palmetto Times* (Columbia, S.C.), September 3, 1970, 1; "United Citizens Party Gets Official Recognition," *Rock Hill (S.C.) Herald,* September 2, 1970, 3; "Broadwater Says His Party Won't Sell Out Its Votes," *Rock Hill (S.C.) Herald,* October 9, 1970, 10, "Schools Main Issue?" *Sumter Daily Item,* October 22, 1970, 1; "Primary Set for August 2," *Spartanburg (S.C.) Herald-Journal,* July 8, 1972, 1. Broadwater received only 3,315 votes. See "GOP Made Biggest Challenge in 1970," *Florence Morning News,* December 20, 1970, 12-C.

31. "Vote for a Winner, Victoria DeLee for Congress," and "Mrs. DeLee Starts Drive for S.C. Seat in Congress," *Baltimore Afro-American,* February 16, 1971, 1 and 2, folders 14 and 24, DeLaine Papers, SCL. In the 1960s, DeLee and her children filed the first federal court action to desegregate schools in Dorchester County.

32. "S.C. Negroes May Vote Republican," *Atlanta Daily World,* January 4, 1972, 1.

33. "Remembering Modjeska," *Point,* January 1995, reel 1, Simkins Papers, SCPC.

34. Simkins attended the South Carolina International Women's Year State Meeting in 1977. See M. Jones and Reynolds, "Final Report of the State Meeting," 44.

35. Burton, "South Carolina," 199; "Klan Terror, Apathy, Slows Down Vote Drive," *Chicago Daily Defender,* November 3, 1965, 10; "U.S. to Spur Voter Registration of Negroes in South Carolina," *New York Times,* November 2, 1965, 20.

36. Lawson, *Black Ballots,* 338–39; "South's Negroes Slow to Register; U.S. Help Sought," *New York Times,* October 25, 1965, 1.

37. Burton, "South Carolina," 199; "Drive in 11 States Spurs Negro Vote," *New York Times,* February 17, 1964, 22.

38. "Negro Leader: Court Ordered," *The State,* December 26, 1965, 3-D.

39. Ibid.

40. Ibid.; "NAACP Names 3 to Field Staff," *Chicago Defender*, January 23, 1960, 2.

41. "Negroes Gaining in Carolina Drive," *New York Times*, January 7, 1968, 58.

42. Edgar, *South Carolina*, 541; "Negro Voter Registrations Double in Dixie," *Chicago Defender*, October 22, 1966, 5; "What Happened in the South," *New York Amsterdam News*, December 12, 1970, 60.

43. "South Carolina: Supreme Court Rejects Ethnic Difference Plea," *Southern School News*, November 1964, 1.

44. "Columbia Students Apply for Grants," *Southern School News*, November 1964, 2; "Now All States Have Some Integration," *New York Times*, September 6, 1964, 8.

45. "Richland County Board Votes against Grants," *Southern School News*, December 1964, 7.

46. *Southern School News*, January 1965, 8.

47. "Furman Admits 3 Negro Students," *Southern School News*, February 1965, 7; Newby, *Black Carolinians*, 332.

48. Christian Social Relations Resolution, Board of Managers, United Church Women, May 2, 1962, box 24, folder 652c, SCCHRP, SCL.

49. Bagwell, *School Desegregation in the Carolinas*, 58.

50. According to Andrew Secrest, during this time South Carolina newspapers generally failed to offer any editorial leadership to the racial problems confronting the state. They also failed to meet the standards of professional responsibility generally accepted in American journalism. The three leading daily newspapers in South Carolina are the *News and Courier* of Charleston, *The State* of Columbia, and *The News* of Greenville. The *Cheraw Chronicle*, of which Secrest was editor, often offered a more liberal view of events occurring in the state. Secrest, "'In Black and White,'" iv–v.

51. Alice N. Spearman to Camille Levy, January 21, 1960, box 24, folder 652, SCCHRP, SCL.

52. Mrs. Fred M. Reese Jr. to Mrs. John W. Sinders, July 25, 1969, box 1, folder 5, Spearman Wright Papers, SCL.

53. Alice N. Spearman to Sarah Daniels, January 21, 1960, box 24, folder 637, SCCHRP, SCL.

54. Rebecca Reid to Alice N. Spearman, January 20, 1960, box 24, folder 652, SCCHRP, SCL.

55. Esther Peterson, "The Ugly Facts of Discrimination Dare not Be Ignored," *The Church Woman*, March 1962, 14–15, 1222-3-3:26, GCAHUMC.

56. Harvey, *Freedom's Coming*, 200. "United Church Women Declare War on Bias," *Jet Magazine*, November 16, 1961, 53. Meares was also a member of the Association of Southern Women for the Prevention of Lynching in the 1930s. See "7,000 Women Represented at Two-Day Meeting Here Pledge Vigilant Effort for Lynchless South in 1933," *Atlanta Constitution*, November 20, 1932, 19. She also received a master of arts in "Faculties of Education and Practical Arts" from Columbia University in 1926. See "List Of 3,908 Graduates Who Will Get Columbia Degrees in Course," *New York Times*, June 1, 1926, 30.

57. Interview with Edith Mitchell Dabbs, October 4, 1975, Interview G-0022, Southern Oral History Program Collection (#4007), SHC.

58. "Report on Localities Approached for United Church Women Workshops, March 29, 1957, 1224-4-2:03, and Summaries of Reports from CWU State and Local Councils, 1957–1959, 1225-2-3:03, GCAHUMC. The reports do not specify which council it was.

59. Church Women United, Resolution adopted for 1969–70, LPASC.

60. Shannon, *Just Because*, 138.

61. Weiner, *The Story of WICS*, 2, 8.

62. Helen Turnbull, CWU/WIC Staff Liaison, to CWU State and Local Presidents in South Carolina, July 26, 1968, box 3, folder 12, Church Women United of Columbia Records, LPASC; "WICS Marks 7th Year of Service," *Chicago Daily Defender*, October 17, 1972, 4; "Women in Community Service Meet Area Head," *Chicago Daily Defender*, June 20, 1970, 21; Dorothy Height, "A Woman's Word," *New York Amsterdam News*, April 24, 1965, 33.

63. "WICS Organize Local Chapter," *Charleston News and Courier*, May 21, 1965, 10-C; Collier-Thomas, *Jesus, Jobs, and Justice*, 451.

64. Alice N. Spearman to Mrs. Herbert McAbee, May 26, 1965, Church Women United in South Carolina, box 1, folder 3, LPASC.

65. WICS was temporarily headquartered at Neighborhood House, later known as the Lady of Mercy Welfare Center, which was located in a predominantly poor and black neighborhood on the east side of the Charleston peninsula. Sister Mary Anthony Monaghan of the Sisters of Charity of Our Lady of Mercy, a registered nurse, had supervised the center since 1953. She was known citywide for her support of the welfare rights movement and for her participation in the southern segment of the Poor People's March on Washington. "Women's Service Group Organized at Meeting Here," *Charleston Evening Post*, May 20, 1965; "Mrs. Greene Installed as WICS Director," *Charleston News and Courier*, June 19, 1965, 12-B; Minutes, 1964–1981, box 1, folder 5, South Carolina Council of Catholic Women Papers, Diocese of Charleston Archives; "Welfare Union Efforts Press," *Charleston News and Courier*, December 1, 1967; "Negroes Don't Even Think of Her as Being White," *Charleston News and Courier*, June 20, 1968, 10-C; "400 Washington-Bound Marchers Spent Night," *Charleston Evening Post*, May 13, 1968.

66. Wiggins, "United Church Women," 4; Hartmann, *The Other Feminists*, 98.

67. Minutes, February 2, 1967, Church Women United of Columbia Records, LPASC.

68. Beardsley, *A History of Neglect*, 103.

69. Representatives Meeting, September 27, 1968, Church Women United of Columbia Records, LPASC.

70. "Goodwin to Speak on Rural Missions," *The State*, January 29, 1971, 16-A; "Volunteers in Adult Basic Education," box 15, folder 67, Edwards Papers, LPASC; "Migrant Ministry Continues," *S.C. Church Women*, Spring 1969, 1, box 1, folder 3, and "State Executive Board Meeting," *South Carolina Church Woman*, June 1974, 3, box 6, folder 8, Church Women United of South Carolina Records, LPASC.

71. "Resolution Adopted at the 1969 Annual Meeting, Church Women United in South Carolina, February 21, 1969," box 24, folder 652c, SCCHRP, SCL.

72. *South Carolina Church Woman*, January 1971, 2.

73. In 1970, Ada Campbell was president of Church Women United in Charleston. "Volunteers in Adult Basic Education: A Report on Action in Ten Cities in Eight Southern States by Church Women United, During the Months of April–June 1970," box 15, folder 67, and Carolyn E. Frederick, South Carolina House of Representatives, to Johnette Edwards, November 8, 1971, box 17, folder 75, both in Edwards Papers, LPASC.

74. Barbara H. Stoops, "Church Women Observe World Day of Prayer," *The State and Columbia Record*, March 2, 1969.

75. "Introduction—Purpose of Conference," box 15, folder 67, Edwards Papers, LPASC.

76. Leppert, *Guidelines for Adult Basic Education Volunteers*, 4–5.

77. Mrs. G. M. Howe to Mrs. Casper Jones, December 11, 1967, Church Women United of South Carolina Records, LPASC.

78. "In Celebration: The 25th Anniversary Celebration: Church Women United in Orangeburg, Orangeburg, South Carolina, May 24–25, 1991," SCSUHC. There was one white member, Ann Johnson from Orangeburg Lutheran Church. She served on numerous committees and as secretary and chaplain for many years. I suspect there were other members, but I have not been able to find any information about them.

79. "Church Women United of Columbia, Triennial Report (1971, 1972, 1973)," box 2, folder 2, Church Women United of South Carolina Records, LPASC. Witherspoon was also the area's supervisor of the National Association of Ministers' Wives. Other African American women, Mrs. C. A. Gibbs and Mrs. B. C. Cunningham, also appear on the list of members of the board of representatives for CWU Columbia in September and December 1967. See also President's Report, South Carolina Council of Catholic Women, March 1972–March 1973, Presidents' Reports, box 1, folder 8, South Carolina Council of Catholic Women Papers, Diocese of Charleston Archives.

80. "In Celebration: The 25th Anniversary Celebration: Church Women United in Orangeburg, Orangeburg, South Carolina, May 24–25, 1991," SCSUHC, Miller F. Whitaker Library; "Valiant Woman Award Honoree Presented," *Atlanta Daily World*, April 6, 1984, 3; Jan Boylston, "Our Churches," *Aiken (S.C.) Standard*, February 2, 1979.

81. In the mid-1970s, another black woman, Dr. Agnes Hildebrand Wilson, was vice president for cultivation for CWU South Carolina. She was also the first female and the first black president of the newly integrated South Carolina Education Association. See *The South Carolina Church Woman*, June 1974, 2; Minutes of the Executive Board Meeting of Church Women United of South Carolina, Friday, February 15, 1974, box 6, folder 8, Church Women United of South Carolina Records, LPASC. In 1969, Wilson, a graduate of Allen University, a former Fulbright Scholar, and a French and journalism teacher at Sumter's Lincoln High School, was the first African American to be named State Teacher of the Year in South Carolina. See "Black Teacher Honored," *New York Amsterdam News*, November 8, 1969, 12; "Negro Woman Chosen as Teacher of Year in

S.C.," *Chicago Daily Defender*, November 19, 1968, 8; and interview with Agnes Hildeb-rand Wilson, WNSC-TV Channel 30, Rock Hill, South Carolina, July 3, 1981, in *Women Leaders in South Carolina: An Oral History*, 166, 167, 168.

82. UCW Columbia Minutes, Representative Meeting, December 21, 1967, Church Women United of South Carolina Records, LPASC. By 1976, Catholic women were attending CWU meetings. See "Church Communities Commission, 1976," Concerns, Church, 1966–2006, box 1, folder 17, South Carolina Council of Catholic Women Papers, Diocese of Charleston Archives.

83. Collier-Thomas, *Jesus, Jobs, and Justice*, 408, 422.

Bibliography

Manuscript Collections

Avery Research Center for African American History and Culture, College of Charleston, South Carolina
  Septima Poinsette Clark Papers
  Ruby Cornwell Papers
  Anna DeWees Kelly Papers
  Bernice V. Robinson Papers
Clemson University Libraries—Special Collections, Clemson, South Carolina
  J. Strom Thurmond Papers
Diocese of Charleston Archives, Charleston, South Carolina
  South Carolina Council of Catholic Women Papers
General Commission on Archives and History of the United Methodist Church, Drew University, Madison, New Jersey
  Church Women United Records
James B. Duke Library, Furman University, Greenville, South Carolina
  Laura Smith Ebaugh Collection
  Greenville County Council for Community Development Papers
Louise Pettus Archives and Special Collections, Winthrop University, Rock Hill, South Carolina
  American Association of University Women, Rock Hill, South Carolina Chapter, Records
  Church Women United of Columbia Records
  Church Women United of South Carolina Records
  Johnette Edwards Papers
  Mary E. Frayser Papers
  Rock Hill Council on Human Relations Papers
  Winthrop Student YWCA Papers

Miller F. Whitaker Library, Orangeburg, South Carolina
    South Carolina State University Historical Collection
Sisters of Charity of Our Lady of Mercy, James Island, South Carolina
    Sisters of Charity of Our Lady of Mercy Papers
South Carolina Historical Society, Charleston
    Harriet Porcher Stoney Simons Papers
South Carolina Political Collections, University of South Carolina, Columbia
    Modjeska Monteith Simkins Papers
    Modjeska Monteith Simkins: In Her Own Words, Digital Collections, http://www.sc.edu/
    library/digital/collections/simkins.html.
South Carolina Room, Greenville County Library, South Carolina
    Hattie Logan Duckett Biographical File
    Phillis Wheatley Center File
South Caroliniana Library, University of South Carolina, Columbia, South Carolina
    Edith M. Dabbs Papers
    J. A. DeLaine Papers
    Wil Lou Gray Papers
    Greenville YWCA Records
    John H. McCray Papers (microfilm)
    John B. Morris Papers
    Claudia Sanders Paper
    South Carolina Council on Human Relations Papers
    Sumter NAACP Records
    Eunice Temple Ford Stackhouse Papers
    Cornelia Dabney Ramseur Tucker Papers
    Annie Bell Weston Vertical File
    Alice Norwood Spearman Wright Papers
    Columbia YWCA Records
YWCA of Greater Charleston Records, Charleston, South Carolina (presently located at the
    Avery Research Center for African American History and Culture, College of Charleston)

Microfilm Collections

Association of Southern Women for the Prevention of Lynching Papers, 1930–1942. New
    York: NYT Microfilming Corporation of America, 1983.
Commission on Interracial Cooperation Papers, 1919–1944, and the Association of Southern
    Women for the Prevention of Lynching Papers, 1930–1942: A Guide to the Microfilm
    Editions. Ann Arbor, MI: University Microfilms International, 1984, Series 7.
John H. McCray Papers. South Caroliniana Library, University of South Carolina, Columbia.
National Board of the YWCA of the USA Records. Sophia Smith Collection, Smith College,
    Northampton, Massachusetts.

Papers of the NAACP. Frederick, Md.: University Publications of Maryland.

Records of the National Association of Colored Women's Clubs, 1895–1992, part 1. Edited by Lillian Serece Williams. Bethesda, Md., University Publications of America

Southern Regional Council Papers. New York: NYT Microfilming Corporation of America, 1983.

Interviews

Brown, Jessica Pearson. *South Carolina Voices of the Civil Rights Movement*, November 5–6, 1982, Avery Research Center for African American History and Culture, College of Charleston.

Clark, Septima Poinsette. Interview by Jacquelyn Hall, July 25, 1976. Interview G-0016. Southern Oral History Program Collection (#4007), Southern Historical Collection, Wilson Library, University of North Carolina at Chapel Hill.

Dabbs, Edith Mitchell. Interview by Elizabeth Jacoway Burns, October 4, 1975. Interview G-0022. Southern Oral History Program Collection (#4007), Southern Historical Collection, Wilson Library, University of North Carolina at Chapel Hill.

Kelly, Anna DeWees. Interview by Edmund Drago, Charleston, South Carolina, August 20, 1984, Avery Research Center for African American History and Culture, College of Charleston.

Moultrie, Mary. Interview by Jean-Claude Bouffard, Charleston, South Carolina, July 28, 1982, Avery Research Center for African American History and Culture, College of Charleston.

Siceloff, Elizabeth, and Courtney Siceloff. Interview by Dallas A. Blanchard, July 8, 1985, Interview F-0039. Southern Oral History Program Collection (#4007), Southern Historical Collection, Wilson Library, University of North Carolina at Chapel Hill.

Simkins, Modjeska. Interview by Jacquelyn Hall, November 15, 1974. Interview G-0056-1. Southern Oral History Program Collection (#4007), Southern Historical Collection, Wilson Library, University of North Carolina at Chapel Hill.

———. Interview by Jacquelyn Hall, July 28–31, 1976. Southern Oral History Program Collection (#4007). Southern Historical Collection, Wilson Library, University of North Carolina at Chapel Hill.

———. Interview by Ann Y. Evans, July 3, 1981. WNSC-TV Channel 30, Rock Hill, South Carolina.

———. Interview by John Egerton, May 11, 1990. Interview A-0356. Southern Oral History Program Collection (#4007), Southern Historical Collection, Wilson Library, University of North Carolina at Chapel Hill.

Thurmond, Strom. Interview by James G. Banks, July 20, 1978. Interview A-0334. Southern Oral History Program Collection (#4007), Southern Historical Collection, Wilson Library, University of North Carolina at Chapel Hill.

Wilson, Agnes Hildebrand. Interview by Mary Jeanne Byrd, July 31, 1981. WNSC-TV Channel 30, Rock Hill, South Carolina.

Wright, Alice Spearman. Interview by Ann Y. Evans, July 3, 1981. WNSC-TV Channel 30, Rock Hill, South Carolina.

Published Books, Articles, and Theses

Aiken, Charles S. *The Cotton Plantation South: Since the Civil War*. Baltimore: Johns Hopkins University Press, 1998.

Ames, Jessie Daniel, and Bertha Newell. *"Repairers of the Breach": A Story of Interracial Cooperation between Southern Women, 1935–1940*. Atlanta: Commission on Interracial Cooperation, 1940.

Azbug, Robert H., and Stephen E. Maizlish, eds. *New Perspectives on Race and Slavery in America: Essays in Honor of Kenneth M. Stampp*. Lexington: University Press of Kentucky, 1986.

Babcock, Fern. "The Contribution of the National Student YMCA and YWCA in the United States to Better Race Relations." *Student World* 44 (1951): 373–76.

Badger, Tony. "From Defiance to Moderation: South Carolina Governors." In *Toward the Meeting of the Waters: Currents in the Civil Rights Movement of South Carolina during the Twentieth Century*, edited by Winfred B. Moore Jr. and Orville Vernon Burton, 3–21. Columbia: University of South Carolina Press, 2008.

Bagwell, William. *School Desegregation in the Carolinas: Two Case Studies*. Columbia: University of South Carolina Press, 1972.

Baker, R. Scott. *Paradoxes of Desegregation: African American Struggles for Educational Equity in Charleston, South Carolina, 1926–1972*. Columbia: University of South Carolina Press, 2006.

Barnett, Bernice McNair. "Invisible Southern Black Women Leaders in the Civil Rights Movement: The Triple Constraints of Gender, Race, and Class." *Gender and Society* 7, no. 2 (June 1993): 162–82.

Bartley, Numan. *The New South, 1945–1980*. Vol. 11 of *A History of the South*. Baton Rouge: Louisiana State University Press, and the Littlefield Fund for Southern History, 1995.

———. *The Rise of Massive Resistance: Race and Politics in the South during the 1950s*. Baton Rouge: Louisiana State University Press, 1969.

Beardsley, Edward H. *A History of Neglect: Health Care for Blacks and Mill Workers in the Twentieth-Century South*. Knoxville: University of Tennessee Press, 1987.

Bethea, Margaret Berry. "Alienation and Third Parties: A Study of the United Citizens Party in South Carolina." M.A. thesis, University of South Carolina, 1973.

Blumberg, Rhoda Lois. "White Mothers as Civil Rights Activists: The Interweave of Family and Movement Roles." In *Women and Social Protest*, edited by Guida West and Rhoda Lois Blumberg, 166–79. New York: Oxford University Press, 1990.

Bodie, Idella. *South Carolina Women*. Orangeburg, S.C.: Sandlapper, 1978.

Brown, Millicent E. "Civil Rights Activism in Charleston, South Carolina, 1940–1970." Ph.D. diss., Florida State University, 1997.

Bryan, G. McLeod. *These Few Also Paid a Price: Southern Whites Who Fought for Civil Rights*. Macon, Ga.: Mercer University Press, 2001.

Bryan, Mary L. *Proud Heritage: A History of the League of Women Voters of South Carolina, 1920–1976*. Columbia: League of Women Voters of South Carolina, 1978.

Bunche, Ralph J. *The Political Status of the Negro in the Age of FDR*. Chicago: University of Chicago Press, 1973.

Burton, Orville. "South Carolina." In *Quiet Revolution in the South: The Impact of the Voting Rights Act, 1965–1990,* edited by Chandler Davidson, 11–232. Princeton: Princeton University Press, 1994.

Burton, Orville Vernon, Beatrice Burton, and Simon Appleford. "Seeds in Unlikely Soil: The *Briggs v. Elliot* School Segregation Case." In *Toward the Meeting of the Waters: Currents in the Civil Rights Movement of South Carolina during the Twentieth Century,* edited by Winfred B. Moore Jr. and Orville Vernon Burton, 176–200. Columbia: University of South Carolina Press, 2008.

Byrnes, James F. *All in One Lifetime.* New York: Harper and Brothers, 1958.

Calkins, Gladys Gilkey. *Follow Those Women: Church Women in the Ecumenical Movement, A History of the Development of United Work Among Women of the Protestant Churches in the United States.* New York: Office of Publication and Distribution, 1961.

Carawan, Guy, and Candie Carawan. *Ain't You Got a Right to the Tree of Life? The People of Johns Island, South Carolina, Their Faces, Their Words, and Their Songs.* Athens: University of Georgia Press, 1966, 1989.

Carretta, Vincent. *Phillis Wheatley: Biography of a Genius in Bondage.* Athens: University of Georgia Press, 2011.

Carson, Mina. *Settlement Folk: Social Thought and the American Settlement Movement, 1885–1930.* Chicago: University of Chicago Press, 1990.

Carter, Dan. "Civil Rights and Politics in South Carolina: The Perspective of One Lifetime, 1940–2003." In *Toward the Meeting of the Waters: Currents in the Civil Rights Movement of South Carolina during the Twentieth Century,* edited by Winfred B. Moore Jr. and Orville Vernon Burton, 402–21. Columbia: University of South Carolina Press, 2008.

Catsam, Derek. "Into the Maw of Dixie: The Freedom Rides, the Civil Rights Movement, and the Politics of Race in South Carolina." *Proceedings of the South Carolina Historical Association* (2005): 1–18.

Chappell, L. David. *Inside Agitators: White Southerners in the Civil Rights Movement.* Baltimore: Johns Hopkins University Press, 1994.

———. *A Stone of Hope: Prophetic Religion and the Death of Jim Crow.* Chapel Hill: University of North Carolina Press, 2004.

Charron, Katherine Mellen. *Freedom's Teacher: The Life of Septima Clark.* Chapel Hill: University of North Carolina Press, 2009.

———. "We've Come a Long Way: Septima Clark, the Warings, and the Changing Civil Rights Movement." In *Groundwork: Local Black Freedom Movements in America,* edited by Jeanne Theoharis and Komozi Woodard, 116–39. New York: New York University Press, 2005.

Chepesiuk, Ronald J., Ann Y. Evans, and Thomas S. Morgan, eds. *Women Leaders in South Carolina: An Oral History.* Rock Hill, S.C.: Louise Pettus Archives and Special Collections, Winthrop University, 1984.

Clark, Septima. *Echo in My Soul.* New York: Dutton, 1962.

———. *Ready from Within: Septima Clark and the Civil Rights Movement.* Navarro, Calif.: Wild Trees Press, 1986.

Clayton, Cranston. "College Interracialism in the South." *Opportunity: Journal of Negro Life,* September 1934, 267–69, 288.

Cohodas, Nadine. *Strom Thurmond and the Politics of Southern Change.* New York: Simon and Schuster, 1993.

Collier-Thomas, Bettye. *Jesus, Jobs, and Justice: African American Women and Religion.* New York: Knopf, 2010.

Collier-Thomas, Bettye, and V. P. Franklin, eds. *Sisters in the Struggle: African American Women in the Civil Rights-Black Power Movement.* New York: New York University Press, 2001.

Coryell, Janet L. *Beyond Image and Convention: Explorations in Southern Women's History.* Columbia: University of Missouri Press, 1998.

Cousins, Ralph E. *South Carolinians Speak: A Moderate Approach to Race Relations.* Dillon: n.p. 1957.

Cox, Ron M., Jr. "'Integration with [Relative] Dignity': The Desegregation of Clemson College and George McMillan's Article at Forty." In *Toward the Meeting of the Waters: Currents in the Civil Rights Movement of South Carolina during the Twentieth Century,* edited by Winfred B. Moore Jr. and Orville Vernon Burton, 274–85. Columbia: University of South Carolina Press, 2008.

Crawford, Vicki. "African American Women in the Mississippi Freedom Democratic Party." In *Sisters in the Struggle: African American Women in the Civil Rights-Black Power Movement,* edited by Bettye Collier-Thomas and V. P. Franklin, 121–38. New York: New York University Press, 2001.

Crawford, Vicki L., Jacqueline A. Rouse, and Barbara Woods, eds. *Women in the Civil Rights Movement: Trailblazers and Torchbearers, 1941–1965.* Bloomington: Indiana University Press, 1993.

Dailey, Jane, ed. *Jumpin' Jim Crow: Southern Politics from Civil War to Civil Rights.* Princeton: Princeton University Press, 2000.

Daniel, Pete. *Lost Revolutions: The South in the 1950s.* Chapel Hill: University of North Carolina Press, 2000.

Davidson, Chandler. *Quiet Revolution in the South: The Impact of the Voting Rights Act, 1965–1990.* Princeton: Princeton University Press, 1994.

Drago, Edmund L. *Initiative, Paternalism and Race Relations: Charleston's Avery Normal Institute.* Athens: University of Georgia Press, 1990.

Drake, Joseph Turpin. "The Negro in Greenville, South Carolina." M.A. thesis, University of North Carolina, Chapel Hill, 1940.

Dudley, Julius. "A History of the Association of Southern Women for the Prevention of Lynching." Ph.D., diss., University of Cincinnati, 1979.

Edgar, Walter. *South Carolina: A History.* Columbia: University of South Carolina Press, 1998.

———. *The South Carolina Encyclopedia.* Columbia: University of South Carolina Press, 2006.

Egerton, John. *Speak Now Against the Day: The Generation Before the Civil Rights Movement in the South.* Chapel Hill: University of North Carolina Press, 1994.

Erskine, Heather Jean. "'This Fellowship without Barriers of Race': The Desegregation of the Young Women's Christian Associations in Greenville, Columbia, and Charleston, South Carolina, 1946–1970s." M.A. thesis, University of South Carolina, 1998.

Fairclough, Adam. *A Class of Their Own: Black Teachers in the Segregated South*. Cambridge: Harvard University Press, 2007.

Farmer, James O. "The End of the White Primary in South Carolina: A Southern State's Fight to Keep Its Politics White." M.A. thesis, University of South Carolina, 1969.

———. "Memories and Forebodings: The Fight to Preserve the White Democratic Primary in South Carolina, 1944–1950." In *Toward the Meeting of the Waters: Currents in the Civil Rights Movement of South Carolina during the Twentieth Century*, edited by Winfred B. Moore Jr. and Orville Vernon Burton, 243–51. Columbia: University of South Carolina Press, 2008.

Fields, Mamie Garvin. *Lemon Swamp and Other Places: A Carolina Memoir*. New York: Free Press, 1985.

Findlay, James F., Jr. *Church People in the Struggle: The National Council of Churches and the Black Freedom Movement, 1950–1970*. New York: Oxford University Press, 1993.

Foster, Kayla. "We Cannot Be Still: The Story of Claudia Sanders." M.A. thesis, Graduate School of the College of Charleston and the Citadel, 2008.

Fraser, Walter J., Jr. *Charleston! Charleston! The History of a Southern City*. Columbia: University of South Carolina Press, 1989.

Frederickson, Karl. "'As a Man, I Am Interested in States' Rights': Gender, Race, and the Family in the Dixiecrat Party, 1948–1950." In *Jumpin' Jim Crow: Southern Politics from Civil War to Civil Rights*, edited by Jane Dailey, Glenda Gilmore, and Bryant Simon, 260–74. Princeton: Princeton University Press, 2000.

———. *The Dixiecrat Revolt and the End of the Solid South, 1932–1968*. Chapel Hill: University of North Carolina Press, 2001.

Frystak, Shannon. *Our Minds on Freedom: Women and the Struggle for Black Equality in Louisiana, 1924–1967*. Baton Rouge: Louisiana State Press, 2009.

Galeone, Mary. "The Role of Church Women United in the Civil Rights Movement." M.A. thesis, Union Theological Seminary, 1989.

Garris, Susan Page. "The Decline of Lynching in South Carolina, 1915–1947." M.A. thesis, University of South Carolina, 1973.

Giddings, Paula. *When and Where I Enter: The Impact of Black Women on Race and Sex in America*. New York: William Morrow, 1984.

Gilmore, Glenda. *Defying Dixie: The Radical Roots of Civil Rights, 1919–1950*. New York: Norton, 2008.

———. *Gender and Jim Crow: Women and the Politics of White Supremacy in North Carolina, 1896–1920*. Chapel Hill: University of North Carolina Press, 1996.

Goldfield, David R. *Black, White, and Southern Race Relations and Southern Culture, 1940 to the Present*. Baton Rouge: Louisiana State University Press, 1990.

Gona, Ophelia DeLaine. *Dawn of Desegregation: J. A. DeLaine and "Briggs v. Elliott."* Columbia: University of South Carolina Press, 2011.

Gordon, Asa. *Sketches of Negro Life and History in South Carolina*. Columbia: University of South Carolina Press, 1929.

Gore, Dayo F. *Radicalism at the Crossroads: African American Women Activists in the Cold War*. New York: New York University Press, 2011.

Gravely, William, "The Civil Right Not to Be Lynched: State Law, Government, and Citizen

Response to the Killing of Willie Earle (1947)." In *Toward the Meeting of the Waters: Currents in the Civil Rights Movement of South Carolina during the Twentieth Century*, edited by Winfred B. Moore Jr. and Orville Vernon Burton, 93–118. Columbia: University of South Carolina Press, 2008.

Gray, William S., Wil Lou Gray, and J. W. Tilton. *The Opportunity Schools of South Carolina: An Experimental Study*. New York: American Association for Adult Education, 1932.

Greene, Christina. *Our Separate Ways: Women and the Black Freedom Movement in Durham, North Carolina*. Chapel Hill: University of North Carolina Press, 2005.

Grose, Philip G. *South Carolina at the Brink: Robert McNair and the Politics of Civil Rights*. Columbia: University of South Carolina Press, 2006.

Hall, Jacquelyn Dowd. *Revolt against Chivalry: Jessie Daniel Ames and the Women's Campaign against Lynching*. New York: Columbia University Press, 1993.

Harris, Carmen. "Grace under Pressure: The Black Home Extension Service in South Carolina, 1919–1966." In *Rethinking Home Economics: Women and the History of a Profession*, edited by Sarah State and Virginia B. Vincenti, 203–28. Ithaca: Cornell University Press, 1997.

———. "A Ray of Hope for Liberation: Blacks in the South Carolina Extension Service, 1915–1970." Ph.D. diss., Michigan State University, 2002.

Hartmann, Susan. *The Other Feminists*. New Haven: Yale University Press, 1998.

Harvey, Paul. *Freedom's Coming: Religious Culture and the Shaping of the South from the Civil War through the Civil Rights Era*. Chapel Hill: University of North Carolina Press, 2005.

Hayes, Jack Irby, Jr. *South Carolina and the New Deal*. Columbia: University of South Carolina Press, 2001.

Hemmingway, Theodore. "'Prelude to Change': Black Carolinians in the War Years, 1914–1920." *Journal of Negro History* 65, no. 3 (Summer 1980): 212–27.

Henderson, Scott A. "Building Intelligent and Active Public Minds: Education and Social Reform in Greenville County during the 1930s." *South Carolina Historical Magazine* 106, no. 1 (January 2005): 34–58.

Hendricks, Wanda A. *Gender, Race, and Politics in the Midwest*. Bloomington: Indiana University Press, 1998.

Hewitt, Nancy, and Suzanne Lebsock. *Visible Women: New Essays on American Activism*. Urbana: University of Illinois Press, 1993.

Hoffman, Edwin D. "The Genesis of the Modern Movement for Equal Rights in South Carolina, 1930–1939." *Journal of Negro History* 44, no. 4 (October 1959): 346–69.

Huff, Archie Vernon, Jr. *Greenville: The History of the City and County in the South Carolina Piedmont*. Columbia: University of South Carolina Press, 1995.

Hunter, Jane Edna. *A Nickel and a Prayer: The Autobiography of Jane Edna Hunter*. Edited by Rhondda Robinson Thomas. Morgantown: West Virginia University Press, 2011.

Janken, Kenneth. *White: The Biography of Walter White, Mr. NAACP.* New York: The New Press, 2003.

Jelks, Randal Maurice. *Benjamin Elijah Mays, Schoolmaster of the Movement: A Biography*. Chapel Hill: University of North Carolina Press, 2012.

Johnson, Joan M. *Southern Ladies, New Women: Race, Region, and Clubwomen in South Carolina, 1890–1930*. Gainesville: University Press of Florida, 2004.

Jones, Cherisse. "'Loyal Women of Palmetto': Black Women's Clubs in Charleston, South Carolina, 1916–1965." M.A. thesis, University of Charleston, 1997.

Jones, Maryneal, and Lessie M. Reynolds. "Final Report of the State Meeting: The South Carolina Woman, Heritage to Horizons," The Carolina Inn, Columbia, South Carolina, June 10–11, 1977. Columbia: South Carolina International Women's Year Committee, 1977.

Jones-Branch, Cherisse. "'To Speak When and Where I Can': African American Women's Political Activism in South Carolina in the 1940s and 1950s." *South Carolina Historical Magazine* 107, no. 3 (July 2006): 204–24.

Joyner, Charles. "How Far We Have Come, How Far We Still Have to Go." In *Toward the Meeting of the Waters: Currents in the Civil Rights Movement of South Carolina during the Twentieth Century*, edited by Winfred B. Moore Jr. and Orville Vernon Burton, 422–32. Columbia: University of South Carolina Press, 2008.

Kittel, Mary Badham. *Cornelia Dabney Tucker, the First Republican Southern Belle.* Columbia: R. L. Bryan, 1969.

Kluger, Richard. *Simple Justice: The History of Brown v. Board of Education and Black America's Struggle for Equality.* New York: Knopf, 1976.

Knotts, Alice G. *Fellowship of Love: Methodist Women Changing American Racial Attitudes, 1920–1968.* Nashville: Kingswood Books, 1996.

Ladd, Everett, Jr. *Negro Political Leadership in the South.* Ithaca: Cornell University Press, 1966.

Lancia, Jessica. "Giving the South the Shock Treatment: Elizabeth Waring and the Civil Rights Movement." M.A. thesis, The Graduate School of the College of Charleston and The Citadel, 2007.

Lander, Ernest McPherson, Jr. *A History of South Carolina, 1865–1960.* Chapel Hill: University of North Carolina Press, 1960.

Lau, Peter F. *Democracy Rising: South Carolina and the Fight for Black Equality since 1865.* Lexington: University Press of Kentucky, 2006.

———, ed. *From the Grassroots to the Supreme Court: Brown v. Board of Education and American Democracy.* Durham: Duke University Press, 2004.

———. "From the Periphery to the Center: Clarendon County, South Carolina, *Brown*, and the Struggle for Democracy and Equality in America." In *From the Grassroots to the Supreme Court, Brown v. Board of Education and American Democracy*, edited by Peter F. Lau, 103–26. Durham: Duke University Press, 2004.

Lawson, Steven F. *Black Ballots: Voting Rights in the South, 1944–1969.* New York: Columbia University Press, 1976.

Leppert, Alice M. *Guidelines for Adult Basic Education Volunteers.* New York: Church Women United, 1970.

Lewis, Abigail Sara. "The Young Women's Christian Association's Multiracial Activism in the Immediate Postwar Era." In *Freedom Rights: New Perspectives on the Civil Rights Movement*, edited by Danielle L. McGuire and John Dittmer, 71–110. Lexington: University Press of Kentucky, 2011.

Ling, Peter. "Local Leadership in the Early Civil Rights Movement: The South Carolina Citizenship Education Program of the Highlander Folk School." *Journal of American Studies* 29 (1995): 398–422.

Little, Kimberly K. *You Must Be from the North: Southern White Women in the Memphis Civil Rights Movement*. Jackson: University Press of Mississippi, 2009.

Lynn, Susan. *Progressive Women in Conservative Times: Racial Justice, Peace, and Feminism, 1945 to the 1960s*. New Brunswick: Rutgers University Press, 1992.

Mack, Kibibi Voloria C. *Parlor Ladies and Ebony Drudges: African American Women, Class, and Work in a South Carolina Community*. Knoxville: University of Tennessee Press, 1999.

Madden, Bianca Tinsley. "'In the Thick of the Fray'": The Professional Life of Mary Elizabeth Frayser." M.A. thesis, Winthrop University, 1995.

Materson, Lisa G. *For the Freedom of Her Race: Black Women and Electoral Politics in Illinois, 1877–1932*. Chapel Hill: University of North Carolina Press, 2009.

Mays, Benjamin E. *Born to Rebel: An Autobiography by Benjamin E. Mays*. New York: Scribner, 1970.

McCandless, Amy Thompson. *The Past in the Present: Women's Higher Education in the Twentieth-Century American South*. Tuscaloosa: University of Alabama Press, 1999.

McClure, Phyllis. *Jeanes Teachers: A View into Black Education in the Jim Crow South*. Charleston: Booksurge, 2009.

McFadden, Grace Jordan. "Septima P. Clark and the Struggle for Human Rights." In *Women in the Civil Rights Movement: Trailblazers and Torchbearers, 1941–1965*, edited by Vicki L. Crawford, Jacqueline A. Rouse, and Barbara Woods, 85–97. Bloomington: Indiana University Press, 1990.

McGuire, Danielle L., and John Dittmer, eds. *Freedom Rights: New Perspectives on the Civil Rights Movement*. Lexington: University Press of Kentucky , 2011.

McMillan, Lewis K. *Negro Higher Education in the State of South Carolina*. N.p., 1932.

McMillan, Neil R. *Remaking Dixie: The Impact of World War II on the American South*. Jackson: University Press of Mississippi, 1997.

Meadows, Karen. "Chapters Never Written, Voices Never Heard: Children as Social Agents during the Era of School Desegregation: The Narratives of Ruby Bridges, Millicent Brown, and Josephine Boyd Bradley." Ph.D. diss., University of North Carolina at Greensboro, 2005.

Mjagkji, Nina. *Men and Women Adrift: The YMCA and the YWCA in the City*. New York: New York University Press, 1997.

Moore, John Hammond. *Columbia and Richland County: A South Carolina Community, 1740–1990*. Columbia: University of South Carolina Press, 1993.

Moore, William Pendleton. "'Tell Them We in the South are Dissatisfied': Politics of Race and Civil Rights Activism in Rock Hill." M.A. thesis: University of South Carolina, 2002.

Moore, Winfred B., Jr., and Orville Vernon Burton, eds. *Toward the Meeting of the Waters: Currents in the Civil Rights Movement of South Carolina during the Twentieth Century*. Columbia: University of South Carolina Press, 2008.

Moore, Winfred, Jr., and Joseph F. Tripp, eds. *Looking South: Chapters in the Story of an American Region*. New York: Greenwood Press, 1989.

Morris, Aldon D. *The Origins of the Civil Rights Movement: Black Communities Organizing for Change*. New York: The Free Press, 1984.

Murphy, Sara Alderman. *Breaking the Silence: Little Rock's Women's Emergency Committee to Open Our Schools, 1958–1963*. Fayetteville: University of Arkansas Press, 1997.

Murphy, Walter F. "The South Counterattacks: The Anti-NAACP Laws." *Western Political Quarterly* 12, no. 2 (June 1959): 371–90.

Murray, Gail, ed. *Throwing Off the Cloak of Privilege: White Southern Women Activists in the Civil Rights Era*. Gainesville: University Press of Florida, 2004.

Muse, Benjamin. *Ten Years of Prelude: The Story of Integration since the Supreme Court's 1954 Decision*. New York: Viking, 1964.

Myers, Andrew H. *Black, White and Olive Drab: Racial Integration at Fort Jackson, South Carolina, and the Civil Rights Movement*. Charlottesville: University of Virginia Press, 2006.

Newby, I. A. *Black Carolinians: A History of Blacks in South Carolina from 1895 to 1968*. Columbia: University of South Carolina Press, 1973.

———. "South Carolina and the Desegregation Issue: 1954–1956." M.A. thesis, University of South Carolina, 1957.

Ogden, Mary MacDonald. "The Making of a Southern Progressive: South Carolina's Wil Lou Gray, 1883–1920." M.A. thesis, University of North Carolina at Wilmington, 1997.

———. "Wil Lou Gray and the Politics of Progress in South Carolina." Ph.D. diss., University of South Carolina, 2011.

Olson, Lynne. *Freedom's Daughters: The Unsung Heroines of the Civil Rights Movement From 1830 to 1970*. New York: Scribner, 2001.

O'Neill, Stephen. "Memory, History, and the Desegregation of Greenville, South Carolina." In *Toward the Meeting of the Waters: Currents in the Civil Rights Movement of South Carolina during the Twentieth Century*, edited by Winfred B. Moore Jr. and Orville Vernon Burton, 286–99. Columbia: University of South Carolina Press, 2008.

———. "To Endure, but Not Accept: *The News and Courier* and School Desegregation." *Proceedings of the South Carolina Historical Association* (1990): 87–99.

Payne, Charles M., and Adam Green. *Time Longer Than Rope: A Century of African American Activism, 1850–1950*. New York: New York University Press, 2003.

Peirce, Neal R. *The Deep South States of America: People, Politics, and Power in the Seven Deep South States*. New York: Norton, 1974.

Pencak, William. *For God and Country: The American Legion, 1919–1941*. Boston: Northeastern University Press, 1989.

Preskill, Stephen, L. "The Developmental Leadership of Septima Clark, 1954–1967." In *Toward the Meeting of the Waters: Currents in the Civil Rights Movement of South Carolina during the Twentieth Century*, edited by Winfred B. Moore Jr. and Orville Vernon Burton, 222–41. Columbia: University of South Carolina Press, 2008.

Quattlebaum, Mary. *Women of the Church Synod of South Carolina Presbyterian Church, U.S., 1800–1973*. South Carolina: Presbyterian Church, Synod of South Carolina, 1973.

Quint, Howard H. *Profile in Black and White: A Frank Portrait of South Carolina*. Washington, D.C.: Public Affairs Press, 1958.

Rauschenbusch, Walter. *Christianity and the Social Crisis*. New York: Macmillan, 1924.

Richards, Miles S. "The Eminent Lieutenant McKaine." *Carologue: Bulletin of the South Carolina Historical Society* 7 (Autumn 1991): 6–7, 14–17.

———. "Osceola E. McKaine and the Struggle for Black Civil Rights, 1917–1946." Ph.D. diss., University of South Carolina, 1994.

Robertson, Nancy Marie. *Christian Sisterhood, Race Relations, and the YWCA, 1906–1946.* Urbana: University of Illinois Press, 2007.

Roefs, Wim. "The Impact of the 1940s Civil Rights Activism on the State's 1960s Civil Rights Scene: A Hypothesis and Historiographical Discussion." In *Toward the Meeting of the Waters: Currents in the Civil Rights Movement of South Carolina during the Twentieth Century*, edited by Winfred B. Moore Jr. and Orville Vernon Burton, 156–75. Columbia: University of South Carolina Press, 2008.

———. "Leading the Civil Rights Vanguard in South Carolina: John McCray and the *Lighthouse and Informer*, 1939–1954." In *Time Longer Than Rope: A Century of African American Activism, 1850–1950*, edited by Charles M. Payne and Adam Green, 972–1052. New York: New York University Press, 2003.

Rossinow, Doug. *The Politics of Authenticity: Liberalism, Christianity, and the New Left in America.* New York: Columbia University Press, 1998.

Rouse, Jacqueline A. *Lugenia Burns Hope: Black Southern Reformer.* Athens: University of Georgia Press, 1989.

———. "Out of the Shadow of Tuskegee: Margaret Murray Washington, Social Activism, and Race Vindication." *Journal of Negro History* 81, nos. 1–4 (Winter–Autumn 1996): 31–46.

Roydhouse, Marion W. "Bridging Chasms: Community and the Southern YWCA." In *Visible Women: New Essays on American Activism*, edited by Nancy A. Hewitt and Suzanne Lebsock, 270–95. Champaign: University of Illinois Press, 1993.

Secrest, Andrew McDowd. "'In Black and White': Press Opinion and Race Relations in South Carolina, 1954–1964." Ph.D. diss., Duke University, 1972.

Shankman, Arnold. "The South Carolina Council for the Common Good." Paper presented at the annual meeting for the South Carolina History Association, April 1982.

———. "The South Carolina Council for the Common Good." *Proceedings of the South Carolina Historical Association* (1982): 90–99.

Shannon, Margaret. *Just Because: The Story of the National Movement of Church Women United in the U.S.A., 1941 through 1975.* Corte Madera, Calif.: Omega Books, 1977.

Shattuck, Gardiner H., Jr. *Episcopalians and Race: Civil War to Civil Rights.* Lexington: University Press of Kentucky , 2000.

Simon, Bryant. "Race Relations: African American Organizing, Liberalism, and White Working-Class Politics in Postwar South Carolina." In *Jumpin' Jim Crow: Southern Politics from Civil War to Civil Rights*, edited by Jane Dailey, Glenda Gilmore, and Bryant Simon, 239–59. Princeton: Princeton University Press, 2001.

Simpson, Ethel. *The First Fifty Years of the Young Women's Christian Association of Greenville, South Carolina.* Greenville: n.p., n.d.

Sims, Lois. *Profiles of African American Females in the Low Country of South Carolina.* Charleston: Avery Research Center for African American History and Culture, College of Charleston, 1992.

Sims, Mary S. *The YWCA: An Unfolding Purpose.* New York: Woman's Press, 1950.

Sitkoff, Harvard. "African American Militancy in the World War II South: Another Perspective." In *Remaking Dixie: The Impact of World War II on the American South*, edited by Neil R. McMillen, 70–92. Jackson: University Press of Mississippi, 1997.

Skinner, Leslie. "Sibling Institutions, Similar Experiences: The Coeducation and Integration Experiences of South Carolina's Clemson and Winthrop Universities." Ph.D. diss., University of South Carolina, 2002.

Solomon, W. E. "The Problem of Desegregation in South Carolina." *Journal of Negro Education* 25, no. 3 (Summer 1956): 315–23.

Sosna, Morton. *In Search of the Silent South: Southern Liberals and the Race Issue.* New York: Columbia University Press, 1977.

Southern, David W. "'Beyond Jim Crow Liberalism': Judge Waring's Fight against Segregation in South Carolina, 1942–1952." *Journal of Negro History* 66, no. 3 (Autumn 1981): 209–27.

Southern Regional Council. *The New South.* Millwood, N.Y.: Kraus Reprint Company, 1975.

Spain, Daphne. *How Women Saved the City.* Minneapolis: University of Minnesota Press, 2001.

Spears, R. Wright. *One in the Spirit: Ministry for Change in South Carolina.* Columbia, S.C.: R. L. Bryan, 1997.

Sproat, John G. "'Firm Flexibility': Perspectives on Desegregation in South Carolina." In *New Perspectives on Race and Slavery in America: Essays in Honor of Kenneth M. Stampp,* edited by Robert H. Azbug and Stephen E. Maizlish, 164–84. Lexington: University Press of Kentucky, 1986.

Sullivan, Patricia. *Days of Hope: Race and Democracy in the New Deal Era.* Chapel Hill: University Press of North Carolina, 1996.

Synnott, Marcia G. "Alice Norwood Spearman Wright: Civil Rights Apostle to South Carolinians." In *Beyond Image and Convention: Explorations in Southern Women's History,* edited by Janet L. Coryell, 184–208. Columbia: University of Missouri Press, 1998.

———. "Crusaders and Clubwomen: Alice Norwood Spearman Wright and Her Women's Network." In *Throwing Off the Cloak of Privilege: White Southern Women Activists in the Civil Rights Era,* edited by Gail S. Murray, 49–76. Gainesville: University Press of Florida, 2004.

———. "Desegregation in South Carolina, 1950–1963: Sometime between 'Now' and 'Never.'" In *Looking South: Chapters in the Story of an American Region,* edited by Winfred B. Moore Jr. and Joseph F. Tripp, 51–64. New York: Greenwood Press, 1989.

———. "Feminists or Maternalists? White Women Civil Rights Activists in South Carolina: Alice N. Spearman, Eunice Ford Stackhouse, and Clarice T. Campbell." The Citadel Conference on Civil Rights in South Carolina, March 2003.

Taylor, Frances Sanders. "'On the Edge of Tomorrow': Southern Women, the Student YWCA, and Race, 1920–1944." Ph.D. diss., Stanford University, 1984.

Terry, Robert L. "J. Waties Waring, Spokesman for Racial Justice in the New South." Ph.D. diss., University of Utah, 1970.

Theoharis, Jeanne, and Komozi Woodard, eds. *Groundwork: Local Black Freedom Movements in America.* New York: New York University Press, 2005.

Tilton, J. W., William S. Gray, and Wil Lou Gray. *The Opportunity Schools of South Carolina: An Experimental Study.* New York: American Association for Adult Education, 1932.

Tolbert, Marguerite. *South Carolina's Distinguished Women of Lauren's County.* Columbia, S.C.: R. L. Bryan, 1972.

Trolander, Judith, Ann. *Professionalism and Social Change: From the Settlement House Move-*

ment to Neighborhood Centers, 1886 to the Present. New York: Columbia University Press, 1987.

Tushnet, Mark V. *The NAACP Legal Strategy against Segregated Education, 1925–1950.* Chapel Hill: University of North Carolina Press, 1987.

Tyson, Timothy B. "Dynamite and 'The Silent South': A Story from the Second Reconstruction in South Carolina." In *Jumpin' Jim Crow: Southern Politics from Civil War to Civil Rights*, edited by Jane Dailey, Glenda Gilmore, and Bryant Simon, 275–99. Princeton: Princeton University Press, 2001.

Wadelington, Charles W., and Richard F. Knapp. *Charlotte Hawkins Brown and Palmer Memorial Institute.* Chapel Hill: University of North Carolina Press, 1999.

Webb, Clive. *Fight against Fear: Southern Jews and Black Civil Rights.* Athens: University of Georgia Press, 2001.

Webb, Ross A. *The Torch Is Passed: A History of Winthrop University.* Mansfield: Bookmasters, 2002.

Weiner, Josephine. *The Story of WICS.* Washington, D.C.: Women in Community Service, 1979, 1986.

Weisenfeld, Judith. *African American Women and Christian Activism: New York's Black YWCA, 1905–1945.* Cambridge: Harvard University Press, 1997.

West, Guida, and Rhoda Lois Blumberg. "Reconstructing Social Protest from a Feminist Perspective." In *Women and Social Protest*, edited by Guida West and Rhoda Lois Blumberg, 3–36. New York: Oxford University Press, 1990.

———, eds. *Women and Social Protest.* New York: Oxford University Press, 1990.

White, Deborah Gray. *Too Heavy a Load: Black Women in Defense of Themselves, 1894–1994.* New York: Norton, 1999.

White, John W. "The White Citizens' Councils of Orangeburg County, South Carolina." In *Toward the Meeting of the Waters: Currents in the Civil Rights Movement of South Carolina during the Twentieth Century*, edited by Winfred B. Moore Jr. and Orville Vernon Burton, 261–73. Columbia: University of South Carolina Press, 2008.

Wiggington, Eliot. *Refuse to Stand Silently By: An Oral History of Grass Roots Social Activism in America, 1921–1964.* New York: Anchor Books, 1991.

Wiggins, Martha Lee. "United Church Women: A Constant Drip of Water Will Wear a Hole in Iron: The Ecumenical Struggle of Church Women to Unite across Race and Shape the Civil Rights Century." Ph.D. diss., Union Theological Seminary, 2005.

Williams, Cecil J. *Freedom and Justice: Four Decades of the Civil Rights Struggle as Seen by a Black photographer of the Deep South.* Macon, Ga.: Mercer University Press, 1995.

Woloch, Nancy. *Women and the American Experience: A Concise History.* 2nd ed. Boston: McGraw-Hill Higher Education, 2002.

Woods Aba-Mecha, Barbara. "Black Woman Activist in Twentieth Century South Carolina: Modjeska Monteith Simkins." Ph.D. diss., Emory University, 1978.

Woods, Jeff. *Black Struggle, Red Scare: Segregation and Anti-Communism in the South, 1948–1968.* Baton Rouge: Louisiana State University Press, 2004.

Wright, Marion A., and Arnold Shankman. *Human Rights Odyssey.* Durham: Moore, 1978.

Yarbrough, Tinsley E. *A Passion for Justice: J. Waties Waring and Civil Rights.* Oxford: Oxford University Press, 1987.

Index

Cherisse Jones-Branch, a native of Charleston, South Carolina, is associate professor of history at Arkansas State University, Jonesboro. She recieved her BA and MA from the College of Charleston, South Carolina, and a doctorate in history from The Ohio State University, Columbus. She is the coeditor of *Arkansas Women: Their Lives and Times.*

The University Press of Florida is the scholarly publishing agency for the State University System of Florida, comprising Florida A&M University, Florida Atlantic University, Florida Gulf Coast University, Florida International University, Florida State University, New College of Florida, University of Central Florida, University of Florida, University of North Florida, University of South Florida, and University of West Florida.

FEB 0 5 ENT'D

CPSIA information can be obtained at www.ICGtesting.com
Printed in the USA
LVOW11s1504140116

470661LV00008B/867/P